www.crystalcleanbook.com

First edition

IBSN 9 781480 0800010

This book is a memoir. The events in this book have been
reproduced from the author's memory, extensive journals, letters,
various medical records and court documents.

Certain names have been changed.

"Let enough people into your closet and there's no room left for your skeletons."
~ Kevin Smith

For anyone who's ever said, "I can't."

Chapter 1

There are precious few things in this life of which I am certain. One is the love I have for my son, Andy.

I was just shy of my twenty-third birthday when Andy was born. My pregnancy was intentional. My son was no accident, but my brief marriage was.

I was two months pregnant and decided I should marry the "sperm donor" and make an honest woman of myself. Three weeks after the ceremony, he hit me and I threw him out. The divorce was final a couple of months after Andy was born. I told my ex that if he left us alone, I would never go after the child support, and that was fine with him. We never saw him again.

As certain as I've always been about being a mother, I was unprepared for the depth and breadth of my love for my son.

Andy was born with Down syndrome, and there were medical problems. He had esophageal atrasia, meaning there was no connection between his esophagus and stomach, so there was no way to feed him. He was in neo-natal intensive care for the first month and a half of his life, and he was two days old when he underwent his first surgery to put a gastrostomy tube in his stomach so that he could eat. He was five days old when Dr. Curnow repaired the atrasia.

For six hours, I sat envisioning Andy's delicate skin being sliced open with gleaming surgical steel, and of hands the size of my son's torso removing one of his ribs and repositioning his tiny organs.

The first time I held him was just before that operation. As I was savoring the moment, holding the six and a half pound person I'd been waiting so long to meet, a nurse clipped a lock of his hair and made prints of a hand and foot. "Just in case," she said. No one had to explain. I knew how serious the situation was.

The feeling I had as I held him to my chest was almost indescribable. My heart felt so full, I thought it might explode. A wave of love, so pure it made my bones ache, washed over me. I couldn't hug him tight enough. I wanted to slip him under my skin so I could get him as close to me as possible.

Even attached to monitors and machines, he was perfect. There was a feeding tube hanging from his recently sawed open tummy and he smelled like a hospital: all adhesive tape, antiseptic and iodine. And he was perfect. He was the yummiest baby I'd ever seen.

When I finally was able to bring him home, I would spend hours just staring into those eyes. Like pools of cerulean. We would stare into each other's souls, and I knew that he had always been a part of me.

Andy spent the first three years of his life in and out of the hospital. There were complications with the initial repair of his esophagus. It was stricturing, trying to close again. He had a hiatal hernia, causing his stomach to creep up into his chest. At final count, Andy had fifteen surgeries, twelve of which occurred before he was two years old.

The constant hospitalizations and anesthesia compromised his immune system and he would get sick which, of course, meant more time spent in the hospital. He had two complete blood transfusions.

Between stays, when he was home, I fed him through the G-tube that hung out of the furious red scar in his tummy, and wheeled an oxygen tank around everywhere we went.

And he was perfect.

But those first three years were hell, and if someone had told me I would have to live through all of that, I would have said they were crazy. No way was I strong enough to handle all of that, especially as a single mother.

But I was. And I did. And it was worth every horrifying minute.

I tell Andy he's my bug in a boy suit, my perfect person and the best human I've ever known. I tell him this every day, because he is. One of the only things I'm certain of in this life is the excruciating love I have for my son.

The other thing of which I am certain is this: no one wants to be an addict.

Nobody wakes up one morning and says, "This is the day I will begin to destroy my life and the lives of those who love me. Today, I will begin my suicide. I'll start taking poison. Not all at once, but a little at a time, so I can experience a long, slow agonizing death."

I've heard it said, that if you drop a frog into a pan of boiling water, it will flop around and do anything to escape. But if you put that same frog in a pan of cool water, place it on the stove and heat it up ever so slowly to the point of boiling, the frog won't realize what's happening to it and will stay there until it's dead. That's how it is with addiction. Death comes slowly.

I doubt anyone has ever said to themselves, "My goal in life is to lie, cheat, steal and beg to get my poison and I will sacrifice everything I have in pursuit of my own death. I will give up my life and give up my hope. I will give up my dreams and my self-respect. I will give my soul."

No one wants to be an addict. Especially a meth addict. Meth is dirty and disgusting. The media shows us that it's made by shady characters with facial sores and no teeth in trailer houses and sheds. Everything we hear and see tells us that meth is a low class drug for low class people like white trash and Mexicans. In my city, there are towering billboards of the ugliest, scariest people you've ever seen: teeth rotted out, lips cracked and infected, skin hanging from the sharp angles of their bones, matted, dirty hair and body sores.

Disgusting people, disgusting drug. How easy it is to dismiss them and categorize them as an almost different species because, after all, there's no way in hell you or I would mess around with meth. We're not those kinds of people. We're not stupid. We have lives and dignity and no one with any self-respect would even *think* of sinking to such murky depths.

That's what I thought, too.

At the time of my arrest, I'd been using meth for over five years. Every single day. All day long. Without exception. I was what's known as a "functioning addict." I worked two legitimate jobs, was raising my son by myself, had a house and a man I thought I was in love with. On the outside, everything seemed fine. But barely scratch the surface, and the chaos of my living hell was frightening.

I started using meth to study on the weekends. Then more often during the week to get through my workday and still have the energy to do what I needed to do in the evening: laundry, dishes, dinner, therapy with Andy and my own studies. I was an honor student, a teaching assistant and a research assistant at the state school and hospital.

It wasn't long before I needed meth. Once I started, I was trapped. If I quit using, I'd fall asleep for days and I'd get behind. I couldn't let that happen. I couldn't fail, so I just kept going.

The flip side of this is that I didn't like myself very much. To be honest, I hated myself. Altering my reality with drugs took me outside of my own head so I didn't have to deal with the constant looping voice of negativity: *not good enough, not smart enough, not pretty, not a good enough mom, stupid, lazy, ugly...*

No one could ever make me feel worse than I could. I'd perfected my self-loathing for most of my life. Meth took me away from all of that. With it, I could do everything I wanted and needed to do. I lost weight, I felt smarter and funnier than I ever had before. My self-confidence was off the chart. Meth made me feel like a whole person. It made me feel normal.

It also robbed me of all my ambition. Everything else quickly became moot. All I wanted to do was get high.

Chapter 2

I call Allan from booking after being fingerprinted, photographed and processed. "You need to call Jill for me."

"You want me to wake her up?"

"Yes! I'm on call and someone has to take the phones. Will you make sure Andy gets ready in time for the bus?"

"Yeah. Are you okay?"

Of course I'm not okay! Why can't you take care of me for a change? "I'm okay. I'll be arraigned tomorrow, and then we'll know more." I don't expect him to say, "I love you." He never has, but it would mean everything to me just now. As I hang up, the desk sergeant calls my name. I can't believe this is happening to me. I'm thirty-eight years old, and I've just been arrested for felony possession of methamphetamine with intent to distribute.

I'm embarrassed. I want to tell the officers I'm different. I'm not like the other people in here. I'm educated, own a home and pay taxes. I'm a bail bondsman. I don't belong here. I should get to go home. A female guard takes me to a room and tells me to strip. This is the worst part for me. I'm completely humiliated. Standing naked in the cold room, ashamed of being on display in front of this woman, I'm sobbing like a sniveling child. It's the first time I've cried since this whole thing started. Everything I'm facing, everything I've been through tonight, and this is what undoes me. With my stretch marks showing and thirty-eight-year-old breasts hanging unsupported, the guard tells me to turn around and bend over.

"Squat and cough," she says. This series of routine procedures is more humiliating than the arrest. Stripped of all facades, all the outer layers that protect me, I'm vulnerable and exposed. Standing here naked, it's just me and I hate myself. I'm ashamed of my nakedness and ashamed that I'm crying. The officer looks at me as if I'm a slug on a sidewalk: something she'd rather not see, but here I am anyway. When I finally get my blue jail uniform, I stop crying, grateful that I'm covered again. A guard leads me and two other women down a long hall. One of them is talking non-stop to the guard. Long, rambling tweaker sentences, with no punctuation, about who's still here and who just got out. She's obviously been here before.

The guard leads us through locked doors and down corridors where overhead fluorescents glare obscenely. I have no idea what to expect in county jail. I've worked for Jill, writing bail bonds, for three years, so I know my way around, but it's different on this side. It's the difference between driving by an asylum and admiring the landscape, and being on a ward in the same asylum. I'm used to talking to defendants through a glass partition, getting their signature on the dotted line, posting their bond at the window and chatting with the sergeants at the front desk, but I've never seen the inside. Walking down the concrete corridor feels like walking into the abyss.

Do not show fear. I tell myself. *And don't cry.* I can't cry. That would be even more humiliating than being strip-searched. We stop at a door, and a guard on the inside buzzes us in. The lights are dim in the dormitory. It's the middle of the night, but everyone is awake. There are two levels of double bunk beds. I have no idea how many women are here. I can feel their eyes sizing me up. I look past the sea of faces.

The guard is male, and he's telling me the rules, though I barely hear his voice. I get a plastic cup with a toothbrush, trial size bar of soap, plastic spoon, sweatshirt, blanket and a sheet through which I could easily read a book. He points me to my bunk.

Jesus. This is worse than I imagined, I think, looking down at the skeleton of metal that is my bed. I start to lay my sheet over the criss-crossing metal straps, when a woman comes over and stops me.

"You need to get your mattress," she says. "Hey!" She yells at the guard. "She didn't get no mattress!"

"It's okay," I tell her. "I can get it." But she's already dragging a thin, worn mattress up the stairs. She smiles at me and I can see she's only got one front tooth. She shows me how to slip the mattress into the sheet the same way I'd slide a sandwich into a baggie, and before retreating to her bunk a few feet away tells me if I need anything just ask her.

Despite the guard's intermittent warnings to shut up and go to sleep, the hushed chatter is constant. I take off my oversized sneakers. They've removed the laces. They don't want anyone hanging herself in here, although I don't know how it would be possible. There's absolutely no privacy. Even the toilet is exposed with only a half wall on one side so the male guards can't watch the women drop their pants and squat down on the cold plastic.

I fold the sweatshirt into a makeshift pillow and lie down. I'm still in shock from the arrest. I can't get my mind around the fact that I'm actually in jail. Lying there with my face in my arms, all I can think about is Andy. I wish I were at home. I wish I could crawl into bed with him until morning. It's cold here, and I feel so alone. How easy it would be to get lost in the system and erased from the outside world. I know it's silly. I know that's not going to happen, but that's how anonymous I feel. My tears flow silently into my folded sweatshirt, and I drift into sleep thinking, "My God. What have I done?"

High-pitched giggling wakes me up. There's a woman a couple of bunks away cackling insanely. Other women are telling her to shut the fuck up, but she just keeps on in a way that makes my skin crawl.

"Shut up, Lisa 'ya fucking bitch!"

"What the hell's wrong with her?"

"Fuckin' tweaker."

All of this drama plays in the background as I fade in and out of sleep with no concept of time. Lisa's laughing that crazy laugh and the women are still trying to get her to stop. In the morning, she's gone. I've slept through breakfast, and the others are back at their bunks talking loudly or pacing back and forth across the length of the dorm. I sit up and listen without looking at anyone. I found out a long time ago that listening provides me far more information than if I were to ask questions.

I hear that the guards have taken the laughing girl to the psych ward early this morning. I discover that many of these women have been here for months awaiting either trial or transport to prison. Most of them are young but there are women here who look as if they're in their 50s or 60s. In jail there's no makeup allowed. Nor are hairdryers, curling irons or tweezers. It's easy to tell which ones are in here on drug charges. They're skinny, with sucked-in, scarred faces, sores on their arms and rotting teeth. They twitch and jerk because of damage to their nervous systems and pace back and forth like caged animals.

With some, it's more difficult to guess why they're here. They look normal, whatever that means. I overhear one of them talking about her impending deportation back to the Czech republic. There's a woman in the bunk next to me who looks like she's in her sixties. She keeps mostly to herself, reading a tattered Harlequin Romance – the only type of book available other than the Bible and the Alcoholics Anonymous handbook. Eventually, someone else asks my name.

"Kim," I say.

"Wadja do?"

"Possession of meth with intent, possession of paraphernalia and possession of marijuana."

"Cool. How much did they get?"

"Just two rocks, my personal stash, my pipe and a little hash. I think they were disappointed they didn't get more."

A guard yells my name and takes me down to booking. Jill's there on the other side of the glass waiting for me. I pick up the phone to talk to my boss.

"What happened?"

"I got pulled over last night right after I got gas. I was on my way to collect money from that guy. You know, the one whose girlfriend skipped out on her bond? They pulled me over and said they saw something on the floor under my feet. They wouldn't tell me what it was, but they dragged me out, brought in the dogs and searched the whole car."

I don't tell her about the drugs they found. Or the $1250. Or my ledger. Or my scale. Or the list of undercover cops and paid informants they found in a pocket of my bail bond bag. She doesn't ask, so I don't tell her.

"You're going to be arraigned at 10:00 this morning. I called your parents and Larry and they'll be there in court. I assume you want Larry, right? That's who you used for Kilo and Allan."

"Yeah, thanks."

"Good. I'll post your bond as soon as they set it. Are you okay?"

"I'm okay. The cops were assholes last night, and it's pretty weird in here, but I'm okay."

"Kim, you have to be straight with me. Right now. Are you guilty? I need to know before I post bail."

I think for a split second before I answer. I don't know about the popcorn yet. What I do know is that it is impossible for me to have anything on any floor in my car, unless someone planted it there, and it's for this reason that I'm able to say with confidence, "No. I don't know what they think they found on the floor. They wouldn't show me. But I swear to God, there was nothing there."

She thinks the whole reason for my arrest is because of something they saw in the car, but she's owned the bail bond business for eight years. She has to sense that something doesn't add up, but she doesn't want to know, and I don't want to shatter her illusion of me as someone who's way too smart to be involved with meth. She's also the only shot I have at getting out of jail. I know my parents would never bail me out. Just like I know that Allan isn't even thinking of how he could post bail even though I've bonded him out twice: once for possession of marijuana and once for failure to pay child support. All I know is that my son's birthday is in a few days, and Jill is my only hope for being home with him. Right now, he's all that matters to me.

When I get back to my bunk, a couple of the women come over to talk to me. "Was it a bondsman? Are you getting out?"

"It was my boss, and yes, as soon as we find out what my bail is, she'll get me out of here."

"Lucky. What do you do?"

I'm a drug dealer. "I'm a bail bondsman."

"What! Are you serious? Which company?"

It's a badge of honor for people here: which bond company they use, who knows which bondsman's name, which company is most lenient and which ones will hunt you down mercilessly. I tell them and word spreads quickly. Soon, they're asking me all kinds of questions about my job. Everyone has a story about their bail or a friend's or that of someone in their family. I answer some of their questions, then lie down and drift off again. I'm coming down from meth. I haven't hit the pipe in twelve hours. This is the longest break I've had from it in over five years, other than when I was in Mexico, but I had coke then. Right now, I'm crashing.

I barely stay awake through my arraignment and when I get back to the dorm, Morpheus seduces me. Just before lunch, a guard calls "Commissary! Line up! Bottom tier first!"

The place buzzes with excitement. Two women come back with huge cardboard boxes filled with soda, noodles, packaged cookies, paper, shampoo and even underwear. Peanut butter seems to be a real coup. Another inmate walks back with one pre-stamped envelope, three small sheets of blank paper and a pen. It's the same kind of pen I had to use in booking – rubbery, small and very hard to write with.

"Where did you get all that?" I ask the woman in the bunk across from mine. She eyes me suspiciously and shoves her loot into the plastic bin. Opening a tepid Diet Coke, she says, "Weekly commissary. You can order stuff off the list if someone puts money on your books."

"What kind of stuff?"

"All kinds of shit. Here."

She hands me a sheet of paper with all the available items. On the front there's a list of food: crackers, cookies and all kinds of snacks. The back is divided into three sections. One is for toiletries: everyday items like shampoo, soap, toothpaste, toothbrushes, combs and tampons. The next section is clothing: nightshirts, underwear, bras, socks, shoes, pants, shirts and sweatshirts. The last section is for miscellaneous items like writing paper and pre-stamped envelopes. There are prices and check boxes next to each item.

I turn to the older woman who's reading and ask her about the list and why some people have so much while others have next to nothing. She puts down her book and sits up on her bunk.

"If you got someone to put money on your books, you can order stuff once a week. If you don't got no one, the county keeps you in soap and that crappy toothpaste you got there." She points to the trial size toothpaste in my plastic cup. "About once a month they'll give you a little paper and envelope so you can write someone. If you got someone to write to."

"What's the deal with the peanut butter?"

"You new here, aincha? Well, you spend some time here, you find out how shitty the food is. Even the peanut butter sandwiches are shit. They use that government peanut butter and you can't hardly chew it. Fuckin' food. You wait. You'll find out quick." She looks me up and down. "You look like you got people."

"Do you have to buy clothes, too? Shampoo? Tampons? What if you can't?"

"Other than what they give you last night, everything else you gotta buy. Or do without. You can't afford panties, you got but one pair. If you bleed in 'em you gotta just wash 'em out and hang 'em to dry. Laundry's only once a week. If you can't buy tampons they'll give you these huge fuckin' pads. You gotta ask the guard every time you need a new one. So you watch out. Make sure nobody don't steal your shoes, or you gotta wait until next commissary day – if you got money on your books."

"Thank you. I have no idea how this place works."

"What are you doin' here anyway?"

"Felony possession."

"Of what?"

"Meth."

"You? Never would have guessed that."

"What did you think?"

"Well, I kinda was thinking you was a narc. You know, put here to spy on us. They do it all the time."

Great. This is just what I need. In my head I'm picturing a midnight mob stealing my shoes, shanking me and writing 'Narc' on my forehead with one of those wobbly little pens.

"No," I say. "I mean, I'm sure that's what a narc would say, too, but I'm not a narc."

"Why'd you get arrested for meth?"

What do you mean why did I get arrested for meth?

"What do you mean?" I say.

"You use?"

"Yeah."

She's squinting at me suspiciously. There seems to be a lot of suspicion in here. Probably because everyone here is a criminal. "How'd you keep all your teeth?"

"I brush a lot." Meth mouth is rampant among users. It's normal for people to be missing teeth. Any teeth left are usually gray and black around the gums. It happens when people are on a steady diet of chemicals, have poor hygiene and don't drink enough liquids. I've seen people with meth mouth. From the beginning, I knew I didn't want to end up that way, so I brush multiple times a day, use fluoride rinse and drink liquids constantly.

"Do you mind if I ask why you're in here?" I feel like I may be starting to get on her nerves, but I ask anyway.

"Third time D.U.I. I'll get prison this time 'cause I don't got no family. No money neither." Her hair color has grown out. From the scalp about four inches down is pure gray. The rest is brownish red.

"How long have you been here?"

"Five months. Still waiting on the courts." She lies back again with her book. Clearly, that's enough talk for now.

My bail has been set at $75,000. Jill posts the bond, and my parents drive me home. We barely speak of the arrest, but my father has brought me red licorice. Mom and Dad don't want to believe I'm a drug dealer any more than Jill does. The licorice is my dad saying, "Aw, Kimbo. Everything will be okay as long as we don't

speak about what all of this implies. Have some licorice, honey."
It's his way of saying they love me, I suppose.

I'm home again and alone. Allan is at work and Andy is at developmental therapy. They won't be home for another hour or two. The police have taken everything: my money, my drugs, my bail bond bag and my keys. All of it is being held as evidence, and may or may not be released to me later in the week. I break into my own house with my driver's license. That and my two cell phones are the only things the deputies in booking gave back to me. I don't even have cigarettes. The police left my car on the side of the road where they pulled me over, so I can't get downtown to where my office is, where all my drugs are. I've been off meth for almost 24 hours so I need to make some phone calls.

"Johnny. Can you come over? Do you still have anything left from what I gave you yesterday?" Johnny is Kilo's cousin. I've been working with him since Kilo went to prison, and he moves at least as much meth for me as Josh does.

"Shit! I saw your picture on the Internet. What happened? You okay?"

"I'm okay, but I need to get high and I don't have anything. They took it all. Are you still holding?"

"I only have my personal, but I'll help you out." This means he has the best of what I sold him yesterday.

"Will you come over? I don't have my car."

"Yeah, I can be there in about an hour."

"I need you to come right now. Allan and Andy will be home by then, and I don't want Allan to know I have to get high. I don't want to deal with it right now."

He comes right away. Of course he comes right away. He's almost out. He needs to re-up and I'm his source, so he wants to make a good impression. He probably thinks I'll give him a break in price for doing this good deed but he's wrong. I don't tell him that, of course. In the first place, he still owes me $2500. In the second place, I need to get high RIGHT NOW. He brings me a pipe and loads it. He lets me take the first hit. It's a respect thing. He puts a huge rock in the bowl and I smoke and smoke until it's almost gone, then I hand him the pipe. The smoke makes its way to the center of my soul. I feel serene and much more relaxed. I feel normal again. I feel nourished. I lean back against the couch and tell him the whole story.

"What about your guy? Have you told him yet? Are you still going to work?"

"I'll call him tonight. I'll have to see what he says. I don't know what he'll want to do."

"Well, I'm out of product and I have people blowing up my phone. Can you at least get something?"

"Christ, Johnny! I just got out of jail. I'll do what I can when I can, okay? It would probably help if you had money for me. They took everything last night. All my money. And I'm not getting it back. I collected from Mitt and one of my other guys too and now I have to eat the loss myself." Mitt is another of Kilo and Johnny's cousins.

"I don't have it all. I got $1500."

I take the money he owes me and smoke the rest of the meth he has with him. Then I dismiss him with the warning "Do NOT call me. I'll call you when I know something."

I have to call Mario, but I'll do it later. Right now, I want to take a shower before Andy and Allan come home. God, I feel so good right now – like I'm back in my own skin. The horror of last night begins to fade away. I have twenty-three messages on my phone – all since last night. I don't want to deal with anyone right now. It feels so good to feel good again.

Allan comes home as I'm getting out of the shower. I want him to wrap his arms around me and take care of me. I want him to tell me everything will be okay, but he doesn't. Of course he doesn't. Instead he asks about the hash: a present I got for him. He stopped doing meth two years ago, but he smokes pot daily, so the hash was a treat. My heart sinks. I don't know why I still feel disappointed. I should know by now what to expect, but every single day I hope against hope that something will change.

"I had the hash with me, and they took everything."

"Bummer. Can you get any more?"

"I'll try," I say. *You bastard*, is what I think. I don't want to talk to him anymore right now. He's ruining my high.

Andy comes home. I can't wait to hold him and hug him. He doesn't know what's going on. At fifteen, all he knows is that Mom wasn't here this morning to get him up for school. Again. He knows I'm gone most nights and usually get home just in time to help him get ready. He doesn't understand or have any interest in where I was last night – only that I'm home now.

"Hey, bug!" I wrap my arms around him before he even takes his coat off.

"Mom!" I kiss his cheeks and nose and the top of his head. He kisses me back and hugs me.

"I missed you, sweetheart. I'm sorry I wasn't here this morning. Did you have a good day at school and program?"

"Oh. Yeah."

"What did you have for lunch?"

"Doh know. Enna watch Star Wars?"

"Sure, honey. I'll make you dinner. I love you, Andy."

"Auya you."

And for some reason those two words flood me with guilt. After dinner, Allan takes me to my car; I go to my downtown office and hop right back on the rollercoaster. There isn't much of a choice. Not only do I still need to make a living, but now there are legal fees as well.

Chapter 3

Meth kicked my ass. I'd done my share of drinking and drugs before I started using it, so I'd been around a block or two, but by no means was I prepared for the unique insidiousness of methamphetamine. That may seem unrealistic, but in 1999, the year I started using, there were no anti-meth campaigns like there are today. Looking back, though, I don't know if the information available now would have deterred me. It certainly hasn't seemed to put much of a dent in the nationwide pandemic.

Meth reaches across all socio-economic strata, from those living in extreme poverty to middle class soccer moms, college professors, doctors and CEO's. Many of them are people you would never imagine to be involved with, let alone addicted to, methamphetamine. I know these people because I've used with them and sold to them. I know them because I'm one of them. For years, I led a double life, and no one outside of the drug world had any idea what was going on with me. But the fact is, I'm an addict, and meth was my vehicle to self-destruction.

Although I'd done drugs in the past, I was sober when I had my son and I'd been sober for four years when I decided to become a foster mother for the state of Idaho. People asked me then, and sometimes now, whether I was crazy at the time. After all, I was a single mother of a son who has Down syndrome and I worked full time. I remember the decision to foster being a spontaneous one. The idea popped into my head one day, I looked into the licensing process and before I knew it, I had my first placements. Over those three years, I took care of eighteen children, including respite care I did for other families. The oldest child I had was seventeen when she came to me. My youngest was five hours old.

When I think about that time in my life, I don't know how I pulled it off: daycares, schools, and visitations with parents and social workers, meetings, middle of the night arrivals, therapists and doctors. One child at a time whose life was being ripped apart in its own unique way. On top of that, I worked full time and my son, Andy, went to school and attended developmental therapy five days a week. It was chaos, it was heartbreaking and it was worth every minute of it, although there's no way I could do it again. It drained everything out of me, which is probably the reason I started fostering in the first place.

It's likely that I was in a manic episode of my bi-polar disorder. I was diagnosed years ago and although for me the mania is rare – I'm definitely on the depressive side of the spectrum – I believe that was one of those episodes.

I was in over my head. I'd taken on too much, which is a pattern in my life. I tend to overextend myself and try to take care of everyone and everything. Except myself. I've never been very good at taking care of me. All these years later, it's clear that being bi-polar was a catalyst for another reason I decided to become a foster mother: it was a substitute for drugs. Another way for me to numb out. When being alone with your demons is the last place you want to be, you'll do anything to distract yourself. Being a foster mother was a good thing, and I was a wonderful temporary mother to all of those children, but for me it was a lot like drugs. I made sure I had plenty of mayhem going on around me, all in an effort to avoid the way I felt on the inside. I've spent most of my life neglecting and avoiding myself in one way or another.

I was always an emotional child. A few years ago, I came across a note sent home to my parents from my pre-school teacher requesting a meeting with them. "Kimmy shows undue anxiety during normal activities like taking walks. She seems to worry that something will happen to her. Please call so we can meet to talk about this."

When I asked my mother why she never called, she said she didn't think it was a big deal.

When I reached adolescence things got worse until one day, when I was in the seventh grade, the school district psychologist asked my parents to come in for a meeting.

I was seeing my counselor often for what I thought were typical things that bother adolescent girls: my best friend moved away, my new friends were being mean to me, I felt fat and ugly, nobody asked me to the Christmas dance. But I knew I saw my counselor more than the other kids did and I knew I was always sad. It was embarrassing, getting so many call slips to the front offices, but secretly, those little slips of paper felt like love letters. Someone wanted me. Someone wanted to talk to me. Regardless of the fact that I'd initiated those requests, for a few moments I felt nurtured, and entering my counselors office was like crawling up into a mother's lap.

But I was ashamed of my emotions, which felt like my broken insides were smeared all over my outside where everyone could see. I would cry at the most unlikely times at school and at home for no apparent reason: Tears of such despair and sadness that it was as if my soul had turned to liquid and draining from my eyes. I was also terribly afraid something was going to happen to me. There were enormous gas storage tanks across the street from the school and I would imagine them blowing up. Some days, it was hard to concentrate in class because I'd be imagining the bloody aftermath of the explosion, caught up in the thoughts of death and destruction that sabotaged my thoughts.

Walking home after school to our empty house, I was afraid of getting shot. There was no basis for my fear. There is nothing "inner-city" about Boise. The City of Trees, was, and still is, a nice little suburbia with a strong Mormon base, and regardless of what you may have heard, Mormons do not run amuck with Tech-9's shootin' up the hood. I knew this, but I couldn't shake my fears, unfounded and irrational as they were. At home, alone everyday after school, I would draw the drapes and duck when I walked past windows afraid that some unseen someone might be laying in wait to pop a cap in my white, middle-class ass.

So I would talk to my counselor who finally decided she couldn't help me anymore and referred me to the district psychologist. After my initial meeting with her, she spoke with my mother, referring us to a professional psychologist. "If you ever want her to go to college," she told my mom, "you need to get her some professional help now."

The first woman we met with had me do the "house, tree, person" test: a projective personality test where the subject draws houses, trees and people providing a measure of self-perception. My drawing of the tree disturbed her the most. She said that the fact that my tree had no leaves and no outward branches was indicative of someone who lives inside herself. My mother thought that, although not a typical tree for a twelve year old, it was a nice picture. The psychologist didn't agree and so I began seeing her twice a week. After two sessions of doing nothing but stare at each other, we decided that I would switch to another therapist.

Iris was more personable. She was matronly and actually engaged me in conversations. She referred me to a psychiatrist who prescribed anti-depressants. It took a while to find the right medication at the right dosage. In the early '80's, anti-depressants were mostly tri-cyclic and carried more side effects than their modern day counterparts. The first one I tried plunged me into a nearly catatonic depression. After a few adjustments though, they did seem to help.

A couple of months into therapy, Iris deemed it necessary to have a family session with both herself and the psychiatrist present. I looked forward to having my parents and brother there with me so we could finally talk about things that we never talked about as a family. We rarely spoke about my therapy or the fact that I was on medication other than when my parents would ask how things were going. "Fine," I would tell them, and that was that. Being the identified patient, I felt separate - apart from the rest of them. It seemed like everything was fine in our family except for me because I was depressed. So, one bright sunny afternoon my family and I met with my therapist and psychiatrist.

No one said a thing. There were a couple of questions asked but the overall tone of the session was, "We're fine, we don't know why we're here, Kim's depressed and we don't know what to do."

Afterward, in the car on the way home, they laughed and joked about being there. "What a waste of time," they said. "No need for that again." I felt ashamed and humiliated for the hope I'd had of the session as a metamorphosis for our family. I'd envisioned us emerging from the cocoon of Iris's office united in a journey toward truth and healing. When they laughed and made fun, I knew I was definitely in this alone, whatever this was.

This, it turned out, was major depression. Over the years, my diagnosis has evolved, along with the DSM, now known as the DSM-IV: Clinical depression, major depression, chemical depression and finally, bi-polar disorder type II. That's my diagnosis, although my tendencies run to the depressive side of the pole.

Mental illness. I'm forty-four now and it's still a delicate subject for me. As an adolescent, it was horrifying. I'm not sure which would have been worse: the other kids finding out about my "condition," or starting my period at school in a pair of white jeans with no hygiene products.

Imagine you're in an enormous vat of peanut butter. You're immersed, though somehow, still able to breathe. Try to walk. Try to move your head or blink. Try moving your arms and hands. You can do it, but it will take forever and everything you try to do is exhausting. The peanut butter fills your mouth and ears. Talking is a chore and aural sensory, dim.

Oh dear. You just dropped your car keys, and you're late for class/meeting/work/whatever. All that peanut butter is heavy, pressing against you from all sides. By the time you pick up those keys, it will be too late even to try to keep your commitments. So tired. So fatigued and frustrated.

Fuck the keys. Leave them on the floor. Who cares now? Lie down. Even that requires herculean effort and when you're finally lying there, it's too much effort to move so you lay there like a lump. With the pressure of the peanut butter against your body, it feels like it's all you can do to breathe.

Now imagine there's another giant vat right next to yours, except that one is filled with cool, clear water. Your friends and family are in it. You can see them and they can see you, but they can't see the peanut butter.

What the hell is wrong with you? They ask. You missed your class/meeting/work/whatever because of *what*? They do not understand why you are lying there like a lump, barely able to blink, in the middle of the day, having blown off your responsibilities. Snap out of it. What the hell's the matter with you? You know, if you exercised more/ate right/got out of the house more often/cheered up/looked at the bright side of life/took the right pills, you might...

Take the right pills. The right medication. Yes, indeed. The right combinations of chemicals that will make me feel "normal." The magic formula to wash all this peanut butter away so I wouldn't have to try and explain it to people.

So when people asked:

What? You live in big vat of invisible peanut butter?

I could respond:

Whaddaya, think I'm crazy? No, I was just joking about that. Hey, pass me the bottle/joint/straw/pipe, would you, please? Because I know my doctor said I'd feel better soon, when we get the medications adjusted, but I need to feel better *right now*.

When I wasn't abusing substances, I was manically chasing my feelings away using other methods. Like overloading my life taking care of other people.

After three years, I decided to stop fostering children. It was too stressful both emotionally and physically, and I wanted my former life back with just Andy and myself. So when my last child left for his new adoptive family, I closed my foster home.

I was fine for a while, working and taking care of Andy, but my parents suggested going back to school. What a splendid idea! With the foster children gone, I now had oodles of time on my hands, what with working full time and raising Andy. To be fair, the decision was mine. I really did feel abruptly empty with too much space, both inside and out, to fill.

I was in my late twenties at the time and I know I shouldn't have cared as much as I did about what they thought, but I craved their approval. More than anything, I wanted them to be proud of me, and I figured that maybe if I finished my degree in psychology, I would finally win their hearts and become the daughter they'd always wanted.

So I dove in. I took classes during the day while Andy was at school, and I had him with me at night when I worked at a hospital daycare from three to midnight. A van service would drop him off after his therapy, and we would go home when I was done with my shift. Then we would get up at six-thirty in the morning and start all over again.

I started feeling angry. I thought I was angry with my parents for always pushing me and never letting me just *be*. I was perfectly fine working and raising Andy. I didn't care about finishing my degree. When I was working on it the first few years after Andy was born, I was an honors student doing research and planning on going to graduate school. But I started falling apart. I had flashbacks during class of when Andy was a baby - of performing CPR on my son, of that time in the hospital when they called code blue on him (the first code blue ever called on the pediatric floor at that time) and all the times I called the ambulance to the house. I kept picturing him dead. I didn't know what was going on and I didn't tell anyone what was happening because I was ashamed. I was mortified that these thoughts and images were so dominant in my mind all the time. What kind of mother fantasizes about her child dying? Especially in the middle of an American Lit class. I was worried it might be a sign that deep down I wanted to hurt him. How could I possibly tell anyone that I was having such sick thoughts?

Finally, I reached the point that I stopped going to classes because the flashbacks came so often and I couldn't keep myself from falling apart in front of everyone. Embarrassed as I was, I was more worried about the connotations for Andy. I was terrified there might be a dark part of me that wanted to hurt him. Why else would I be having these horrible thoughts and images? Finally, I was in such agony that I talked to a professor I'd done independent study with in the area of adolescent psychology. I sobbed into my hands as I explained what was going on, and told her how worried I was about what it all might mean. She recommended I talk to someone who had experience treating post-traumatic stress disorder, or PTSD.

Huh?

PTSD is something soldiers have when they've seen heavy combat, right? Men and women who were in the Vietnam War or Desert Storm. PTSD is a serious condition that stems from having witnessed trauma and death and man's inhumanity to man. I'm a middle class white chick from Boise, Idaho whose son was born with a few problems. What the hell do I have to complain about? There are millions of people in the world in significantly worse situations. I don't *deserve* a diagnosis like PTSD, I told the therapist I'd started seeing.

I did go through a major trauma with Andy, she pointed out. At one time, his medical situation was so bad that I started thinking about what I would do for his funeral. How big would the casket be? Would I rather have him cremated? What would I do with the ashes? But that's not what caused me to have all the flashbacks and other problems. The post-traumatic stress occurred years later because I didn't deal with my feelings when I was having them. I never stopped to allow myself to feel scared, angry, sad or helpless. Anytime I came close, the people around me were there to tell me that I was overreacting. "You're strong. You can do this. Andy needs you, Kimbo. You can't fall apart. You can't get upset every time the doctor talks to you. You can't get mad at the doctors. I'm worried about you. You're crying too much. Cheer up, things could always be worse." It's the same message I've heard since I was a little girl. I feel too much, I cry too much, I need too much, there's no reason for me to feel the way I do.

So I stuff my feelings as far down as I can rather than dealing with them as they come, because I'm afraid of them. I don't want to be an oversensitive mess of a woman. I want to be like other people, and when I look around, everyone else seems to have it all together.

I dropped out of school when Andy was little because, in light of everything that was happening, working toward something I wasn't sure I wanted in the first place didn't make sense. Leaving seemed the right decision for me.

When I decided to stop fostering children, I did go back to school, but I was angry. I thought I was angry with my parents, but that wasn't true. I was mad at myself for doing something that I didn't really want to do. And I was doing it because I was still seeking validation. Mostly I was mad because I was aware how pathetic it was that, as an adult, I was still such a child. Pathetic or not, though, that was how I came to enroll in school for the third time.

I was exhausted. A psychology degree is useless unless you intend to go to graduate school, and since I knew I didn't want to do that, the only goal I had was to obtain a piece of paper that said I'd graduated: Tangible proof that I'd finally done something worthwhile. Even so, I obsessed about my grades. I studied every chance I got, but uninterrupted study time was next to impossible. When first semester finals loomed, I started to panic, and on a Saturday afternoon, I made a phone call to my brother that changed my life forever.

Chapter 4

Chuck, who's two years younger than I am, lived a somewhat bohemian lifestyle. My brother spent most of his twenties wandering the streets of San Francisco and following the Grateful Dead around in his weathered VW van. Just before Andy was born, he lived on a beach in Hawaii.

By the time I decided to go back to school again, he'd settled back in Boise and lived with a woman and their two small children just around the corner from Andy and me. He delivered pizza and still led a hippie lifestyle, so when I decided I needed something to keep me going during finals, I figured he'd be able to help me. We'd partied together in the past, so it wasn't a big deal for me to ask him to get me some crank. "I just need to get through finals," I told him.

He got me a quarter of a gram and it lasted me the whole week. I would snort a line or two after Andy was in bed, study all night and take a nap during the day between classes and work. Things went along swimmingly. I aced all my finals and felt like Wonder Woman. I've always loved the rush of speed. I had plenty of energy to clean my house and I could get more done at work. I also lost a few pounds, and I don't know of a woman alive, no matter how thin or fat, who wouldn't count that as a huge bonus.

Weight loss. For women especially, that's one of the biggest draws to meth. Whether it's the reason they try it in the first place, or if it's a welcome side effect, losing weight becomes powerful reinforcement to continue using. It seems so easy at first: no appetite, tons of energy. You're a Goddess. You can do everything: take care of your family, run errands, cook and clean, work, shop for groceries, take the kids to practice and lessons. Until it's too late, and too late comes too quick. For some people, it only takes one time. Others may use for a few days or a week before it turns on them, but it always does. And the result is always the same. One hundred percent of the time. Meth will rip you apart and destroy you, no matter who you are, and by then it won't matter how thin you are or how clean your house is because the whole picture is uglier than anything you can possibly imagine. But right then, it worked for me. I got exactly what I thought I wanted that first week. Then the week was over and the crank was gone.

And I crashed.

Although I slept every day while I was doing it, for at least a few hours, when I ran out of drugs, I became lethargic. All I wanted to do was sleep. I couldn't stay awake at work. Driving was scary because my eyelids were like lead. I started wearing rubber bands on my wrist, snapping them to stay alert. I couldn't stay awake to play with Andy and had no energy to do anything around the house. I felt awful, and I didn't want to feel awful, I wanted to feel good again. I wanted my super powers back so I could do all the things I'd been doing when I had the drug. I wanted to be a Goddess.

So I called my brother again.

"It's different this time," he told me.

"What do you mean?"

"It's called meth. It's just like crank, only better. Much cleaner and a way bigger high."

A better high for the same price. Who would turn down that?

Again, I bought a quarter of a gram, the smallest amount you can buy, that cost twenty-five dollars. He was right. I fell in love with the first line I snorted, and that was the end for me. The end of everything I knew and cherished for a long time to come.

The only reason I never started using needles is because I knew I would never go back. Shooting up is the end of the line, and since I didn't shoot up, it was easier to convince myself that I wasn't really an addict.

I loved meth, and I loved the ritual of snorting lines: chopping it, crushing it, making intricate patterns. But the day someone showed me how to smoke it, I never went back to snorting. When that rush hit my brain, a single tear dropped. I was finally home. The exact words I said when I called my brother were, "I want to do *this* drug in *this* way for the rest of my life." Those words will haunt me to my grave.

Meth, in the form of an opaque, white cloud of smoke, entered my brain and my soul at the same time, filling the emptiness inside me. It was as if I'd finally found what I'd been searching for my whole life. All my insecurities evaporated, and I was finally the woman I wanted to be. I was funnier, smarter, more confident and enormously productive. Every addict I know says the same thing, in one way or another: their drug of choice filled that empty space in their soul that nothing else could touch. It's the same thing as the creepy man in the van offering candy to a child. Who doesn't want candy? When you take it, though, it's too late and everything you knew and loved will vanish in the back of that dark van. The man with the pretty candy that tasted so good only wants you for his own dark, sinister pleasure, and just as the sweetness starts to melt in your mouth, it's too late.

For me, the man with the candy was meth. The day I smoked my first bowl was the day I climbed in the back of the van, and it took me years to find my way home again.

Within a week, getting high became a daily habit. I started buying in larger quantities. Meth is a commodity like any other product, and the more you purchase, the lower the price.

I would pool my money with my brother or someone else, and split the meth between us.

That's how most people start dealing. If enough people contribute to the buy, you get your drugs free, and that's how it started for me. Chuck didn't want to be involved with buying larger quantities, and eventually introduced me to his dealer, Garnett.

Garnett was a lanky man with horn-rimmed glasses and a mess of loose curls that fell to his shoulders. He was soft spoken when I first met him, ducking his head beneath his hair when he wasn't wearing a battered Fedora. He seemed almost fragile. We met in May, and when spring melted into summer, his knobby knees and pointy elbows occasionally peeked from beneath his Bermudas or short-sleeved shirts. He was bright, interesting and funny, and we became friends immediately, spending more and more time together over the next couple of months. There was nothing about him, initially, that indicated the destructive malevolence behind the meek façade. Nothing that indicated the true Garnett. The one I would, unfortunately, become well acquainted with in the near future.

He was a drug dealer. That was his full time job. Prior to that, he and his friends from high school worked at the same pizza parlor as Chuck. They were all close friends with my brother, playing poker, Ultimate and Frisbee golf in their free time. Garnett started spending more time with me and before long, I met all the guys, occasionally joining in the card games, or hosting all night bull sessions. Among them, I felt like a queen. I was one of the guys, separated only by sex, and therefore treated like both a lady and a pal. I was elite in an exclusive club whose books were closed. I felt special.

Meanwhile, I started buying meth more often. People I knew who used preferred the quality I could get as well as the lower prices I offered. I wasn't out to make money; I just wanted to get high. As long as my share was paid for, I didn't charge any more than I had to in order to get the lower price. Word got out, people I knew started buying for their friends, and I began buying larger quantities. By the end of summer, I was making a couple hundred extra dollars per month on top of what I was using myself. As a single mom always struggling to makes ends meet, it felt good to be able to afford extra things for Andy. I paid the bills on time and in full. We could buy name brand food and fresh produce. There was extra money so we could go to the movies occasionally and have our picture taken together at a studio for Christmas presents for Grandma and Papa. I had the money Andy needed for field trips at school, so he never had to miss out on activities with his peers. I also had the energy and stamina to do everything I needed to do. That's how I started seriously dealing meth. It wasn't as much a conscious decision as it was an evolution.

I was out of school for the summer. Andy qualified for extended school year (summer school) due to his disability, and he still went to developmental therapy as well. Since I didn't have to go to work until three, I had most of the day free and it was then that I went about the business of dealing drugs. I always had all the meth I wanted, so once I started dealing, I never experienced the crash that comes with sudden withdrawal. Occasionally, Garnett would run out and we would have to wait a day or two before he could pick up again, but I usually had some stashed away. I never went more than a day without being able to use. It was simple: I loved getting high, I had unlimited access, and for the first time since Andy was born I was able to take care of us both without worrying about whether or not we could pay the electric and the gas bill each month.

I realize, now, how unreal this sounds. Now that I'm in my right mind, the way I rationalized what was happening is ludicrous. The constant influence of meth and the seduction of easy money made everything seem worth the risk. Sitting here sober, telling you about the woman I was then, I'm embarrassed and disgusted. It's obvious now that I was addicted to meth the first time I tried it, but it wasn't clear to me then. I was Charlie Bucket and I'd just found the last golden ticket. At the time, meth seemed the answer to all my problems when, in fact, it was just the beginning of them.

About that time, two things happened almost simultaneously. My brother broke up with his girlfriend and then disappeared without a trace, leaving his two young children behind. Soon after that, I lost my job.

Chuck and I were close. Our bitter sibling rivalry during childhood mellowed to deep friendship in our adult years. When he vanished, it was easy for me to use the heartbreak of the situation to validate my increasingly erratic behavior.

I started showing up late to work. At first, it was only a few minutes, a day here and a day there. Then I started coming back from lunch late. My chronic tardiness became an almost daily event, and a few minutes turned to half an hour or more. I was distraught over my brother's unexplained absence, I told my boss and co-workers. He left behind a mess. Between trying to help his family, everything I had going on with Andy's therapy, school and everything in between, I was overwhelmed. I was doing my best to stay afloat in a sea of obligations. I was a martyr.

Maybe people bought the sob story for a while, but I was never quite able to convince myself completely. I remember rushing around the house at the last minute, or later, out of breath, looking for my keys, taking one last hit off the pipe, and then another. And all the while, I would think to myself, "*Why* am I late again? I have so much on my plate trying to deal with everything that's going on in my life. People just don't understand." Poor, poor me. As hard as I tried to make myself believe that my brother's disappearance had such a grave effect on me, the real truth was this: I could never get high enough to leave my house.

I'm not sure when that knowledge hit me. Today I can see it clearly. All those times I was late or blew people off entirely were because I could never get my high right. Sunday dinners missed. Ruined Christmases and Thanksgivings, Mother's Day's, birthdays, and weddings. I was late for my grandmother's funeral where I was to give the eulogy I wrote. They couldn't start without me.

I'm not sure if I knew it back at the beginning, but I suspect that somewhere very deep inside me, I did. That's a frightening concept, though, and one that speaks to something much bigger than, "I just like to get high." Even if I'd had any inkling, the thought would have been inconceivable, as it nearly is now. It was easier to blame someone or something else for my troubles, and my brother's vanishing act coincided perfectly with the beginning of my downward spiral.

I would smoke and smoke, as fast and deep as possible, desperately trying to take as much of the drug with me as I could. I would get irritated when I had obligations to meet. I could feel my stomach tighten, my heart race and my muscles tense. The world and everyone in it expected too much from me. Why couldn't they just leave me alone?

Addicts are great at shunning responsibility. Nothing is ever our fault. The universe has conspired to make our lives miserable. Ask any addict, especially an active one, and they'll tell you the same thing. We try, man, we really try, but the system's got us down. The landlord's an asshole. Fuckin' boss is prejudiced. Cop pulled me over. Long line at the store. Battery died. Ran out of gas. Alarm didn't go off. Up all night with the kid. Left my woman and kids because she's a bitch. No, *she* cheated on *me*. Locked myself out of the house/car/office. The goldfish died.

Addicts excel at blame, but the truth always boils down to the fact that in one way or another, we just can't get high enough to leave the house.

So I told myself, and anyone who asked, that I lost my job because I was so distraught over my brother that I fell apart. I was worried about him and his family and damn it, as his big sister, I by God had to *do* something.

Like stay home and get high.

Meth was everything to me. And every*one*: My lover, friend, parent, sibling and shrink. It took the place of everyone I've ever wanted or needed.

Wake up in the morning and see a beautiful sunrise? Smoke a bowl. Bad day at the office? Smoke a bowl. Time for celebration? Feeling down? Smoke a bowl. Want to go out dancing on a Saturday night? Smoke a bowl. Curl up under the covers and watch movies all day? Don't forget your dope. Entire family coming for Sunday dinner? *Damn* sure, don't forget your dope.

After my brother disappeared, I started spending even more time with Garnett. Most of the time, he would come to the house late, after Andy was asleep, and we'd listen to music, get high and talk. Occasionally, though, Andy would spend the night with Mom and Dad and I would go to his house instead. That was my introduction to the Gentleman's Club.

The Gentleman's Club was simply Garnett's basement, but the name stemmed from the fact that no women were allowed. It was where "the boys" hung out, played cribbage or cards, smoked, did drugs, played guitars, and mostly, hid from the women in their lives. When he first moved into the house, the basement was nothing but the unfinished, dirt-floored, spider-infested bowel of the house. The boys told me it took him a while to turn it into his own private Idaho. The result was impressive. The dirt floor was compact with rugs laid down, and the walls were clear of debris. Personal items hung here and there, as they would in any home. He built a table that stretched from the rear wall far into the room, dividing the basement into what eventually became part laundry room, part Gentlemen's Club. Tiny Christmas lights lined the beams of the low ceiling creating a lovely, intimate lounge-like atmosphere. A little table and a few chairs sat beneath a small window at the back of the room, alongside the table he'd built. There were a couple of bookshelves with a mish-mashed collection of literature and videos, and another shelf with a TV and VCR.

I was the only woman ever allowed in the Club, including Garnett's wife, who'd lived in the house prior to their recent divorce. She was a taboo subject. The boys told me never to bring it up, and I never did. I figured if he wanted to talk about it, he'd let me know.

When I was there, he never invited anyone else. The two of us played cards sometimes, but mostly we talked. An evening shared will turn a stranger into a soul mate when you're using meth. Meth lowers inhibitions, and that combined with lack of sleep, often leads to all night talk marathons where people will unabashedly offer up their deepest fears and darkest secrets. More often, the mundane feels like extraordinary bonding.

"Have you ever read this book?"

"Oh my God. Yes! You have, too?"

"Yeah, but no one else I know has read it."

"Did you get the part about..."

"When the guy..."

"I know! Have you read..."

"I was just thinking the same thing. The one by that other guy? Where he talks about kind of the same thing?"

"I can't believe you were thinking that, too."

"Well, it's so *obvious*."

"To people like us, I guess. Ha ha ha ha."

"There's a movie out right now based on the book. Want to go see it?"

"No. Let's just stay down here in the basement. I don't want to leave."

"Cool! Me either!"

"Want to smoke another bowl?"

"Hell yes!"

That's what it's like. You talk and talk and talk and share all these drugs and pretty soon you realize you've finally found the one person on the face of the earth who understands you and doesn't judge you, and you feel the same about them. My God! How did we make it this far in life without each other, and isn't it fabulous that we're finally together?

That's what happened with Garnett and me down in that basement. Too many hours, too much meth and zero interruption from the world outside. I felt a bond with him that I'd never shared with another human, let alone a man. That's what the meth told me, and I believed it because I so desperately wanted to. It told me I was special enough to take precedence over everyone else in someone's life and it wasn't because he wanted sex. He was truly interested in me as a person. He told me I was smart, he laughed at my humor and he made me feel pretty, complimenting me when I wore something new or fixed my hair in a different way.

My history with men is one of mistrust. There were incidents throughout my childhood: brothers of friends, fathers of friends, friends of my brother, and once, a friend of my parents. These were not incidents of rape, but of inappropriate touching and teasing, or a mid-night awakening to a cold, rough, unwelcome hand in my panties when I was nine.

One night when I was sixteen, my parents and another couple came home late at night after being out doing whatever it was they were doing that involved drinking. They were drunk when they got to the house. They came into the living room, talking and laughing in that sloshy way that people do on late Saturday nights. I don't remember how it started, but the man began to tickle me. One minute, I was sitting on the fireplace hearth, and the next, I was on the floor in the living room and this man is on top of me. He's stinking of whiskey and tickling me, working his stiff fingers into the flesh of my stomach while the backs of his hands brushed against my breasts. My parents and his wife, who'd been sitting on the sofa, adjourned to the kitchen for another drink, leaving me on the floor with this man. A couple of minutes later, his wife called to him, yelling at him for being immature. He got up and left me there on the floor like a used condom.

I felt ashamed and wanted to cry. I wanted to go into the kitchen, slap him across the face, and make him leave the house and never come back. Actually, I wanted my dad to do that, but he didn't. It was as if nothing out of the ordinary had happened. Maybe it wasn't a big deal. No one else thought it was. I remember laying there for what seemed like forever, confused, not knowing what to do, listening to the four of them laughing and talking in the other room, feeling ashamed that my parents had seen what had happened.

I learned long before that, though, that men and boys are not to be trusted and will always hurt you. I was eleven years old in the sixth grade when a group of my classmates, all boys, and our teacher, who was also male, taught me lessons I will never forget.

There was never anything "cool" about me. I wasn't the dorkiest kid in the room, I was just there, craving popularity and boyfriends just like all my other members of the not-the-dorkiest-kid-in-the-room club. My best friend and I spent hours after school at her house daydreaming about boys and wishing we were as pretty and well liked as some other girls in our grade.

Why couldn't we be like those girls? Why couldn't we have perfect hair and afford cute clothes? Why couldn't we be Sandy and find our Danny and live happily ever after? I loved the movie *Grease* and I fantasized about one day breaking out of my geek-shell and showing everyone how cool I really was by wearing black leather, teasing my hair and dancing in the Shake-Shack at the school carnival. Well, maybe not that exactly, but I dwelled on the metamorphosis fantasy. One day, something would happen that would make people, boys in particular, notice me and say, "Holy shit! Where did *she* come from? That's Kim? Why didn't we notice her all this time? She's gorgeous. And just look at how cool she is."

So there I was: a typical pre-teen girl with stars in her eyes and dreams of one day becoming homecoming queen.

To this day, I don't know why the following events took place. Maybe I wear my heart on my sleeve. Maybe it had something to do with the fact that I was one of only four little girls in an all male class taught by a male teacher in a school with a male principal in the late '70's. Whatever the reason, I became a target.

It started with a note passed to me from the cutest boy in my class who I'd had a crush on since fifth grade. He was one of the most popular boys of all three classes that made up the sixth grade. He passed a note, folded and smudged, to his friend who flicked it onto my desk. I had to double check the name on it to be sure it was for me. Taking care to keep it out of view of the teacher, I unfolded it in my lap and read it.

<u>Will you go with me?</u>

<u>Yes</u>

<u>No</u>

It happened! My wish came true. I looked at the sender to see him flashing a million dollar smile, and in that smile I saw junior high dances and roller skating dates, football games, Saturday night movies, high school pep rallies and bon fires.

I checked the yes box and sent it back, barely able to contain my excitement. I couldn't wait to tell my best friend at recess. Would he kiss me? Would he sit next to me at lunchtime? Would he want me to sit with him and his friends? I wasn't clear on the rules of "going together," but I was anxious to learn.

I looked over to smile at my very first boyfriend - who was laughing and passing the note around to his buddies who were all laughing with him. "Aaa ha ha ha ha! She fell for it. Hey, stupid, you really fell for that, huh? You really thought he wanted to go with *you?* Aaaa ha ha ha ha!"

I'd like to say I was humiliated, but there are no words that describe exactly how I felt. Those boys confirmed what I'd only suspected all along: I was an ugly, dorky little girl, just like I thought, and now I was stupid enough to fall for their trick to boot. I should have known better. How could I be so stupid? Why would any boy, let alone one of the elite, want to be my boyfriend?

But it didn't end there.

The group of boys took turns writing those notes with the stupid check boxes, and I kept falling for it. The note from the next boy would be longer, apologizing for his friend, saying he would never do that to me. I would get what was left of my hopes up, only to be smacked back down. In retrospect, the reason I continued to fall for their asinine game is the same logic that's caused me a lot of trouble in my life. I want so much to be liked that I'll do things for acceptance that are not in my best interest. I think I knew that none of those boys would want to be my boyfriend. I just wasn't in their echelon. But maybe there was a chance that one of those notes would be genuine, and maybe if I just stuck it out and kept taking it in the chin, everything would pay off eventually.

Finally, the embarrassment was too painful and I stopped checking the yes box. When it became harder to get a rise out of me, they started calling me at my friend's house, sweet-talking over the phone only to bash me the next day at school. When I stopped falling for their bullshit altogether, that's when the abuse began.

Standing in line to go to lunch or to recess, I heard the stage whispers and hisses. "Bitch. Stuck up cunt. Slut." Walking in the hallway to the library or to music class, a hand would reach out and grab my chest or sometimes my crotch. The grabbing turned to pinching and twisting and I would go home some nights and look in the mirror at the yellow and green bruises on my budding, little girl breasts.

I had terrifying, reoccurring nightmares of men dressed in black turtleneck sweaters, pants and ski hats coming over the backyard fence to get me. In my dreams, they would carry machetes and knives to stab me with, or catch me and drag me into the garage where they would pour scalding hot water down my shirt while laughing. These dreams went on for years and while I don't know when they stopped, I remember them vividly to this day.

It started happening all the time: recess, lunchtime, music, during class, in the hallways, during class films when the lights went out. The abuse was blatant. I knew everyone saw what was happening to me, but no one tried to stop it. No one stepped forward to say it was wrong, so, ashamed and confused, I laughed it off at school and cried myself to sleep at night. It felt like everyone not directly involved, including the teachers, just pretended not to notice. Maybe that's why I never told my parents what was happening. No one at school seemed to think it was a big deal, so it must not have been. But I felt dirty and ashamed. If I cried, they made fun of me and the pinching and twisting and grabbing and name-calling got worse. I didn't understand why it was happening. I was confused, and the worst part may be how I felt about it at the time, because I still wanted those boys to like me. I wanted the other kids to like me, too. I wanted everything to stop, but I didn't want people to think I was un-cool or a bitch, so I never stood up for myself the way I should have. I guess I thought if no one else was going to protect me, I wasn't worth protecting.

I hated that year. I hated that teacher and hated those boys, most of whom I would spend the next six years going to school with. I tried to block it all out and never think of it again. But inevitably, those memories would sneak up on me, catch me off guard and hurl me into a black hole of self-hatred and fury so overwhelming, it was all I could do to lock it all away again. During those times, I would think about those boys. Those mean little fuckers with smug looks who were popular all through high school. The asshole pricks that played football, always had dates to the dances and to movies on Saturday nights. The guys who were honored at pep rallies, whooped, and hollered during the school bonfires. I never went to any of those things. I never dated anyone I went to school with. No parties, no kisses, no fooling around. I watched from a distance as those boys grew into young men, and I wondered how they treated the girls they dated.

I would often think about that group of boys throughout high school and even into my twenties, and I would pray harder than I've ever prayed for anything that they would all have daughters. And I would pray that their daughters would go through what I went through and suffer the way I suffered, and that those boys-turned-dads would one day feel a little of my agony. For a long time, the thought that this indeed might someday happen was the only thing I had to help me keep those memories from engulfing me. Jagged thoughts of long, cold revenge were the only thing that would chase the self-loathing and fury away.

I'm five years clean now and I know that some of those boys did grow up to have daughters, and some of those daughters are the age now that I was then. What I think now is this: I hope that those little girls have people in their lives that are looking out for them, because every little girl is worth protecting. Even the daughters of douche bags.

So it was in the sixth grade that I learned two important lessons. A) When a boy/man shows interest, beware, and never believe anything they tell you, and B) Boys/men hold the power in the world.

To this day, I have no idea when a man is flirting with me. I assume it never happens, although people tell me otherwise. If I do happen to notice when a man shows interest in me, I go straight into bullshit mode. I immediately establish myself as "one of the guys," which gives me instant protection from rejection with the "friend" label, and diminishes my sexuality. "No, of course I'm not interested in you, we're friends, and that's why you're not interested in me." No mess, no fuss, no chance of heartache. This is the way my mind works.

I never said I didn't have issues.

So with Garnett, I felt fabulous. We were close friends, but he treated me like a lady rather than just a buddy. I'd never had a relationship with a man that was so intense and didn't include sex. I knew he respected me and was interested in what I thought. I felt special.

Until the night I saw Ron Jeremy suck his own dick.

Chapter 5

Garnett was moody. Sometimes he was funny, bright and a joy to be with. Other times, he would get agitated for no apparent reason, pacing back and forth beneath the beams of the basement's ceiling and mumbling to himself. At those times, he would leave me alone while he went to meet someone to sell them drugs. Fifteen minutes, he'd say. Two and a half hours later, he'd come back with no explanation. Sometimes he was extremely calm and gentle. Other times he'd be amped up, pacing the basement floor and talking to himself again. I never knew what to do when that happened because he was between the staircase and me, blocking my exit, and something told me that it was in my best interest to be as invisible as possible while he worked through whatever was haunting him. Usually, I just quietly wrote in my journal and got high, waiting for him to calm down.

Occasionally, he'd return with a surprise for me: Imported chocolate, some trinket I'd had my eye on, or a video for us to watch.

"Miss Kim," he would say. "I hope you haven't seen this one already." Then he'd slide in the tape, arrange the table with our chairs on either side, turn off all but the Christmas lights and begin the movie.

Then, one evening, he called to tell me he would be home soon. A couple of minutes later, he walked down the stairs with a tape in his hand. He stood next to the TV, looked at me, opened and closed his mouth twice, popped the video in and sat down in his usual spot across the table from me. No formalities, no lights, just wham-bam-thank-you-ma'am. I had no idea why he was acting so strange, but figured a ninety-minute break from talking wasn't a bad idea.

I sat there, calmly getting high and staring at the infamous porn star, Ron Jeremy in his Penishead costume. I was raging inside. Same shit, different day. Garnett was just another man playing games.

I could never quite figure out what his objective was. He never made any advances toward me, and our relationship was platonic, but he was obsessed with pornography. We never talked about it, but he would occasionally show me a movie or give me a book of erotic stories and have me read a particular one to myself. I think he just liked to watch me. I have no other explanation.

He started taking me with him to certain places to meet people. He would introduce me as his lady friend, and would give me a rock of meth to smoke while I waited for him to take care of his customer in another room. After a few visits, he was more comfortable about conducting business with me in the room, speaking in hushed tones and he weighed and packaged the product. People trusted me. I never looked anyone in the eye until they spoke to me, and I smoked meth in great, huge hits that impressed even the most seasoned tweaker. Garnett and I knew a man who blew glass and would make beautiful, sturdy, long lasting pipes and innovative bongs for smoking. People were envious and looked forward to our visits. Most people who smoked did so using light bulbs or tiny glass tubes sold at the counter in convenience stores.

We were rock stars. He only took me to two places, and neither of them was too bad. I'd heard of places akin to meth dens that were filthy: families whose children went unattended and unfed, apartments and trailers with a rotating cast of seedy characters, covered in open sores, crouched in corners shooting up or nodding off on sofas and dirty mattresses. I heard about these places from Garnett and his friends, and from some of the people I sold to. I suspect some of them dwelled in places like those, but I never saw it, so it was easy to dismiss. They were the great unwashed. The addicts. The tweakers. They were the ones who couldn't handle their drugs. Poor, poor pathetic creatures. As long as I never sank to those depths, I didn't have a problem. I was different. I could handle my high. I told myself that for years, and it was the belief in that lie that played a huge part in not only the duration, but the depth of my addiction. Appearance is everything. I'd learned that growing up. As long as everything looks okay on the outside, what's going on underneath doesn't matter.

Garnett's dealer, Kilo, was like some exotic myth to me. All I knew was that he was Asian, younger than we were and that he drove a Lexus. I also knew that Garnett was in awe of him. I would listen to him talking on the phone in the basement, arranging a meeting to which I was specifically excluded. Garnett would gather his things, eager to get to the rendezvous. He was usually in a good mood when he returned, and we'd sample the new batch: bright, shiny crystals of meth the size of a piece of Chiclets gum. We would test it using bleach, even though we knew the product was excellent. When you've seen the best, worst and everything in between hundreds of times, you know good product when you see it. Like an appraiser of diamonds, only you don't need a monocle.

We always did the bleach test because it was fun. Fill a glass halfway with bleach and drop a little meth into it. It doesn't have to be much, just a pinch. If it's good, it will fizz. Pure stuff will "dance," or spin around on the surface of the liquid. Anything that's not meth will sink to the bottom of the glass.

So we'd do the bleach test and ooh and aah while we smoked bowl after bowl, and he would weigh the amount I was picking up from him and we would smoke some more. The nights he came back from seeing Kilo were always a celebration, like Christmas or your birthday. We'd talk and laugh and joke about the people we sold to who were spun – the ones who had gone over the edge. We joked about the losers who couldn't handle the drug, and congratulated each other because we could. Then he'd whip out the porn. And I would sit there, getting high, watching the movie, while he watched me. And I would think to myself how good it was that I didn't have a problem, and how lucky I was to have all the meth I wanted, and that it was a small thing - probably not a big deal -that the tradeoff was hanging out with this weird fetishist, who I was beginning to not like very much.

The other tradeoff was that I was spending less time with Andy. I was asking my parents to watch him for the night or have him spend the night with them, more often. I rationalized by telling myself that I had to take care of business, keep making money, and I didn't want him anywhere near the drug or the people involved in the meth world. I told myself I was a good mother, and that I was sacrificing time I would rather be spending with him was for his own good.

The truth is I began to choose meth over my son.

I look at those words on the page, and they nauseate me. To come to terms with that, to be able to admit it, has been far and away the most difficult part of my recovery. Andy. My bug in a boy suit. He's the best thing that ever happened to me and the best thing I've ever done with my life, and I chose methamphetamine over spending time with him.

I knew, somewhere deep inside, that something was happening to me; that I was changing into someone I didn't want to be. I could feel myself being sucked into Garnett's world, and it didn't so much frighten me as it did disgust me. I was trading my soul - the very essence of who I am - for meth, and the more I sold out, the more I tried to smoke away my guilt and shame. The guilt was all about my son. The shame was about spending all the time I could in a basement either watching dirty movies or tip-toeing around a man whose behavior was becoming more erratic each day. His mood swings and "pace and mumble" sessions increased, and they scared me, but I tolerated them. I tolerated it all so that I could have my precious drug.

It was also getting harder to lie to my parents about where the money was coming from when I wasn't working. The house that Andy and I rented belonged to them, and they were worried that I wouldn't be able to pay the rent if I didn't find work soon.

Then, my brother called.

When he disappeared, he'd hopped in his VW and, like Kerouac and Cassady, hit the road with no destination other than away from the responsibilities he decided he'd had enough of. The van broke down in Nevada, about 40 miles south of the Idaho border, in a speck of a town called Jackpot. Population: 1,500.

The town sits, surrounded by desert, at the base of a hill that rises up out of dull, dead sagebrush, at the end of a lonely stretch of a two-lane highway. From the top of that dirt mound, just before swooping down on the town like a vulture, you can see that the gambling oasis is less than two miles long. Jackpot may be a speck in the middle of nowhere, but it's also collectively the biggest employer in southern Idaho. People commute from nearby rural towns to work at one of the five casinos. There's also a post office, general store, gas station, school and liquor store. One of each.

It was in this gambling Mecca, at one of the casinos, that my brother was working as a cook and living with the woman who was his supervisor. He was even considering seeing his children again. Life was good for Chuck, as it usually was. He has a habit of breezing from one situation to the next with little effort on his part, simply ignoring whatever or whomever he leaves in his wake.

As pissed off as I was at him for leaving his family in Boise, let alone me, without a word of explanation or goodbye, I was relieved to hear from him. I was worried about him, of course, but the other reason, the main reason, was because of Garnett.

Garnett's behavior was becoming even more erratic. He wasn't showing me movies anymore. Instead, he started giving me books with stories in them about bondage and sado-masochism. He would talk about how his ultimate fantasy was to be dominated and that so far, he hadn't found anyone willing to indulge him.

He was also becoming more agitated and secretive about his increasing trips when he'd leave me in the basement alone, getting high.

Since Garnett was the only person I spent time with, it was easy to forgive and forget with Chuck, if only to have a confidant who could perhaps shed some light on what was going on in the Gentlemen's Club.

I drove down and spent a weekend in Jackpot, mostly staying in my hotel room with the curtains drawn, sitting on the bed getting high, but also seeing and talking to my brother. He seemed content, and more than that, he seemed peaceful. I stayed for two days and at the end of those two days, with my head in a cloud of meth smoke, my brain steeped in chemicals and an overwhelming desire to get away from Garnett, I went home, sold half of everything I owned and moved Andy and myself to Jackpot, Nevada. Population: 1,502.

Chapter 6

I told my parents and Garnett that I just had to get away from the craziness of the city, that I was disillusioned with people, that I'd lost faith in humanity. I needed a simpler life and I needed my brother. I'd lost my job through no fault of my own, I told them, and I simply didn't know what to do. Moving my son and myself to a desert town where there's nothing to do except gamble 24/7 was just what I needed to rejuvenate myself and get a fresh start.

I got a job tending bar, though I'd never done more than pour beer at the local race track. Chuck watched Andy for me, and from midnight to seven am, I worked solo in the only bar in town that had no gambling. Not even machines. It was the bartender's bar. The place all the other bartenders came after their shifts were over to play pool or darts, listen to the jukebox and drink. No out-of-towners ever went there, because there was no gambling, so it was their own. The place they could unwind, untuck and let loose. A few of them were born and raised in that speck of a town, the most current generation of bartenders and craps dealers. Almost all of them were alcoholics, and most of them liked drugs. In a 24/7 town with nothing to do but gamble and drink, there was a bottomless well of desire for drugs.

Busses shuttled workers back and forth from surrounding areas. Cars were uncommon in Jackpot. Residents could take the shuttle into Twin Falls, the closest town, to shop just to get the hell out of Dodge, but they were stuck in the middle of the desert. Escape, in whatever form, was a commodity.

When I say that many of the residents of Jackpot were alcoholics, particularly the ones born and raised there, I'm not exaggerating. I met Chris my first night on the job. He was sloshed, acting like a complete ass. I had to ask some of the guys to escort him out of the bar because he was so disruptive. I only stayed in Jackpot for four months, but in that time, I got to know Chris and saw him try to quit drinking three times. I also heard from his friends about his previous attempts. He worked doing hard count, collecting all the coins from the machines, at the graveyard shift at one of the casinos. More than once, he tried to quit drinking cold turkey. He would show up to work with DT's, his skin and eyes yellow with jaundice, sweating and throwing up, but he never missed a night, and was a hard working son-of-a-bitch. When he was drinking, though, he was so bad, he would pour whiskey on his corn flakes in the morning.

I got to know and love Chris. He was tough and my heart shattered every time he fell off the wagon. He was in such late stages of alcoholism that one drink would turn him into a raging drunk. He was Nicholas Cage in <u>Leaving Las Vegas</u>. He was Jim Morrison in his last days in Paris. The last time I saw him was shortly before I left Jackpot. I was at his apartment and he was trying to get sober again, taking Antabuse but still unable to quit drinking. He showed me pictures of him and his friends, many of whom I served shots and beer to after midnight, when they were in high school. He gave me some of those pictures, smiling, saying he wanted me to remember him the way he was in happier times.

About a year after I moved back to Boise, I went back to Jackpot for a weekend. His long-time girlfriend told me Chris was dead. He died alone in his apartment of acute liver failure. He was twenty-six years old.

Living in the middle of the desert was akin to living on an island. The people there counted on outsiders to bring drugs into town, and were at the mercy of the dealers who determined price, quality and frequency. The first time someone offered to get me high, I accepted even though I had my own with me. I was curious to see what the people in Jackpot had access to. I was stunned. They were being overcharged for a product that was light in weight and cut with who knew what. It didn't get me high and I couldn't understand how they put up with paying good money for so little in return. They had no choice, they told me. One main guy came regularly and made his rounds. It was a take or leave it situation.

Ka-ching.

I began making runs between Boise and Jackpot two or three times a week, during the day while Andy was in school. Before long it was almost every day and sometimes twice in one day. I mainly sold meth out of the bar where I worked. I collected cigarette packs, the box kind, and specified a brand for different weights. A Marlboro light was a half gram. A Camel was a gram. A Marlboro red was an eight ball, and so on. I was the only employee in the only bar in town where there were no cameras (because there was no gambling) and the cigarette packs flew. I brought them in a bag that I kept behind the counter and as people came up to order their drinks, they'd tell me what they wanted and tip me accordingly. Then I'd either slide them a pack - Here you go. There's only a couple left. You can keep the pack - or I'd leave one on the table as I cleared the empty bottles and dumped the ashtrays. I sold to five guys, Chris being one of them, and they took care of everyone else. I was in heaven. I didn't have to deal with Garnett anymore, other than brief visits to pick up meth and deliver cash, and the cash flow was infinite.

The casinos own everything in town, with the exception of the post office and school. When you work for the casino, your living expenses, rent and utilities, are withheld from your paycheck. You keep the remainder. The hefty amounts of excess cash came from tips. The bartenders and games dealers I knew made between fifty and three hundred dollars in tips each night, and a lot of that money made its way to me.

Once again, I was special. I was a queen and I had a huge amount of power and control. I could make an entire town happy, or an entire town miserable. Meth affects the lives of everyone connected to the user. If someone is used to getting high every day before work, then suddenly can't, job performance suffers, if the employee even bothers to show up. Spouses and children can't understand why the user is sleeping all the time, and is irritable and depressed. Children of meth addicts may go to school hungry because mom or dad couldn't wake up to fix them lunch or even to go shopping. Drug and alcohol abuse always affect more than just the user, but meth is especially destructive because of the extremes: The energy and desire to do everything, or nothing at all, from stellar employee to a waste of space. It's the difference between having a living, breathing human in the home, or a corpse.

So although I didn't wield this power, I felt it and it fed me. It made me feel important. I had control then, where I had lacked control so often in my past, and it felt almost as good as the drug itself. And I had money. Enough money that when I was fired from bartending for, you guessed it, excessive lateness, it didn't even faze me. After that, I don't remember much except for flashes, like brief scenes in a movie.

Here's what I remember.

I remember what my apartment looked like. I remember Andy's bathroom because it was huge, and I decorated it with brightly colored fish. I remember cooking chicken nuggets and green beans for him for dinner. I remember drug runs to Boise and back. I remember picking Andy up sometimes an hour and a half late from school because of those runs. I remember meeting with his teacher and realizing that the school wasn't the right place for him because he was basically shut away with two other kids, who were severely disabled. I remember feeling nauseated with guilt because of that. I remember sitting in my dark bedroom at night after he'd gone to sleep, getting high, smoking all night until it was time to get him up in the morning.

Here's what I don't remember.

I don't remember playing with him. I don't remember feeding him those chicken nuggets and green beans. I don't remember tucking him in at night, and I don't remember what we did on the weekends.

What kind of a mother doesn't remember those things?

I have little snippets of holding his little square hand and walking him to school, of a school program I went to and of eating lunch with him once in the school cafeteria, though I don't remember why. He didn't have any friends and I don't think he was happy there. I don't remember if he was happy at home. It was my love of and my addiction to meth that robbed Andy of a mother who was present for him, and on some very deep level, I knew that. My meth use caused me to do, or not do, things I felt guilty about, and the only thing that eased that guilt was smoking meth.

I paid a high price for my addiction. I continue to pay, and I accept that. Whatever the reasons for my addiction may be, I'm the one who picked up the pipe, and I'm responsible for everything I've done. My son didn't have a choice, and he's the one who suffered. I could smoke away my guilt, but he couldn't do anything about the way he was feeling and what I was putting us through.

He spent Thanksgiving break with my parents in Boise. I told them I couldn't get time off from work. As far as they knew, I was still a bartender. When Christmas rolled around, I used the same excuse, so Andy went to stay with Grandma and Papa for the two-week winter vacation from school. Except for Christmas day, I spent those weeks making drug runs. I celebrated Christmas by staying in my apartment and getting high all day.

I tried to sleep at least a little every night, but time slips away like smoke from the pipe, and I would sometimes realize it had been two or three days since I'd had any sleep at all. Driving became dangerous. I found myself nodding off and started using rubber bands on my wrists again and ice cubes down my shirt - anything to try and stay awake on that lonely stretch of road between Jackpot and Boise.

It was early morning, about 2:00 am on the first day of 2001 and I was making a run from Boise to Jackpot. The freeway was covered in ice and everything around it shone eerily white in the cold night. I'd been up for few days and was exhausted, but I had to get to Jackpot to pick up money. As always, when I traveled, my loaded pipe was my only passenger. I set the cruise control at seventy-five, took three long hits, filling my lungs each time, then opened all the windows and cranked the radio to keep myself awake. When I couldn't stand the cold, I closed the windows.

The rumble tracks on the side of the road woke me and I panicked when I realized I was only partly on the freeway and headed toward an embankment. I grabbed the steering wheel and over-corrected to the left, nearly rolling the car. I couldn't figure out why I wasn't slowing down when I remembered the car was still on cruise. I cranked the steering wheel back to the right and stepped on the brake, which sent the car spinning. When the tires caught the edge of the road, the car flipped into the air. Everything went into slow motion as the car tumbled through the still night. I was upside-down at least twice while thinking this was exactly like a recurring dream I'd had of rolling my car into a field. The only difference was, in the dream, it was day and the field was green rather than the middle of the night headed into a sea of snow. I had a second to think about that when WHAM! The car landed right side up, down the embankment a few yards from the freeway.

I blacked out for a couple of minutes and when I came to, I thought heavy rain was beating down on the car until I felt the snow and dirt on the back of my neck. It wasn't raining. The back windshield had shattered and the dirt and snow I had displaced with the car was filling the backseat. The engine was still running and the radio blaring. My seat was crooked but the seatbelt was still strapped across my chest. "Why didn't the air-bag deploy?" I thought, and then, "Where the hell is my pipe?"

All I could think was, "I have to get back on the road and keep going." I would worry about the damage when I got to Jackpot. When I tried to drive up the embankment, the tires just spun in the snow. I turned the steering wheel both ways trying to find the traction I needed to get the car moving again. The last thing I needed was for someone to stop, especially a cop, since I still hadn't located my pipe. A single-car accident would mean investigation, sobriety tests and a detailed search of the scene.

The wheels only spun, digging deeper into the snow. I dug through the mess in the backseat and grabbed the blanket I always carried. My mother always said, "You never know when there might be an emergency and a blanket could come in handy." She was right. I got out and went to the front of the car. Christ, what a mess. The hood was buckled and the left front tire had popped but I figured I would take care of that later. Maybe at the next town I could drive the car to a gas station and have some friendly local change my tire for me at three in the morning.

I crammed the blanket between the ground and the good tire, half-buried in snow thinking this would give me enough traction to get going. It didn't work. The tire wouldn't grab the material and wet with snow, the blanket froze to the ground.

I started looking frantically for the pipe, knowing that when a passing car happened to notice me, the police wouldn't be far behind. I-84 was always desolate at night except for the big rigs, but that morning I hadn't seen anyone since shortly after leaving Boise. I knew my luck wouldn't hold out and I had to find that damn pipe, quick.

About twenty minutes later, I saw the first headlights. In the dark, there was no sign of the accident, and with all the lights off in the car, I crouched there trying to buy more time. I had no coat and the blanket was stuck to the snow. I was freezing cold and the only thing I could think of was finding the evidence before the police arrived. Two more cars passed and I still hadn't found it. Shivering and teeth rattling, I knew I had to get out of the cold. I was in the middle of nowhere and couldn't get a signal on my phone. I prayed the pipe had shattered or was buried. I'd looked everywhere using the dim light of my phone with no luck.

Someone in a truck finally noticed my car and pulled over. I plowed through the snow up the embankment and a man opened the passenger door for me. "Thank you so much!" I said, climbing up into the cab.

"You must be freezing," he said, turning up the heat. "What happened?"

"I don't know. I think I caught a patch of ice and slid off the road." My teeth wouldn't stop rattling.

He used his C.B. to call the state police and give them our location.

"Thanks so much for stopping. I can't get a signal on my phone."

"They'll be here in a minute. They're coming from Mountain Home. You can wait in here for them." He seemed so nice – and straight. Sitting there in the cab of that truck, I felt dirty. Not from the wreck but from the chemicals in my body. I couldn't look at the man who had possibly saved my life because I didn't want him to see me. I felt ashamed - as if my presence would somehow taint him.

A single police car came and I thanked my rescuer as the lone cop escorted me to the front seat of his cruiser. I was scared shitless. This was it: The beginning of the big investigation leading to my arrest and incarceration in a small town jail on the first day of the new year.

He asked me what happened and I told him I had fallen asleep while driving, rolling my car. "That happens a lot out here. This stretch of road is so long and there aren't many rest stops. Hell," he said, "I've fallen asleep at the wheel dozens of times. Best thing to do is pull over to the side and take a nap if you need to."

I was stunned. He was acting as if this was no big deal – like he was going to help me because he understood that, hey, shit happens. Bummer way to start out the new year. He called for a tow truck and asked me where I wanted the car towed.

"I guess back to Mountain Home. I'll figure out what to do from there."

"Alright. As soon as we get your car on its way, I'll drive you back into town. You have someone to come get you?"

I couldn't believe this was happening. Not only would there be no investigation and no sobriety tests but he wasn't even going to cite me. And he was going to chauffer me back to town in the front of his cop car. What the hell was going on here?

"I can drop you off at the all night diner for you to wait for someone, but I can't take you all the way to Boise. Sorry."

Sorry? He was sorry he couldn't be of more service to me. This was crazy.

"I'm sure I can find someone to come get me. This is so nice of you. Thank you."

"Sure. It's my job. It's just sad how many people die on this stretch of road every year. We get reports of probably thirty or forty people a month falling asleep at the wheel out here. I'm just glad you're not hurt – or worse. You ever notice all those markers on the both sides of the freeway? Those are memorials put there by families of people who have died in accidents out here."

I knew what he was talking about. Little makeshift crosses, sometimes covered with flowers, dotted both side of the freeway. I saw them all the time, but never realized, until he said that, how many there actually were. I wondered how many had died from road fatigue and how many had died from being too wasted to drive.

The edges of the sky were just starting to turn from black to purplish-blue when the officer dropped me off at the all-night diner.

"You gonna be okay? You sure you got someone coming?"

"I'm sure, and thank you so much for all your help."

Garnett came and drove me back to Boise. A few days later, I went back to Mountain Home to sign the totaled car over to the wrecking yard, and I found the pipe - still loaded and intact on the floor beneath the back passenger seat.

If I hadn't been so loaded, I might have seen the whole incident as a giant red light. Then again, if I weren't loaded, the whole thing never would have happened. It scared me, but more than that, it added to my sense of invulnerability. I earned a kind of folk hero status for having gone through such an incredible ordeal. By all rights, I should have been dead or at least in jail, but I wasn't. I remember praying, to some unidentified something, that if I could just get out of this, I wouldn't drive when I knew I was too tired ever again. Every addict I know has been there. You're in a bad situation or a close call so you pray to whatever or whoever you pray to, saying, "If you'll just get me out of (fill in the blank), I'll never (fill in the blank) again." Then, when you get through whatever it was, you think, "We didn't shake on that, did we?"

I knew I was tired. I knew I shouldn't have been driving. That was my mistake. Addiction is a disease of denial, though, and it honestly didn't occur to me that I had a problem with drugs. I didn't see it for the hazard sign it was. I viewed it as a driving problem. I drove when I lacked sleep. Simple as that. The only drug related thoughts were the fear of getting caught with drugs or paraphernalia and, more importantly, being scared that I'd lost my pipe. It was my best pipe and it was loaded with really good shit.

That was how my mind worked at the time, if you can call that working.

Coming through the accident unscathed, other than losing my car, confirmed my belief that I didn't have a problem. A little sleepy, but as the cop said, it happens to lots of people on that stretch of road. It really had nothing to do with me. It's that kind of denial that kept me trapped for so long.

Chapter 7

In a town with a population of less than 2,000, a person who doesn't work may as well be wearing a sign that says, "Shady character. Please investigate further." Since I no longer had transportation anyway, it was time for us to leave. I rented a storage unit for my belongings, and Andy and I moved back to Boise and in with my parents. I enrolled Andy in school and set about the task of pretending to find a job.

I did half-heartedly look. I sent out resumes on the Internet and circled help wanted ads in the classified section of the newspaper every morning. I went through the motions, but I couldn't picture myself working a nine to five. I told myself it was because I didn't work well with people, that I'd lost faith in humanity. That was a favorite saying of mine. I saw myself as a victim. I was fired from the last two jobs I'd had for being chronic lateness. In my drug-addled mind, though, I was convinced that people just didn't understand my special circumstances. I was, after all, a single mother of a child with a disability. Shouldn't that afford me extra privileges? No one understood me and of course, this provided the perfect excuse for my drug use, as well.

I honestly don't know what I thought I was going to do, but I was in no hurry to find a job. All I cared about was spending time with Andy when he was home, and getting high the rest of the time. As generous as they were about taking us in, I resented my parents. I felt stifled by their sterile home and rigid routine, which was much different from when I was growing up.

When I was younger, my parents drank. Canadian Mist and 7-Up was the beverage of choice, especially when we were with Mom's side of the family. My family and I would sometimes spend the weekend with my two uncles - Mom's brothers - and their wives, at my grandparents' house in Hailey or Fairfield, little rural towns in southern Idaho. They would play cards, or watch a football game on TV, but drinking was always the backdrop for family get-togethers.

At home, Mom and Dad would have an occasional cocktail after work, but there was less restraint on the weekends, especially when my grandparents would visit. The four of them would drink all evening and if they went to dinner or a football game, they drank there too. Drinking was part of spending time with family. At Thanksgiving and Christmas, it was common to bring a half gallon of booze to the celebration. That being the custom and with the size of our family, it was normal to have three or four half-gallon bottles and plenty of beer.

My parents both drank back then, but with Dad it was different. Sometimes he would get falling-down drunk. He wasn't a mean drunk, at least not around the extended family; he was a happy, silly drunk. To me, it seemed that he was the clown, the buffoon that everyone laughed at. I hated him for letting himself be treated that way. Once, when my parents and grandparents came home from a ball game, Dad attempted to take the babysitter home, but he passed out behind the wheel in our driveway. We never saw that babysitter again.

When I was in junior high, my father's drinking got worse, or at least that's when I started to notice what was happening. Sometimes he would go for a drink with a friend after work on a Friday afternoon and we wouldn't see or hear from him for two or three days. Mom was very quiet on those weekends, sitting at the dining room table by the phone, chain smoking. To this day, I have no idea where my father was during his AWOLs. I do remember one weekend he called on a Sunday and my mother spoke with him briefly. She told us he woke up three hundred miles away in Winnemucca, Nevada alone and had no idea how he got there. That was all we were told. Other than that, all I knew is that he sometimes just didn't come home.

Children of alcoholics tend to abuse alcohol, just as children raised in violent households tend to become abusers themselves. You would think that seeing the effects of alcohol on my father would prevent me from ever touching a drop, but aside from the outrageous, I learned something else about alcohol. It relieves stress and it's required for socializing. Those are two reasons I drank and did drugs, at least in the beginning.

There was another side to my dad, a thing that lived inside him. It was never directed at anyone but Chuck and me. He never did it to Mom and he's never been that way with his grandchildren. I saw it a lot growing up. Maybe it had something to do with his drinking, although he didn't have to be drunk for us to see it. I haven't seen it for five years now, but I remember it vividly and the recollection provokes intense memories.

I hated the thing and I hated my father when it consumed him. His face would change and he would almost snarl. His eyes would flood with hatred. He was threatening and gruesome when he was like that and to this day, even thinking about it - that thing - causes rage to boil up in my throat and makes me want to scream and rip out my hair. When he would get that way, I hated the fucking prick. I hated my father with everything I was. He wasn't my dad when he was that way. My brother and I refer to it as The Thing That Lives Inside of Dad. I wonder sometimes if that Thing was his internal rage. The sum total of his own demons from his life that he tried so hard to suppress and only came out when, for whatever reason, he felt rage toward Chuck or me.

It's difficult to explain how something as simple as a look could make me feel so hated...so small...like some slimy bug he would just as soon squash as look at. I can't fathom looking at Andy like that, just as I can't imagine slapping him in the face or whipping him with a belt for not falling asleep on time. Those are things you do to people you hate. Those are the kinds of things that vicious, evil people do to dogs. I've never asked him why he was like that. I've never asked my mother how she could stand by and watch. I don't think I ever will. I don't want to know.

I was still using and dealing meth after the car accident, which caused terrific tension between my parents and me even though they didn't know what was going on. One night, I was using Mom's computer and felt a presence behind me. When I turned, I saw The Thing That Lives Inside of Dad for the first time since he'd stopped drinking. It not only scared me, it infuriated me. I felt rage build inside me and I remember thinking, *"He can't do this. I'm an adult. He can't do this to me."*

I didn't say anything and neither did he. Maybe he was pissed off because I was in his office and he didn't want me there. Maybe it was because I was using my mother's computer. Maybe he was mad because I didn't have a job. I don't know. All I know is that I saw that Thing and I had to get away from it.

With limited options - I had no real job, so I couldn't get an apartment and I didn't want to stay with my well-meaning friends (who were usually only well-meaning if they thought they could get free drugs) - I packed my things in the middle of the night and moved into my VW van. I left Andy behind. It killed me to leave him, but it was February and the temperature at night was in the teens. I couldn't make him live like that and I couldn't disrupt his routine: school, developmental therapy and a home. A home without me.

I didn't say anything to anyone. I packed my bags in the middle of the night while they were sleeping, and left a note for Andy.

Dear Andy,

Momma's going away for a little while. You stay with Grandma and Pappa. I'm going to get a job and find us a place to live. I love you, bug. Be a good boy.

That was it.

I knew Dad would never show the Thing to Andy. I still don't know what *it* is, or what I ever did to deserve it, but my parents were different with Andy then they'd ever been with me. Mom and Dad did the best they could with what they had when raising Chuck and me. Despite any flaws, I will tell you they are stellar grandparents. As shitty as I felt about leaving Andy, I never had a second thought about leaving him with them.

I thought about him every day and being away from him tore me apart. I had abandoned my son - the worst thing a mother can do - and I told myself I didn't deserve him. I fell into a depression matched only by guilt in its depth. It carved a canyon through my soul and I filled it with self-loathing. *Smoke it away. Smoke it away.* I thought that with enough meth, I could make myself numb. With enough distractions - buying meth, selling meth, looking at it, cleaning the pipe, loading the pipe, lighting it, hitting it, cooling it off, finding a place to stash everything and starting all over again - I could avoid looking at the mess I was making of my life.

This wasn't me. I wasn't meant to be this person. But I'd gotten myself into the situation, and I was going to get myself out. My main priority was getting an apartment for Andy and me. And still, with all this going on, I didn't think of meth as my problem. I never considered quitting. What I needed to do, I decided, was get my shit together, get back on my anti-depressants and everything would be all right. My depression was the cause of my problems, and meth was merely a means to an end. It helped with my illness and I loved the high. I needed the high. It didn't occur to me to live without it.

I did actually find a job, but when I found out that not only did they drug test urine but also hair, I never showed up. I might have been able to fake a urine analysis, but I had no clue how to get around a hair test. Especially one scheduled for the following day. Hair can show drug use for up to ninety days prior to the date tested.

All I did was drive from place to place, park the van and sit inside with the curtains drawn, getting high and sobbing about the disgusting person I was. Aside from that and selling or buying drugs, I would curl up in a dirty down comforter Garnett had given me and sleep on the foldout bed in the van. Sleep offered me escape from the empty existence I had chosen. I tried to pretend it was a big adventure, living in my van. How lucky I was, I thought, that I had a van and not just a car. I told myself it wasn't so bad, living the way I did, but I knew it was disgusting. I used a big insulated mug - the kind you can buy at convenience stores and refill with soda - to urinate in, discreetly emptying it into gutters when it became full. Since I ate very little, I rarely had bowel movements. When I needed to, I would find a Wal-Mart or Fred Myer and use the facilities. I used baby wipes for spit baths. I brushed my teeth using bottled water or occasionally accepted an offer to shower at a friend's house. I lived that way for two months: cold, lonely, depressed and despising the person I had become. Without my son, I was nothing, but I felt I had no options. There was no way I was going back to my parents. I needed to find a place for Andy and me to live. I fantasized about killing myself. My meth soaked brain made rational thinking nearly impossible.

Most days I would sit in my van at some random park. In the early months of the year, Boise is nothing but gray days where the sun only shines high above the ever present inversion that covers the valley like a damp wool blanket. I would watch parents with their children, pushing them on swings and playing catch. I would think about Andy, my heart and guts twisted with the guilt. I would imagine it was us out there with me pushing him on the swing and him yelling, "Oh no! Oh no!" and laughing so hard his trachea would collapse and make that weird honking sound that was so familiar. (He still has low muscle tone - hypotomia - around the trachea and esophagus, and has always been a big hit with kids his age because of his mastery of the vulgar burping noises little boys love to make.) I took comfort in knowing he was safe, warm and well taken care of, but I felt like the worst mother in the world. I abandoned him and I wasn't worthy of motherhood. Andy deserved so much more than me. He should have had a daddy who adored him as much as I did, and maybe a sister or brother to look out for him when he got older. He deserved a house with a swing set, and a puppy to grow up with and all the things the Beaver had, because that was what I thought a perfect life looked like: white picket fence, paper route, June in the kitchen making cookies for Wally and the Beav. Instead, all he had was me, and I was broken, shattered, living in a van, and while not quite down by the river, only a stone's throw away.

I still sometimes wish for all these things for Andy, wish I could give him the picture perfect life that seems so ideal from the outside. I used to regret that he doesn't have a father or siblings, but, "it is what it is," as they say in recovery. And the thing is, Andy doesn't know there's something he's supposed to be missing. He doesn't understand the concept of "Dad." Sort of like I, as a woman, don't miss having a penis. Never had one. Fine without it. Don't need it, and I don't miss it. I wasn't castrated, it was just never there. The same way there was never a father for Andy. I suppose you don't miss what you've never had.

Now, you can long for something you've never had. You can covet. Although I've never had a penis, I've heard (and seen) good things. It might be interesting. I may discover that it's something I've been searching for my whole life. (It would be such a relief if I could blame all my problems on penis envy.)

But it's different with Andy. When we're with his Uncle Chuck, and his cousins are calling him Dad, Andy will replace "Uncle Chuck" (and sometimes Mom) with Dad. Not a problem. To Andy, it's just a word - a label - and nothing more.

I'm all he's ever needed. He just needed me to be whole. I was well into my recovery when I had this epiphany, and I went from feeling guilty for not giving him what I thought I should have, to feeling guilty for almost destroying the only thing he really ever needed: me. I felt guilty then, I felt guilty in early recovery and I still feel guilty sometimes. I would have made a great Catholic.

One Tuesday night, while getting high, I started looking through the phone book for people I used to know. I sat and smoked, looking up names of people I remembered from grade school, high school and some that I went to college with. I had no intention, really, of calling anyone. I remember simply wanting to feel some kind of connection with people when I was doing it. Like an affirmation that there were others out there who were probably leading normal lives.

I remembered a guy I knew from high school who I'd spent time with in my late 20's, and found his name in the phone book as well. I had thought of him over the years and after a couple of days, decided to call the number listed for Allan in the phone book. When his wife answered, she told me they had been divorced for about a year and a half. She knew Allan and I had spent a lot of time together when we were in our twenties though, and thought he would want to hear from me.

I was nervous as I dialed, wondering if he'd even remember me, but there was a tiny spark inside me. A spark of hope, I suppose, that he would remember and I'd have someone to talk to.

"Hey, Allan. It's Kim. Do you remember me?"

"Kim! Oh my God! Of course I remember you. How are you doing? It's been a long time. How did you get my number?" Allan was possibly the most gregarious person I had ever known. He always seemed happy, even mischievous, with a boyish excitement about him that had always lifted my spirits if I was down and elated me when I wasn't. Hearing his voice that night stirred my heart a little from its atrophied state and I smiled for the first time in weeks. His enthusiasm was contagious as it bubbled over the airwaves.

Allan and I first met in high school. We had a class together our senior year. We knew each other but he was a mullet-haired, partier-jock and I was high all the time, coming to school stoned almost every day.

The next time we met, we were in our late twenties. I was playing pool by myself at a bar and he was there with a friend playing darts. There wasn't anything odd about it. People tend to stay in Boise after high school to attend B.S.U. or enter the work force. Even when people leave to go to school, work or just to find themselves, they often end up coming home. Boise is a wonderful place to raise a family. There's a strong sense of community, relatively low crime rate, and we're surrounded by mountains for skiing and lakes for fishing and boating. It's also the cleanest city I've ever seen. If you see a gum wrapper on the sidewalk, chances are it won't be there the next day.

It's not unusual to run into people you grew up with or to

maintain friendships with the people you went to first grade with. So when I ran into Allan and his friend, it was a nice surprise.

I bought them a pitcher of beer and spent the rest of the afternoon with him, drinking and playing pool. We were instantly attracted to each other. We could talk for hours about everything and nothing. He had a contagious laugh and a penchant for mischief that fit perfectly with my lifestyle. For the next year or so, Allan and I spent as much time together as we could, despite the fact that he was married with a child on the way. With his wife at home pregnant, he spent a lot of time out with his friends, so she was used to his absences in the evenings. I sometimes felt sorry for her, sitting alone night after night, waiting for their child to be born, but I never felt guilty because, after all, Allan and I were just friends. I rationalized our friendship because I felt so good when I was with him. The crush I had on him and my daydreams of what it might be like if he weren't married were harmless, I thought. I had never been an adulteress and did not intend to get involved with a married man.

That's what I told myself in order to shun any guilt I might have had about the situation. The truth is - and this became a pattern during my active addiction - I was disrespecting other women: driving a wedge between my sisters and myself.

I used to say that I didn't get along with other women. *I like men better*, I'd say. For years, I had very little interaction with other females. There were a few I sold meth or pot to, but mostly I saw them as irritants on the periphery of my world. They were the wives and girlfriends of the men I spent time with. They were party-poopers. They wanted their men at home instead of out doing drugs and boozing with me (whether they were aware of me or not.) I was cheating with their men, and I knew that on a not so deep level. Not physically, but cheating doesn't always involve sex.

I knew what I was doing, although I would never admit it to myself, but it wasn't really about the women. It was about control, and men. If the cheating were sexual, I wasn't interested. But there was something extremely satisfying about being constantly surrounded by men who chose me over the women in their lives. If there was sexual tension as well, all the better.

At the time, of course, nothing was this clear, but looking at the situation with sober eyes, it makes perfect sense:

<u>Will you go with me?</u>

<u>Yes</u>

No

Unlike grade school, though, I was in control.

I was into cocaine when Allan and I started spending so much time together, and I charmed him with my ability to write his name in the white powder instead of cutting the boring lines everyone else did. I threw midnight poker parties and he came as often as he could. When we were together, my heart beat faster. I was like a schoolgirl with her first crush. By then he had shed his high school mullet - thank God - and he was breathtaking. He looked like a rugged version of Woody Harrelson. Allan was a man's man - muscular and strong with eyes that saw places inside me no one had ever seen.

One night, we were alone at my house watching a movie. It was around 10:30 when he asked me to massage his back. I had long ago learned that "massage" was a code word for foreplay. Although I told myself it was innocent, I was thrilled at the chance to touch him as I'd wanted to for so long. He lay on the floor and I straddled him. Shortly after I started, he reached back, moved my shorts aside, and touched the upper inside of my thigh. I froze. He rolled over, pushed me to the floor and started kissing me.

It was raw and powerful. He was the most sexually exciting man I had ever known. When he told me he had wanted me since he saw me in the bar that day, my base instincts kicked into overdrive, and I became a whirling, lusting dervish. I discovered a new use for every room in my house. He made me ravenous for sex.

The next day, we talked about what had happened. Our attraction was mutually animalistic, so we couldn't go back to the way we were before. We wouldn't be able to keep our hands off each other. But we also knew we couldn't see each other again the way we had. He was the first to speak.

"Kim, I can't do this."

"I know." I didn't want to know, but I did.

"I've got a baby on the way and I've never cheated on my wife before." He looked away from me. "I cheated on my first wife. Before and during our marriage. We both did. In fact, it happened so much, I don't even remember who cheated first. But this time I wanted it to be different. And it has been. Until last night." He looked back at me. "I didn't think I'd feel guilty like this, but I do."

We were both quiet for a few minutes. What could I say? As much as I wanted him - especially right then - what he was saying made me want him even more. Regardless of what happened the night before, I saw him as gallant.

"I don't think we should see each other anymore, Kim."

I agreed, wanting to seem adult about the situation, but when he left, only fifteen minutes after he'd arrived, I lay down on my bed and cried myself to sleep.

Vagueness lends itself to rationalization, but once a thing is tangible, there's no denying its reality. There can be debate about various forms of infidelity: emotional, spiritual, intellectual, time spent in Internet chat rooms and on porn sites. But when it comes to sex, the line is salient. Sex = adultery.

Just as hitting = abuse. When the man I was briefly married to punched me in the head, I refused to let it happen again. It only took one hit for me to throw him out and divorce him, because hitting is salient. Other types of abuse aren't always as obvious. Emotional and mental abuse, as with infidelity, is more complicated because it's so hard to define. It's vague, and therefore, easy to rationalize. *I'm not really an adulteress if we're not having sex. If I'm not being smacked around, it's not abuse.* I have no problem with saliency; it's in the gray that I struggle.

In recovery, there's a lot of talk about boundaries or, in my case, the lack of them. Having boundaries is all about keeping yourself safe. You say, "No, I will not do this. No, I will not allow that to happen to me. Yes, this is okay, but no, that isn't."

It's about knowing who you are and taking care of yourself. Boundaries are integrity. To be blunt, if you're too chicken-shit to stand up for yourself, you'll allow people to walk all over you. For a long time, I was a chicken-shit. I didn't want to hurt anyone's feelings, even if it meant that mine were.

A lack of boundaries looks like this:

"Hey, Kim. Can you do me this favor?"

Shit. I've got fifty million things to do, I'm late for my appointment, the pot on the stove just boiled over and I haven't brushed my teeth yet today.

"Absolutely!"

Having boundaries looks like this:

"Hey, Kim. Can you do me a favor?"

"Actually, no. I'm late for an appointment and I have to brush my teeth. By the way, can you clean up that mess on the stove?"

But salient boundaries are easy to see, and Allan and I crossed the line. The thing was, whether real or contrived, Allan's regret made me like him even more, and that made losing him all the more tragic.

I replayed our night together a thousand times in my head over the years, and often hoped he would call. Even though we only had sex that one night, I could never get it out of my mind and no one has compared with him since. But I didn't see or hear from him until the night I called him seven years later when my loneliness turned to selfishness. I hoped he would remember me. I hoped he wasn't seeing anyone.

I hoped that, maybe, he'd want to get high.

"I'm good, I'm good. I talked to your wife, well, ex-wife I understand, and she gave me your number. She said she thought you would want to hear from me."

"I can't believe she did that, but I'm so glad she did! Are you in Boise? What are you doing these days?"

"I'm in Boise, yeah. Not doing much. Same old thing I guess. What about you? Are you still in Boise?"

"When I'm home I am. Right now I'm in Florida."

"What? What the hell are you doing in Florida?"

He laughed. "I drive long haul. I'm only in Boise for a few days a month between runs."

"Are you driving now? I don't want to bother you."

"No, I'm at a truck stop. Just about to get a couple hours sleep." I closed my eyes and tried to imagine him in the cab of an eighteen-wheeler, at night, in a truck stop parking lot talking to me on his cell phone. "I'm watching the lot lizards."

"The what?"

"The lot lizards. They're at every truck stop." I envisioned some kind of iguana or gecko. I didn't understand why he would be watching them. I figured there must be some kind of invasion of them, like locusts, and I felt better thinking of him sitting high up in his truck.

"What are you talking about, Allan?"

"The lot lizards." He repeated. "They're at every truck stop." All I could see was a torn up, redneck version of a giant iguana: The kind that haunted trailer parks and cut their teeth on lawn furniture. I could understand why he would be watching them. I was morbidly fascinated, and I was almost three thousand miles away. I wasn't sure of the extent of the invasion in Florida, but I felt better knowing he was safe in his truck, out of reach of the gnashing teeth of the wild beasts.

"Really? Are there a lot of them?"

"Oh, God. They're everywhere. Every truck stop. They're interesting to watch, though. I'm just sitting here smoking and watching them before I catch some sleep."

"I'm sorry. I didn't mean to...I can let you go if you're tired."

"No way! I'm glad you called. Don't you dare hang up on me now."

"So...what are the lizards doing?" I wasn't sure I wanted to know, but I couldn't help myself. You know, the train wreck thing.

"Same as always. Hopping from truck to truck."

Holy mother of God! Those monsters must be rabid!

"What?"

"Well, that's what they do. It's not like they spend the night or anything. When they're done, they move on to the next trucker who'll take them."

"Allan, what are you talking about?" I felt like I sometimes did in social situations where everyone else knows each other and the conversation may as well be in a foreign language because I had no reference point.

"Lot lizards. You know, hookers."

"Ohhhh. I get it now." I felt like such an idiot.

"What did you think I was talking about? Actual lizards?" He was laughing, but I didn't get the feeling it was at my expense. It felt more like the way old friends laugh at some silly misunderstanding.

"No, of course n...well, okay, yeah. I did. I've never heard that term before." I was laughing a little now too, and it felt good. It was as if a valve were being turned just a smidgen to the left, letting out a bit of pressure and making it easier for me to breathe.

We talked for almost an hour about nothing in particular. His enthusiasm for everything was contagious, whether he was talking about cars, skiing, music, or lot lizards. He'd been that way since I remembered him in high school. Allan was by nature an extremely friendly, outgoing person. Sitting there, alone in my van, I felt better than I had in a long time-a little normal. Allan said he'd be back in Boise in four days and asked if he could take me to dinner. At thirty-three years old, I could count on one hand the number of times I'd been asked for a date. Of course, he could take me to dinner. That meant he wanted to spend time with me. He wanted to see me and talk to me and it wasn't all just a façade for getting drugs. Someone was interested in *me*.

That's where the problem started. Not my addiction, but the beginning of what turned into years of a relationship that never should have happened. I see that now, but I certainly didn't see it then. I took what was a normal, friendly catching-up-with-an-old-friend conversation, and turned it into the cornerstone upon which to hang my salvation. I was at the lowest point in my life, and Allan was a beacon in the distance. I scraped together the few remaining shreds of hope I had left and stuck them, like Velcro, onto Allan and our brief conversation because I wanted it all to mean more than it did. Much more. I wanted it to mean a new beginning for me. I wanted someone to care about me for more than just meth. I wanted the words between the lines of our dialogue to mean that he was genuinely interested and couldn't wait to see me. If Allan had known what I was thinking, he probably wouldn't have wanted to see me. If I had been in my right mind, I wouldn't have wanted him to see me either. I would have told him to run as fast as he could in the other direction of that woman he'd been speaking with because yikes! Men should stay away from psycho women like that. Hell, *women* should stay away from psycho women like that. But I didn't realize how warped my mindset was. Nor did I realize how skewed *his* mindset was. On whatever level he was attracted to me, or whether he had other intentions from the beginning, all I saw was what I wanted to see rather than any warning signs of what might be to come.

If I had the clarity then that I have now, I probably wouldn't be an addict.

I cried myself to sleep that night, huddled in the warmth of that dingy comforter, feeling more like a real person. I was so lost, so removed from even myself, that simply talking to another human being, such a tiny slice of humanity, was all it took to nourish me. I hadn't told Allan I was living in my van or that I had abandoned my son. I didn't know what I was going to say when he asked about Andy. All I knew was that I had something to look forward to and, even if only for a few hours, I wasn't going to be alone. Four days. It seemed like forever. I felt like I did when I was a little girl waiting for Christmas to come.

The next morning I drove to the Ameritel Inn, a decent place where I rented a room for a week. I took a long, hot bubble bath. Sinking into the masses of bubbles that overflowed to the linoleum floor was like going back to the womb and I stayed there until the water turned frigid. I watched some T.V. and a little later, I went to the store for Diet Coke, soup, crackers, ice cream...just a few things so I would have something to put in the cupboards and refrigerator. I felt uplifted, hopeful and normal. I had a little home with a kitchenette, sofa, coffee table and sleeping area. I made a few deliveries then called Garnett and arranged to see him later that night.

I curled up on the queen-sized bed and turned one the T.V. with the sound down low, not really watching, just for background noise. I got out my journal and began to write. I wrote whatever came into my head: where I was, what I was doing and how I felt. Mostly I wrote about my desire to get myself out of my current situation. For the next couple of hours I filled page after page as I smoked meth and cigarettes and drank Diet Coke.

Garnett came by and dropped off a couple of ounces and we passed time, getting high and chitchatting for an hour or so. I told him about Allan and he said he was happy for me, though his tone and expression didn't match his words. I didn't think much about it at the time.

When he was gone, I wrote some more, finished what was in the pipe, and then went to sleep. Meth was so much a part of my daily diet, and had been for so long, that I could easily fall asleep after getting high. The room was warm and the bed and pillows felt so nice. It was a safe cocoon. I slept for seven hours that night. It was the most uninterrupted sleep I'd enjoyed in weeks and I felt like a new person in the morning. Within an hour of waking, I was getting high again.

I felt so good, I decided to call my parents. I hadn't spoken to them since the night before I left and I was nervous. I didn't know if they would even talk to me, but I needed to find out how Andy was doing. It was worth risking their wrath and hatred if I could just talk to him for a minute, or at least find out how he was doing. When I heard my mother's voice on the phone, my throat tightened and I couldn't talk for a few seconds. I squeezed my eyes shut to keep the tears from flowing.

"Mom, it's me."

"Oh, Kimbo! Where are you?"

"I'm in a hotel right now."

"Are you okay? We've been so worried. Why did you leave? Where have you been?" Her voice was so warm, it instantly brought home the shame I felt for what I'd done to my parents, my son and myself.

"I'm okay, Mom. How's my baby?"

"He's fine, Kimbo. How's *my* baby?" That did it. I started crying, my tears running down my cheeks and my voice breaking.

"I'm okay, I'm fine. I've been job hunting." This wasn't a complete lie, but it wasn't the complete truth either. "I think I should have one here pretty soon. So I can get an apartment for Andy and me. How is he? Is he there? I miss him so much."

"He's not here. He's still at therapy. He misses you too. He's always asking where Mom is. I don't know what to tell him so I've just been saying you'll be home soon. Will you be home soon?"

"Like I said, I'll be getting a job soon and an apartment for us."

"Kim, just come home."

"I can't, Mom." Jesus, it was so hard talking to her. I wanted to go back. I wanted my momma to wrap her arms around me and rock me on her lap telling me everything would be okay. But even in an ideal situation that would never happen. I'm too emotional, too needy, "too huggy," as my mother once told me. I've always needed reassurance of love and physical affection. I think some people are just born that way. My brother was never like that, but I always have been. I need to be hugged and reminded that I'm loved, but I've always been told that this is unacceptable. *Too huggy.* What I want is not okay. I'm not like other people. I need to be strong. I need to learn to take care of myself because it's not okay to ask for what I need. To do so is weak.

But right then, in that hotel room, talking on the phone, I wanted my mom and dad and I needed my son. I wanted everything to be different but I couldn't see how to make that happen. As much as I wanted to be with my family, I also wanted meth, and I knew I couldn't have both. Meth didn't judge me regardless of how much I needed it. Meth was always there and it always made me feel good. Meth won.

"There was just too much tension between us, Mom. Especially with Dad and me. If we want to be okay, if we still want to be a family again in the future, I can't be there right now. I'm sorry. I'm all right, though. Everything will be okay soon."

"Where are you getting the money for a hotel?"

"I got my taxes back." God damn it. I wanted her to quit asking me questions so I wouldn't have to lie to her. I hated lying.

"Tell Andy I love him if you don't think it will make him feel worse about me not being there. And Mom, thank you for taking care of him."

"You can come see him, you know."

"Really?" In my mind, leaving Andy with them and sneaking off in the middle of the night was unforgivable, and I assumed they felt the same way. It hadn't occurred to me that they would ever let me back in the house. I still couldn't believe my mother was talking to me, saying she missed me. I couldn't believe she didn't hate me. I hated me. I assumed everyone else did too.

"Of course, Kimbo. He needs to see you."

"Okay. Let me figure something out and I'll call you. I love you, Mom. Thanks for not hanging up on me." I was crying again and so was she

"Why would I hang up on you?"

"I thought you guys would hate me and never want to see me again."

"Sweetheart, I could never hate you. You're my baby, and I love you. I just want everything to be okay. I'm worried about you and I want you to be safe. Are you taking your depression medication?" Shit. Again with the questions.

"I'm taking them, but I'm almost out." I hadn't taken my meds in at least two months. My prescriptions ran out. But I was self-medicating as usual. Meth was all I needed.

"You know your father and I told you if you ever need your medication, we'll pay for it."

"I know, Mom." That's the one thing they would always help me with, but I couldn't ask for help. If I were drowning, I wouldn't take a hand offered to me. I'd just keep saying, "I got it. It's okay. I can do this," and I would go under, gurgling the words as my lungs filled with water.

"I love you, Mom. I'll call in a couple of days."

"I love you too, Kimbo. You take care of yourself."

The first thing I did when I hung up was get high, smoking furiously until I was numb. I did little else but stay on that bed smoking meth for the next three days. It didn't occur to me, then and for a very long time, that I was an addict. On some level, I think I knew that meth had a hand in my circumstances, but I was in such denial that I never allowed those thoughts to surface. I convinced myself that all my problems were the result of a string of unfortunate circumstances, and the more meth I smoked, the easier it became to believe my own rationalizations.

I truly thought that if I ever wanted to stop using, I would be able to. There wasn't a doubt in my mind. But I saw no reason to quit. I loved doing drugs and the main fringe benefit of dealing was the never-ending supply. I had all I wanted of the best stuff around. I figured the people who had meth induced psychotic breaks either had inferior product or couldn't handle their high. I thought I was different. I thought I was safe. I didn't shoot up, I took care of my teeth, I ate, although infrequently, but I certainly wasn't emaciated, and I slept almost every day, at least for a couple of hours. I could handle my high because for me, it was my typical state of being. I wasn't like other people. I used meth as medicine so I could feel normal. I didn't see myself as having a drug problem. My problem was depression and always had been. That was my battle. I was just lucky enough to have fallen in with the right people at the right time and I loved getting high.

(There's a term for this in recovery: terminal uniqueness. *All my problems are so much worse than - or not as bad as - anyone else's, and it's because of this that no one will ever understand what it's like to be me.* Dramatic sigh.)

I didn't want to think about any of that. I didn't want to think about the last two jobs I'd been fired from, or the car I'd totaled, or my parents or the fact that I wasn't with my son. Instead, I smoked the bad thoughts away and daydreamed of seeing Allan again. Although I didn't realize it at the time, Allan stepped back into my life at exactly the right time. I needed more distraction than meth could provide.

Distraction from life. Distraction from having to look at what I was doing to my family and myself. The phone call on lizard night was the beginning of three years of the biggest distraction any self-loathing addict could hope for.

Allan called the day he was to take me to dinner to say he would pick me up at the hotel at seven. I was excited and nervous the whole day. I took a long, leisurely bath around noon and spent the rest of the day pampering myself and smoking meth. For the first date I'd had in years, I wanted to spend time doing the "girly thing." I did my hair, painted my nails and applied makeup - something I rarely did. We hadn't seen each other in such a long time, and I was nervous about how the evening would go.

The security guard let him in and I waited in the hallway, wringing my hands the way I do when I'm anxious. When I saw him, electricity raced up my spine and through my scalp. The way he looked at me, as he half walked, half jogged down the corridor, made me feel like the most important person in the world. I've always loved his smile, which is brightly mischievous. He was wearing his favorite worn, floppy Fedora, reminiscent of Indiana Jones. To me, he looked like home.

"Kim! Hey."

"Hey, Allan." He hugged me and I felt so safe in his arms - as if someone had built a strong, secure house around me that no wolf could ever blow down.

We didn't go to dinner that night. Instead, we went to the bar where we met so many years earlier to shoot pool, drink and catch up with each other. I paid the bill.

Back at the hotel, I changed into my sweats and took off my makeup. "Do you still do crank?" he asked me.

"Well, not crank...but meth. You know, crystal."

"Can we do some? I'll buy some from you if you have enough."

"You don't have to buy it. I'm good."

"Do you smoke it?"

"Well, yes. Why? Do you? Or do you still do lines?"

"Lines."

I made a face. "Jesus, why? I hate the burn and the drip. I've never liked the taste of drugs."

"I know. I remember," he said smiling. When he smiled at me with that certain look in his eye, all I wanted to do was throw him on the bed and ride him into the sunset. "I love the burn. And the drip. If you don't mind, I'll do lines."

"Not if you don't mind if I smoke it."

"Nope. I might take a hit or two later if that's okay."

I pulled out my pipe, a credit card for making lines and a straw. Then I took a bag of crystal meth from the hotel safe in the room.

"Holy shit, Kim! How much is that?"

I tossed the baggie on the table. "I don't know. It's my personal. Maybe a quarter ounce?"

He picked it up, looking at it like it was the Hope Diamond. "Fuck, this is good shit, huh?"

"Of course it's good," I said as I opened the bag and handed him a rock about the size of half a grape. "What are you, *new?* I always did have good drugs, remember?" We lay on the queen-sized bed cross ways, did drugs, smoked cigarettes and talked incessantly the way people do when they use meth or coke together. Both drugs have the effect of turning total strangers into best friends within almost instantly, but Allan and I were already friends so for me, it felt like serious bonding. He did most of the talking, as we lay there, he kept inching closer to me. I knew I could have had him if I wanted to, but I was too drunk. I lost count of the number of double Jager shots I'd had earlier, and I was seeing double.

I hit my pipe continuously, trying to counter the effects of the alcohol, but it wasn't working. I closed my eyes and tried not to fall asleep as I listened to him go on about what it was like being on the road all the time. He kept moving closer until our bodies were smashed together and all I could do was lie there, drunk and desperately trying to get high enough to pull myself out of my double-vision stupor. I didn't want him to know what was going on with me, so I just ignored his nudging and listened to him talk about the road.

"I'd love that," I said. "It sounds like heaven to me. Just driving...always being somewhere different. It must be like the ultimate road trip."

He touched my face. "I'd take you with me anytime."

"Really? You would?" Hearing those words made me feel so connected to Allan. I felt like he was my knight in shining armor and that, with him, I would be safe because he would take care of me. He would take me away with him anytime I wanted to go.

It was close to noon the next day when he said he had to go. His son had a football game at 1:00, and he needed to go home, shower and change clothes. Suddenly I was pissed off. Everything was going so well and now he had to leave me. Asshole. I felt like such an idiot. I always did this: got my hopes up, creating this image in my head of how everything would happen, only to be drop-kicked by reality. "Damn it," I thought, "I know better. Why do I always do this?"

Whenever I meet a guy I like, which isn't often, I envision us dating, married and with kids, the whole relationship worked out and already lived in my mind, before dessert. My mind would go, my thoughts racing, and I was powerless to stop them. Usually, by the time the date was over, I was already tired of the guy and didn't really care if I ever saw him again. With Allan, I imagined the two of us living in the cab of his big truck, driving back and forth across the country, just living in our own magic bubble away from the world.

The effects of the alcohol were gone by the time he was leaving for his son's game, and I was in a strange floating place. Wired-tired, I called it. It was the feeling of being sleepy and high at the same time. So I just lay there on the bed trying to appear nonchalant and aloof.

"Do you mind if I come back when the game's over?" Allan asked me. I got up.

"Really?"

"If it's okay. I don't have to leave until tomorrow night." I threw my arms around him. "Of course it's okay. Thank you, thank you..."

"For what?" His arms were around me too, and I felt the same as when he had hugged me the night before. Safe.

"Nothing. I'm just happy. Call me before you come, though, okay?"

"No problem. Do you have any more of that stuff?" Of course I did. I always did.

From that day forward, we were together whenever he was home, and he would call me from the road several times a day. Allan made me feel special. No man had ever showered me with so much attention.

Chapter 8

I rented an apartment using Allan as my job reference. "Why yes. Kim has worked as my bookkeeper for over two years now and she's a fine employee. I know she'll make a great tenant."

I moved Andy in with me and began to feel whole again. I bought a car, a LaBaron convertible, again with Allan posing as my employer. We fell into a pattern. He was usually gone four or five days at a time, home at least two and sometimes three days in a row. We spent almost all of that time together. I hadn't yet gone with him on one of his trips. I was so busy, I couldn't find a good time to leave. Someone always needed drugs and, of course, Garnett always needed money. It was a vicious cycle: keep working to keep paying, keep paying to keep buying in order to meet the never-ending demand for meth.

As much as I sometimes hated dealing with people and the feeling of being a gerbil on a wheel, the lifestyle afforded me the luxury of supporting my son and myself. We didn't want for anything. I wasn't rich by any means, but I never had to worry about having enough money for groceries or bills. I could afford to buy our clothes and didn't have to worry about Andy's school expenses. If his class was going on a field trip, I always had the money and would sometimes send extra in case one of his classmates couldn't afford to go. I never had to worry about getting someone to watch Andy before or after school because I could always be there for him - usually in my bedroom getting high while he watched his *Star Wars* tapes in his room - to play Mario, cook dinner for him, give him his bath and tuck him in every night. It seemed like an ideal situation to me. To be able to have that much time with Andy in the legitimate world I would have to work part time, and I couldn't support us working part time. I had the luxury of being a stay-at-home mom. And I didn't need a husband to be able to do it.

Meanwhile, Garnett's behavior was becoming increasingly erratic. It was obvious that he didn't like me spending most of my time elsewhere. If Allan called when Garnett and I were together, he would make snorting noises under his breath and start pacing around the room. The mere mention of Allan's name would send him into a passive-aggressive fit and he would withhold my drugs or jack up my price. His strange disappearances were more frequent and he talked to himself under his breath when he thought I wasn't paying attention.

He had also begun to collect guns. He traded meth for guns, and started carrying one everywhere he went. He had rifles and handguns, semi and automatic, and was starting to talk about "going out in style." When I asked him what he meant by that, he explained that if the "pigs" ever stormed his house, he'd be waiting in his basement for them, and take out as many as he could before they killed him. But that wasn't the most disturbing thing.

Most meth heads, at one time or another, hallucinate. (For whatever reason, thankfully, I never did.) They see shadow people moving in the corners of their houses and outside in their yards. Shadow people particularly like to hide out in trees. Most meth heads are also paranoid to one degree or another. Garnett was paranoid to another degree.

He decided that there were people who had made it their goal in life to slap his house. At first, he said it was a group of kids who would take turns running up to the front of his house, slapping it and then running away. When I asked him why someone would want to do such a thing, he looked at me as if I was the stupidest person to have ever walked the earth and said, "Are you *kidding*?"

He began referring to the people as monkeys. Before long, his delusion consumed him. Not only were the monkeys slapping his house, but there were people from four different states who switched license plates every hour and followed him wherever he went. Again, I asked him why he thought this was happening. He said, "Kimbo, are you kidding? I'm probably the most interesting thing they've ever seen!"

He was serious.

Everywhere he went, he took long, elaborate routes, attempting to "shake his tails." He started wearing crazy wigs to disguise himself from his imaginary followers. One night he took me with him so he could prove what was going on. As we stopped at a traffic light, he tilted his head toward the car idling next to him. It was a run of the mill, four-door sedan with a middle aged woman behind the wheel and what looked like it could have been her elderly mother sitting next to her in the passenger seat.

Garnett was giddy with excitement. "Watch this, watch this. When the light turns green, they're going to turn left."

"Garnett, it's a turn only lane. Of course they're going to

turn left."

I don't know if he didn't hear me or was ignoring me, but when they turned left, he started a high-pitched giggle that made my skin crawl. "I knew it! I knew it!" His excitement was that of a hardcore sports fan whose team just won the biggest game of the year. "They always turn left!" Pounding on the dash. "Do you see now?" Looking at me for approval. "Do you see what I put up with every day, all day long?"

I nodded and suddenly felt cold. Because when I looked into his eyes, there wasn't a doubt in my mind that he believed everything he was saying.

And even *that* wasn't the most disturbing thing.

The thing that disturbed me the most was when I found the hole in the wall of the basement, underneath the front of his house. Actually, it really wasn't a hole at all. It was a tunnel. It was only a foot and a half deep when I first saw it, but over the next couple of weeks, Garnett dug a tunnel that stretched almost five feet underneath the house. What was he doing? Why, he was going to dig a tunnel all the way under the street to the lawn on the other side so that he could crawl through one night and catch the monkeys in the act of slapping his house.

So when Garnett called me one night to tell me he was being arrested, all I felt was relief.

He'd been pulled over and the cop was back in his cruiser running the license.

"So, why do you think you're going to be arrested?"

"I have a warrant."

"For what?"

"I don't know. Probably my fucking ex-wife. You gotta do something, Kim. You gotta get me outta this."

Huh? "What? Do you have anything on you?"

"I already stashed that. I'm not driving my car, so I think it'll be okay, but I have the Beretta on me. What should I do?"

I wanted to tell him to wave it out the window. I figured that would get him locked up for a while.

"Kim! Hurry up. He's coming back. What should I do?"

"Shit, I don't know! Um," I was trying to think, "take the clip out and kick it under the seat. At least that way it's not loaded."

"Okay."

He left his phone on while they arrested him, but all I could hear were muffled voices.

Garnett was charged with fourteen counts of malicious stalking and harassment of his ex-wife, which explained his strange disappearances.

Scanning the yellow pages of the phone book, I found a bail bond company owned by a woman I'd gone to high school with. Jill met me at the jail and I co-signed for his bond, accepting responsibility for Garnett showing up for all future court dates. It never occured to me that he wouldn't.

Two days after his release, he told me he was going to run.

"What the hell, Garnett? You can't run. I'm on the hook for twenty-five grand."

"Sorry, Kimbo. I just can't do it. I can't take the risk of doing time."

"You can't be serious."

"Sorry. You'll figure something out."

And I did. I called Jill and asked her to revoke the bond.

"He told me flat out. He's going to run. He doesn't care about the money or me. I made a mistake. He shouldn't be out." After a brief discussion, she agreed. "He can't know it was me, though," I said.

"Don't worry. We'll come up with a reason. You just have to let me know exactly where he'll be at a certain time, and I'll have the guys bring him in."

I arranged for them to pick him up at my house; the only place he felt comfortable other than his own. I didn't want anyone to have to deal with a psychotic Garnett hiding in his basement with who knew how many guns.

They dragged him back to jail where he would remain until the court decided to let him out, or someone else co-signed for his bond. No one, not even his family, wanted him out.

His behavior was so odd during his two-month stay in the Ada county jail that they removed him from the regular population and placed in the medical unit under psychiatric watch.

When I was able to talk to him, he told me he was two months behind in his rent, and two weeks away from eviction. If that happened, he would lose everything he owned.

"Please, Kim, please. You're the only one I trust to get things done. Can you deal with the landlord and get my stuff into storage so I don't lose it?" He also wanted me to take care of his people - the ones he sold to - while he was away.

I'll be honest, I was glad he was in jail. I was thrilled that I wouldn't have to deal with his craziness, at least for a while. I'd been feeling trapped by his lunacy and it was getting more and more difficult to conduct business with him because of his paranoia and weird hallucinations. I put up with it because it was through him that I had access to meth. At the time, I thought of it as a business thing. I needed product and he was my supplier. The real reason, the one I never would have admitted at the time, was that I needed a constant supply of meth for *me*, and I was willing to do just about anything to get it.

Spending time with a crazy, paranoid person that I didn't like was nothing compared to what other women have done for meth. I know women who allowed themselves to be traded among men - sometimes groups of them - like baseball cards. The woman went to the highest bidder, so to speak. Whoever could provide the current "keeper" the most bang for their buck became the new owner. And on and on it would go, because once a woman is in that situation...

And the thing is, none of those women wanted to be that way. None of them would ever have imagined, in their worst nightmare that something like that could happen, especially not to them.

No one wants to lose her humanity.

No one wants to be an addict.

When Garnett asked me to handle his affairs, I said yes with no hesitation, because the first thing I thought was that this was my opportunity to move up. I didn't have a clue how that might come about, but something told me that I would somehow profit from the situation.

I knew where he kept his stash and I knew his regular customers, so I went to see each of them and explain the situation. I paid his landlord the back rent and arranged to pay for an additional two weeks so I could get all of Garnett's things moved. I kept track of everything so he would know where every penny went. I paid a couple of his friends, in meth of course, to pack and move everything to my storage unit, which I was about to let go because I wasn't using it anymore.

Then, just as I'd run out of Garnett's stash and was dangerously low on my own, Kilo showed up.

Kilo was Garnett's "guy." His connection. I knew who he

was. Garnett sometimes brought him to my apartment during the day to do deals when his "monkeys" were especially active. Kilo and I had never spoken. So when he appeared on my doorstep one afternoon, I was stunned.

"Can I talk to you for a minute?"

"Of course. Come in."

He and his constant sidekicks, Craig and Billy, sat on the sofa. I sat opposite them in the rocking chair. It was a bit unsettling having those men in my house without the buffer of Garnett.

I sat, trying to keep from wringing my hands, looking at the rainbow across from me. Kilo was Asian, tall, extremely handsome and soft-spoken. Craig was Hispanic, short and stocky and looks tough and hard. Billy, on the other hand, was even taller than Kilo: a long, gangly white boy who can't quite seem to sit still. They were all in their early twenties.

Boise is a melting pot. There's a large Hispanic population, especially in the surrounding areas, due to the agriculture. I've asked my Lao and Bosnian friends, "How on earth did you end up in Boise, Idaho, of all places? What did you do, throw a dart at a map?"

What they tell me is that church and civic groups sponsor refugees. I have no idea how common this is anywhere else. What I do know is that I currently reside in a low-income apartment complex, which in larger cities might be known as a housing project. There are twenty-three different languages spoken here, according to management. As a Caucasian, I'm definitely in the minority where I live. There are families from different countries in Africa, from Bosnia, Turkey, Russia, India, and Laos, to name a few. Most are refugees, sponsored by World Relief. It's nice, really, especially on Sundays when the families stroll the commons visiting one another wearing the most beautiful colors and fabrics: Saris, Babushkas, Dashikis and head wraps.

The elders in the families watch over those too young to go to school while their parents catch the city bus to work. They go for walks. They slide, climb and swing on the playground in the common area. It's lovely, really, the strong sense of family I see here everyday.

Kilo and Craig, however, were a rare oddity. Hispanics and Asians don't typically get along, but somehow they found each other and clicked.

Kilo took me aside. He knew what I'd done for Garnett and

was impressed with my loyalty. He was also beginning to have doubts about Garnett and his bizarre behavior. His obsession with monkeys and increasing paranoia were bad enough. The fourteen counts of stalking and harassing his ex-wife and entanglement with the legal system was dangerous for everyone. That's how I was promoted, so to speak. Loyalty goes a long way in the drug world. It's a rare commodity, particularly in a situation like I'd just been through. The common, the expected, result would have been for me to take the drugs and money and leave Garnett to sort out his own problems. It wasn't pretty, but it happened all the time and no one would have said a thing. Not to my face, anyway, and I would have eventually gone on to find another dealer with no problem. What surprised everyone was how I handled the situation, and I think that's what gave me respect in Kilo's eyes. It was exactly what I hoped would happen.

I started going through Kilo, and when Garnett finally got out of jail, most of his customers stayed with me. I was more reliable and they didn't have to deal with the psychotic bullshit they did with him. It wasn't my decision, but I certainly didn't discourage their choice. That move against Garnett was the first in a series of events that eventually led to my arrest.

I was moving up in the underworld and the additional responsibility brought more money. At the time, I felt good about myself. The recognition and acceptance I received from Kilo and my regular customers went a long way toward building my nearly non-existent self-esteem. In that world, it didn't matter that I hadn't finished college. It wasn't important that I couldn't seem to hold a job. It didn't even matter that I had a drug habit the size of a third world country because, hey, it's a stressful job. We all did it. Smoking meth was so normal, we barely paid attention to our own use. When Kilo and I were together, we never said, "Hey, let's get high." We just loaded the pipe as an ancillary behavior, and when I was alone it was like drinking water. It was just something I did. It's what I did to feel normal.

My brother had just ended his most recent relationship in Jackpot, and moved in with me to get on his feet. In exchange for room, board and, of course, free drugs, he would stay with Andy when I had to go out at night to make my rounds. Everything was covered. When Allan was home, we would spend as much time as possible together at my house. I would sometimes cook for him and do his laundry. "It's no problem," I would say. "It doesn't make any sense to take your clothes to a Laundromat when I have a washer and dryer here. Just let me do this for you."

Allan started calling me Kimpossible because if it was possible, he said, Kim could do it. I took it as a great compliment that someone thought I could do anything.

Co-dependency, a layman's definition: making sure everyone else's needs are met while completely ignoring your own. Co-dependency means never having to say, "I love you."

We would spend our time together talking or sometimes watching movies. Occasionally we would go shoot pool, but mostly we got high and had sex - wild, raunchy, raw sex. I couldn't get enough. We were fabulous in bed together. I felt like I was living a dream life: I was taking care of my son and myself without having some mundane, boring office job, I worked in the daytime when I wanted to, I was there for Andy when he was home and I had a man who...

A man who what? Dropped by on the weekends for sex and drugs, that's what. But I was in denial. If someone had smacked me upside the head and pointed out what was right in front of me, I wouldn't have seen it. It breaks my heart, thinking of the woman I was, selling herself short, selling herself out, for a man. It was easy to dismiss the obvious, using his job as a long haul truck driver for an excuse. So what if he never took me out to dinner? Who was I to hope for flowers or little trinkets from the places he'd been? Why should I care that we never went to the movies? Any time I started to think about what was really going on, or what wasn't, I would push the thoughts aside, telling myself I was being greedy.

Allan's tired from the road, and besides, he doesn't need to spend money on me. I can do it. (I don't deserve it) *I can pay for dinner. I can provide all the drugs and booze and whatever else anyone needs, because* (I don't deserve it) *I'm not worthy of being taken care of. I don't need any help. I'm Kimpossible.* If I were worthy, I wouldn't have to ask. It never occurred to me, as it does in sobriety, that the measure of my own self-worth is in how I treat myself.

Hindsight's a bitch.

I hated it when Allan had to leave. I tried to pretend it didn't bother me, but inside I felt betrayed, as if his leaving was a direct affront to me.

"I want you to start keeping track of what I owe you," he said one day as I handed him his package of meth for the road. "You know I'll pay you back, so start keeping track, okay?"

"Are you sure, Allan?" I felt awkward, but I was also glad he had offered. I was sending a lot of dope with him on the road, and I had a strong feeling it wasn't all for him. I figured he was either sharing with his trucker friends or selling some on the side.

Supporting my habit, Allan's and my brother's was putting a dent in my profits. "I hate to ask, but I really appreciate it. I'll give you good deals, though," I said, kissing his neck. "I promise."

I kept a separate ledger for what Allan owed me. He didn't belong with my customers. He was different. He was special. I thought it was very caring of him to consider the effect his habit had on my bottom line and that strengthened my illusion of our relationship. That's all it ever was: my illusion. My own little fantasy I created in my head. Conveniently, by never defining our relationship, my illusion was secure.

Another reason it was so easy to hide in my fantasy was because of the way Allan treated my son. They adored each other. The only man Andy ever spent any time with was my father and, occasionally, his Uncle Chuck. Seeing Andy with Allan tugged at the corners of my heart. They played Mario Kart together - Andy's favorite video game - and Andy would show Allan things he'd made at school that week, explaining what his class had done. It never bothered Allan that he couldn't understand most of what Andy said. I've always joked that Andy speaks "Andowneese," which is a combination of Andy and Down syndrome with the "eese" denoting, of course, that it's a language. Andy's funny, raspy voice, babbling on and on never fazed Allan. He just acted as if he knew exactly what Andy was talking about, and after a couple of months of me translating, he did.

When Allan was on the road, Andy asked about him. When Allan called, he asked about Andy. I'd be lying if I said there wasn't part of me that wished for Andy to have a daddy someday, and at the time, Allan seemed a perfect fit. I never thought, "I wish Allan were Andy's father." It wasn't like that at all. It was just a warm feeling I got seeing them together and a lovely little tapestry with which to decorate my fantasy world.

Chapter 9

Allan decided to buy a house, and we started house hunting when he was home on the weekends. I admit, there was a twinge of hope in the back of my mind that he was thinking of asking Andy and me to move in with him, but I never gave it serious consideration until he called me one day to tell me he'd found his dream house: a gorgeous log home in the mountains. His exact words were, "Do you want to be partners?"

I believe I quit breathing for a moment. The fact that he qualified the question by explaining his specific intentions did nothing to quash my excitement. What he meant, he said, was that he wanted me to pay a portion of the mortgage in exchange for spending an occasional weekend in the mountains. What I heard, of course, was, "Do you want to be partners?"

He wasn't able to buy that house, but he did qualify for one in the city: four bedrooms, two baths and a huge backyard with an old barn in one corner. It wasn't the dream home in the woods, but it would do nicely.

He was already pre-qualified, and the process was going smoothly when he called me from the road one rainy afternoon to tell me the earnest money had to be at the title company before five o' clock. Would I help him out? He'd pay me back, he promised. Just add it to his books. Keep track of everything. He'd pay me back.

A few days before closing on the house, Allan was on his way to Oregon. He'd found a new job with much better pay and the opportunity to own his own truck. He was flying to Oregon to drive the truck home. That was the plan.

He was pulled out of line at the airport. Most likely profiled because of the way he looked. In addition to his usual rugged appearance, he'd been drinking all night, was unshaven and wore a black leather skullcap. The authorities searched his bag and found a long forgotten pipefitting he'd once used to smoke pot. According to Allan, he simply grabbed a bag from his closet and threw a few things into it for the trip. He never looked inside and had no idea the pipe was there. There was only faint residue in the fitting, but it was enough to land him in jail that Friday afternoon, and keep him there until the arraignment on Monday morning.

Once again, I called Jill, and once again, she met me at the courthouse and then the jail where she posted Allan's bond. It was set at five thousand dollars, meaning I had to pay five hundred, plus fees. This, of course, went on his tab.

While we were waiting for his release, Jill offered me a job. I believe her exact words were, "You seem like you're comfortable around criminals. Would you be interested in working nights writing bonds?"

Why yes, I am. And yes, I would. And that's how I became a bail bondsman.

"Can I take you to dinner?" After thanking me, that's the first thing Allan said when he got out. Afterward, as we cruised down the freeway with the top down on my convertible, he reached over and cupped the back of my head in his hand, running his fingers through my hair. The November air was cool, stinging our faces. The feeling of his strong, warm hand cradling my head washed through me like the first sip of hot chocolate winding its way to your stomach on a chilly day.

This is how you touch someone you love, I thought, and I eased into his hand, feeling safe as I drove Allan to his future house, which he was renting from the current owners pending closing.

The bad news came just as we pulled into the driveway. When Allan hadn't shown to pick up the truck in Oregon, his new boss-to-be did some checking and found Allan's mug shot on the Ada County web site. He was calling to tell Allan not to bother coming. He didn't want a druggie driving one of his trucks. It was two weeks from closing on the house and Allan was suddenly unemployed.

I don't remember the exact conversation, but I'm sure the gist of it was, "I'll take care of it, Allan, if Andy and I can move in. I'll take care of the mortgage until you find a job. I know you'll pay me back. After all, you bought me dinner and ran your hand through my hair. It's the least I can do."

I do recall that Allan was hesitant about accepting my offer, but I didn't want to see him lose the house. That part is true. The real reason I did it, and I think I knew it at the time, was that I saw the opportunity to buy my way into his life. I thought that if we lived together, he would realize he loved me and we'd live happily ever after. That's a hard thing to own up to: that I was so unhappy, I was willing to buy love. With enough meth, though, even the worst idea can seem genius, and if that's true, I had enough meth to qualify for Mensa a hundred times over.

Andy was thrilled. He adored Allan and was excited that we were living with him. We moved in December 2003, just a couple of weeks before Christmas.

I enrolled Andy at the local Jr. High school - no small feat given the transition process. I met with his special ed. teacher and arranged for her to meet with the staff at the receiving school.

Every child in special education has an I.E.P. - an individual education program - that outlines the student's goals for the year. Part of the I.E.P. is to determine the amount of time he or she will spend in the "regular" classroom versus how many hours they'll be segregated in special ed. I've fought long and hard to make sure Andy gets as much mainstreaming with his typical peers as possible, and every year I go through the same thing at the annual I.E.P. meeting, fighting to make sure my son has the same opportunities as any other child to the extent that he is able. It's not easy. Far less effort is required to keep children with developmental disabilities segregated. It's easier for staff and easier for the child. Andy's always thrived among his typical peers, though, and there's no doubt in my mind that the effort I've put into making sure he's mainstreamed has provided a richer experience for everyone involved.

In 2003, I had the not so pleasurable experience of repeating the I.E.P. process with the receiving school. Both old and new teachers assured me he would continue to be included in regular classes, with an aide as necessary.

I felt guilty transferring him again as I'd done when we moved to Jackpot, and again upon moving back to Boise. This was his third transfer in two years, and even though he seemed to take it in stride, I knew that what was best for him was stability. I vowed to myself that he would finish junior high at the new school, move on with his class, and graduate without any more transfers.

I drove him to school on the first day, and walked him to his new classroom. The I.E.P. specified that he would spend first period with the special ed. class, and another in the afternoon so he could receive one on one attention for his specific goals. He would eat lunch in the cafeteria with the general population while an aide stood nearby, supervising until she was sure Andy would be okay on his own. Once he was comfortable, he would go to lunch independently. He was used to the routine of going through the line for hot lunch, getting everything he needed and finding a place to sit. The aide was there to make sure he wasn't harassed, and to help him with his social skills.

Andy is a social guy, with an affinity for blonde chicks. Kids have always liked him. Expressive language is where he has the most trouble. People with Down syndrome tend to have large tongues and/or small mouths, which sometimes makes them difficult to understand. Andy has both to delay his expressive language. Simply put, my son loves to talk, but unless you've been around him for a while, he's nearly unintelligible. I've always been his translator, and he sounds fine to me, but I sometimes have to remind myself that not everyone speaks Andowneese. It's an acquired skill.

So I drove him to school the first day, but when we got there, he didn't want me to go in with him. Of course he didn't. What eighth grade kid wants their parents at school with them? I was concerned, though. About everything, really, but at that moment, I wanted to make sure he could find his classroom.

"Andy, I'm not going to stay. I promise. I just want to walk you to your class."

"Mom, no. Unna go way. Andy do it."

But I was firm. I had to know for sure that he wasn't going to walk into that building and simply disappear among the concrete, linoleum and raging hormones that make up a junior high school. All I could picture was Andy roaming the halls, not knowing where to go and feeling frightened until a bell rang and the between-class stampede began. There's no way I was going to let that happen.

"Andy-bug, you don't have a choice on this one. Come on. I promise I won't stay. I'll leave as soon as you get to your room." I reached out to hold his hand, but he scowled at me, grunted and waited until I started walking, staying about five paces behind me.

I walked him to his class, and he wouldn't say goodbye to me. He was pissed, and I was secretly thrilled with his reaction. It was so typical of kids his age. But the mom in me wanted to protect my baby and make sure everything was okay.

Driving away from the school, I slipped my Mom skin, leaving it behind with the warm glow that was Andy, for safekeeping.

Chapter 10

Back at home, I sat down on my bed and lit a cigarette. I was so tired. I couldn't remember the last time I was horizontal. I knew that sometimes I'd fall asleep at the computer for an hour or so, but I couldn't remember the last time I actually slept in my bed. My practice of sleeping every night was beginning to fall by the wayside. I was drifting in and out when my eyes snapped open.

"Shit," I muttered, picking up my still-lit cigarette. It had burned halfway down, leaving another hole in the increasingly puckered landscape of my new down comforter. It was the second time in a week I'd fallen asleep that way. The puckers were the places where I'd sewn burn holes shut, and now I was going to have to do it again. "Later," I thought and stubbed the cigarette out in the ashtray. As I got up, tiny feathers poofed from the fresh hole. Rather than going to bed, which is what I needed to do, I got high. I had things to do and people to see. Sleep could wait. I knew Shadoe was waiting for me to call.

"Hey. You up?" The question was rhetorical.

"I'm always up. You coming over?"

"Yeah, I'll be there in about twenty minutes." I had him on speakerphone so I could load my pipe and talk at the same time.

"All right. Is it good?" I hated it when people asked me that. I didn't even matter if the meth was good, which it usually was. They'd bitch and moan, but they always bought. Always.

"Goddamn it, Shadoe. I'll be there in a minute." I loaded everything into my rolling briefcase - the same one I used when I wrote bail bonds - and arrived at his house forty-five minutes later.

"You're early," he said, opening the door. He was being sarcastic, but for me, arriving twenty-five minutes late *was* extremely early.

A couch and end table shared the living room with a motorcycle, and greasy engine parts lay on the kitchen floor where a dining table should have been. A thick layer of dust covered everything. I could see the particles, disturbed from inertia by our movement, dancing in the single patch of sunlight bold enough to risk a peek between the draperies as we moved through the forgotten part of the house. He led me through the house to the back bedroom - the only place Shadoe spent his time.

His bedroom was his office. That's what he called it. He dropped his four-hundred-plus-pound self into the plastic lawn chair that barely fit between the queen size bed and the closet. Shadoe always made me feel a little ill. He looked like a fifty-year-old sloth with a greasy, thin ponytail. The tee shirts he wore were old, tired and no longer held their original form. He cut the sleeves and neck line out, so there was no way to avoid seeing all sagging, white flesh when I was with him.

I started getting out my scale and baggies, setting them on the wooden slab he kept for me at the foot of the bed so I had an even surface to weigh on.

"Look at this. I made this last night," he said pulling down a small propane tank connected to a bungee cord suspended from ceiling.

"What the hell is that?"

"I designed it so that when I fall asleep with the flame going, it'll lift up instead of burning me. I think it's a pretty neat little invention," he said, and he chuckled. Shadoe suffered from diabetes and had recently burned his foot so badly that he ended up in the emergency room. He'd fallen asleep holding a propane torch going full blast. Three weeks later, his foot looked like gangrene was setting in, but he refused to go back to the doctor.

An empty coffee can on the bed was full of broken and burned pipe remnants. He blew glass, but badly. He was always showing me his latest, greatest invention or new design for a pipe or bubbler. I knew he wanted to replace Kelly, the guy who blew all my pipes, but that was never going to happen. I hated his work.

It took me a long time to see to it that Kelly made my pipes exactly as I liked them, and I did not intend to go elsewhere. The stem had to be just the right length, the glass an exact thickness and the bowl and hole on top precisely as I liked. Kelly was good, too. He'd started experimenting with different types of glass and using a hotter gas. His designs were becoming quite intricate. If I wanted to smoke out of a piece of art, Kelly was my man. Besides, Shadoe could barely blow his own nose, let alone a good pipe.

I glanced up at the canister hanging from the ceiling. "Nice, Shadoe. That's great. Does it work? Won't it light the wall on fire instead of burning you?"

"No, no. I've rigged it so it's far enough away from the wall and doesn't go all the way to the ceiling. I've worked on this for a while and now I've got it perfected." He was very pleased with himself - cocky even. "So," he rubbed his thick hands together, "whatcha' got for me today? I hope it's different. People kind of complained about that last."

Well if you didn't cut your shit with Fruit Fresh, I thought, *they might not complain so much*. He didn't realize I knew what he did, but I knew a lot more than anyone might have guessed. It was amazing how much information I could get just for getting someone high, or buying them a little food when they were hungry.

"Yeah, it is," I said, and tossed him a small rock. "You'll like it. See what you think."

Despite everything, Shadoe was a really a nice guy. His was the only house I'd stay and get high at, because I felt safe there. God knows why, but I did. It almost made me feel a little guilty lying to him. The shit was the same as it was the day before, but people are easy. They'll believe anything I tell them. It didn't really matter how good it was. I could probably sell bone fragments if that's what I had.

"This is good. Thanks. Can we do an ounce this time?"

"Sure. Do you have all the money?"

"Right here," he says, chucking me a roll of bills wrapped with a rubber band.

Shadoe was a handy-man, doing odd jobs for people here and there, but his main source of income at the time was selling meth. The burdens of his weight, age and diabetes made it hard for him to walk, let alone squat and bend. Sitting in a chair in his bedroom closet was about as much exertion as he could stand.

I knew he was barely getting by, and almost lost his house recently. The previous month, he worked out some kind of deal with a man who sold Shadoe on a crazy scheme that I didn't understand to keep him from foreclosure. Shadoe didn't understand it either, but he scrawled his name and initialed "here, and here." When he began "paying the man back," it was in the form of rent.

Shadoe made enough money selling drugs to keep his utilities on, buy food and make sure he always paid me in full. He enjoyed thinking of himself as a big-time dealer and said that all he cared about was living "the life" and getting high.

For those of us caught up in the drug world, that's all any of us cared about. Most of the people I sold to disgusted me because I wasn't like them, right? They were meth-head tweakers. I simply *used* meth. All of the time.

The truth was, the disgust I felt wasn't so much for them as it was seeing in them a mirror image of what I'd become.

"Do you have any sandwich bags? All I have are quarter-ounce baggies."

"Yeah, yeah," he said, and pulled a box from a shelf in his closet. He was always so eager to please me. Kind of like how I was with Allan, but on a much smaller scale.

It never occurred to me until very recently how Allan must have felt about my "cling-on" ways. My epiphany came in 2009 when I joined Facebook and began the "friending" process. Someone from my past accepted my invitation with a note attached that said, *I can't believe you wanted to friend me. I always thought you hated me in high school. Do you want to have lunch?* Two minutes later, the same person messaged me. *Did I say something to make you mad? You didn't respond to my message.* And when I didn't respond to that (I was a little irritated at that point) they sent me *another* message.

Two thoughts came to me almost simultaneously. *Jesus, God this person is annoying the hell out of me/holy shit, that's probably how I was with Allan.* And, of course, that's exactly what I must have been like. *Want drugs? Want sex? Can I do your laundry? Give you a blow job? Buy you a house?* (pant, pant, pant) How can you have respect for someone so determined to be a lapdog? It took me six years to catch on, but I get it now. I don't know what I would have done if I were Allan, but I'd like to think I wouldn't have moved in with me.

I weighed Shadoe's crystal and threw him the closed baggie. "Do you have a Q-tip?" I asked, counting the bills. "I need to clean my pipe a little."

"Here, use mine. It works really good."

"You know how I am." I could never use other people's pipes. I wouldn't drink out of glasses in anyone's house, either. Even if they were clean. I always carried a bottle of soda in case I got thirsty. Just one more way of separating myself, I suppose.

Shadoe found a Q-tip, and I started cleaning my pipe. "You've put more blankets over your windows, huh?" He had thick, heavy blankets nailed over his bedroom windows from the ceiling to the floor.

"Yeah. Now I think I've got every crack covered." Shadoe was like a lot of people I knew: paranoid as hell that someone was always watching them. Blinds weren't adequate window coverings, they reasoned, because people could see through the tiny holes where the strings threaded through. It was ridiculous. I hated paranoid people and swore to myself when I started this gig that I wouldn't let myself succumb to it. I saw enough twacked out people day in and day out, including Garnett, to remind me of my vow, and somehow that allowed me to escape the paranoia that consumed so many people I knew.

I took a huge hit off my pipe, clouding the room as I exhaled. "Shadoe, has it ever occurred to you that you just aren't that interesting? Why would anyone want to spend their time watching you from rooftops and trees?"

"You never know," he said. "I like to be safe." I rolled my eyes because that's what I always did when we had those conversations.

We sat and smoked, and I listened to him ramble while I updated my ledger.

"You know you shouldn't write things down. I keep everything right here," he tapped his head with his still smoldering pipe. "Writing things down will get everyone you work with in trouble if you ever get popped."

"I've told you, the only person my books would ever incriminate is me. Besides, Shadoe, what you keep in your head isn't anywhere near as accurate as my ledger. I've got everything coded."

I charged Shadoe $1100 an ounce because he thought he was getting a killer deal. The guy he went through before charged him more for product that always weighed light and wasn't nearly as good as what I had. I also charged him that much because I knew he cut it and should have been making bank.

I had all my ledgers in a file cabinet at home. Every nickel I've ever spent on dope and every cent that's ever come in. When it became clear that I was selling more than just quarters and half grams to cover my own habit, I started keeping books. It was how I made sure business was profitable and not just me selling in order to cover the cost of my own drugs. "We don't commit felonies for free," I'd say. Selling meth in the quantity I did was a business, and good business people always know what their bottom line is. It just made sense and it pissed me off when people like Shadoe wanted to lecture me about my bookkeeping.

The side benefit of keeping records, which I didn't anticipate, was that it was impossible for anyone to do the "Dude, I paid you last time. Don't you remember? We're even, I swear to

God," thing. My people all knew I kept records because I wrote everything in the ledger in front of them, unless there was a public transaction. "You think we're even?" I'd ask if they balked at their tab. "Well, let's just compare your notes to mine." Sometimes I'd imitate "The Church Lady," a skit Dana Carvey used to do on Saturday Night Live. "Oh, you don't have anything written down? Well isn't that *special.* I guess all we have to go on is what I have here by your name." I rarely had anyone question me and they all knew I was fair.

As Bob Dylan sang in *Absolutely Sweet Marie,* "To live outside the law, one must be honest."

Josh, my newest "boy," moved more meth than anyone else did for me, but he was irritating as hell at times, so his price was $950. A twenty-two year old white boy, Josh dressed like a wanna-be gangster with his jeans slung low, untied kicks and his hat on backwards. He'd recently bought a Blue Tooth, the latest thing in cell phones at the time, and wore the earpiece constantly. We'd be in the middle of a deal and he would start saying things that didn't make sense until I realized he was talking to someone on his phone. Josh was a pretty boy and quite the ladies' man from what I heard, mostly from him. He had long eyelashes and batted them at me.

"You keep batting those fucking eyelashes at me," I told him, "and I'll jack your price up. That shit doesn't work on me, so quit flirting and give me my money."

"Awww, Kim. Don't be like that."

Josh had a plan. He told me about it one day, as I was weighing a quarter pound of meth for him. He wanted to take over Boise.

"What the hell are you talking about, Josh?"

"I'm talking about taking over. You know, like one day you'll retire and maybe I can meet your guy. Then I'm going to undercut everyone else out there until I'm the only one left. I'll be the man!"

I thought he was joking until I studied his eyes and realized the jackass was serious. "Josh, you're a fucking idiot. You're kidding, right? You know that'll never happen."

"Why not? I'm good at this. That's my dream. I want to be the man."

"Yeah, but Josh, you're *not* the man. You're a fucking idiot."

He started pouting, batting those damn eyelashes at me. "Don't say that. I'm totally going to do it. You just watch."

I'd had it. "Goddamn it, Josh!" I slapped the Blue Tooth out of his ear. "Pull up your pants, tie your fucking shoes, sit up and pay attention!" He leaned over and, looking wounded, picked up the earpiece for his phone. "Do you know why there are several bail bond companies in this town? Do you ever stop to think that there is more than one phone company?" He was sitting there, looking offended, as if I'd hurt his feelings, and that only pissed me off more. "It is IMPOSSIBLE for you to be the only asshole selling meth ANYWHERE, let alone Boise. Who the fuck do you think you are? Get this straight. When and IF I 'retire,' I won't be passing any torches on to you, so get that out of your head right now."

"Why not? I'm a good worker."

"Because, Josh, you're reckless and not particularly street smart. You're a shit for brains kid with visions of sugarplums in your head. Sure, you know people you can sell quantity to, but that doesn't qualify you for anything. You think the guys who work at Best Buy are all scheming to knock Bill Gates off his pedestal? Maybe they dream about it, but they sure as shit aren't serious. You know why?"

"Why?"

"Because they know their place, Josh! There are *banks*, not bank. There are grocery *stores*, not grocery store. Do you understand what I'm saying to you?"

"I understand, but you wait and see. I have a plan. It'll work." He was pouting as he put his Blue Tooth back in his ear. "Why wouldn't you give me to your guy when you retire?"

"Because," I said. "There are a lot of reasons. For one thing, you're dangerous. You've got a different girl with you every time I see you, and even though I've told you I don't want them around, you still have them drop you off."

"I have them park down the street," he interrupted. I glared at him.

"It's not even that, Josh. You run around with these skeezy chicks, get them high and start bragging to them about your big plan. And don't tell me you don't talk about it, because I know you. I've told all you guys: women will always fuck shit up. They are your Achilles' heel, and you will fail because you're stupid. You just don't talk about shit, Josh, except that you do because your fucking ego is so out of control. And as for me retiring? Fuck you. Right now all you need to be concerned with is that I'm *your* man and you need to know your place."

He pouted some, but didn't mention his plan to dominate the drug world much after that. He knew what my opinion was, but every now and then, he'd make a comment about his grand plan. Mostly, I saw Josh as a kid with stars in his eyes who needed to be put in his place once in a while. It was worth it, though. He made me a lot of money.

It's accepted as fact in the drug world that women are trouble. Loyalty went a long way toward securing my position and I took pride in that. I also knew how rare it was for a female to command any kind of respect in the meth world, let alone be successful. Women will rat you out if you piss them off. If caught, women will flip rather than do jail time because they can't handle it. Women are "cop-callers," calling the police anytime they feel like complicating your life. Women are more likely to flip (work with the police when caught) if they have kids...

Then again, most CI's (citizen informants) I've known have been men, but I wasn't about to concede that to Josh.

I was a completely different person with the people I worked with. I wasn't a mother and I wasn't a co-dependent woman desperately seeking love. I kept my worlds separate and there was a different Kim for each. It wasn't acting as much as it was accessing pieces of me that I normally kept hidden. I think everyone has facets of themselves they never explore. There's good and bad in all humans. My behavior in the drug world had a lot to do with acting out rage from my past. There was so much hurt and confusion inside me, and I was afraid of those feelings. Being more aggressive, and sometimes downright bitchy, was how I vented my anger and feelings of helplessness. The power I felt, and the control I had over people - especially men - was as reinforcing to me as the drugs were.

In the book *Drinking: A Love Story*, Caroline Knapp writes, "...the problem with self-transformation is that after a while, you don't know which version of yourself to believe in, which one is true. I was the hardened, cynical version of me when I was with (some people) and I was the connected, intimate version of me when I was with (another.)"

That's how it was for me, except that I knew I was two different people.

Sometimes I wonder which I was more addicted to: the drugs or the life. Obviously, it was meth, but the drug world itself was a very close second and all of it served a greater purpose for me that I didn't understand at the time. In that world, I was important. I had status and people respected me. Around my boys, I felt smart, sexy and self-assured.

I started getting high so that I could get more done. Call it the Superwoman syndrome. But I continued getting high as a way to escape the feelings I didn't want to feel. It wasn't long before getting high was the only way I could function. I'd become entangled in a web of my own creation, and I couldn't see a way out. If I quit using, I'd have to deal with the depression and bi-polar disorder, and that scared the hell out of me. I would crash and be non-functional for who knew how many days. If I quit selling, Allan would lose the house, and if that happened, he wouldn't need me anymore.

I was starting to feel trapped.

Chapter 11

After Christmas, we settled in to our new house and my days, much like my life, were compartmentalized. I was Mommy in the morning, drug dealer during the day, and at five o'clock, I transferred the bond company's phone line from whoever was on shift during the day to the cell Jill gave me to use for work. I was on-call five or six nights a week, five p.m. to six a.m., but I didn't have to sit in the office, which was nice because there were a lot of nights when I would only write three or four bonds. On a good night, I might write eight or ten. I received a flat fee per bond, so the more I wrote, the more I made.

Whatever I'd been doing during the day, when Andy came home, I was Mommy again. We'd go through our usual coming home routine before I made him dinner.

He would come through the front door and announce his arrival. "Oh, hi Mom. It's me. I'm home." He still does the same thing and it makes me smile every time I hear it. He's so deadpan about it, like he's on the five 'o clock news reporting something extremely important. To me, he is.

"Hey, Bug! How was your day?"

I used to get a lot of flack from people, mostly my mother, about all the nicknames I have for him: Andy-bug, bug-butt, bug in a boy suit (there's a pattern there, I know) Mr. Monster, palooka-butt...

The names were just there. I never thought about them, they just came out. Mom would tell me he was never going to know his real name if I kept confusing him by calling him by different ones, but I disagreed.

"Mom," I would say. "He has Down syndrome, he's not an idiot." Sure enough, Andy knows his name.

He's had a communication log between the school and me every year since he was three, and I still have every one of them. So he comes home and shows me his notebook with his teacher's comments for the day or some project he's been working on at school. And everyday, we have basically the same conversation when I ask about his day.

"Oh, uh, essa fine."

"What did you do today?"

"Um..." (long pause as he taps his finger on his chin) "Hmm... doe know."

"Andrew, what did you do today?"

"Oh... pfff," and he'll put his square little hand on my cheek as if to say, *Oh, Mom. You're so blasé*, which is why I have the notebook so I know what he's been doing all day.

I'll grab his hand and kiss the palm. "Sheesh, fine. Are you hungry?"

"Oh, yeah. Um, essa little pizza, whole bunch of peas. OH! Enna jams." The first thing he does when he gets home, after I'm done bothering him, is put on his pajamas - boxers and a tee shirt - and pop in a DVD.

"Alright, sir," I'll say. "Love you, Bug."

"Ayu you."

Between school and developmental therapy, Andy has long days: seven a.m. to six p.m., and he loves it. If he didn't, I certainly wouldn't subject him to that kind of schedule. Long days make for short evenings, though, and after he's done eating, it's time for a shower and then about an hour of free time before bed.

I love that part of the day. It's when I feel most like June Cleaver: uber-mom.

I never went anywhere from the time Andy came home until I tucked him in at bedtime. The only exception was if I had to go to the jail to write a bond, but that rarely happened. Most of the bonds I wrote were late at night or early in the morning: DUI's, FTA's (failure to appears) disturbing the peace, vandalism, urinating in public. They're the crimes and misdemeanors that stem from too much alcohol.

Every night when I tucked him in, I sang Andy a song. A ritual of ours began when he was a baby in N.I.C.U. and I would sit beside his bed just babbling away so he could hear my voice. I made up this silly song. I don't even know where the words came from. Like all the nicknames I have for him, they just came to me one day and I've been singing it to him ever since.

"I love you so much, I'll sing you a song, that says: I love you, I love you, and I guess I'll always love you. 'Cause you're cute, and you're smart, and you're funny, and you're strong. Andy sing."

"Ayu you, ayu you, seesh I ayu you. Essa cute, smart, funny, strong!"

"I love you, I love you, and I guess I'll always love you. 'Cause you're cute and you're smart and you're funny and airplane!" I pretend to forget what comes next and he giggles with that raspy sound his throat makes. "Oh man! I forgot. Andy sing."

"Ayu you, ayu you, seesh I ayu you. Are cute, smart, funny," he thought for a second. "Orange!" He laughed as if this is the funniest damn thing anyone has ever said. "Momma do it." It's become part of the game and we go back and forth until I declare enough is enough.

After our song, I would kiss his cheeks and forehead and he'd wrap his skinny arms around my neck and do the same. Leaving his room, taking one last look at him curled up under the covers with his thumb in his mouth, I always felt a sweet sadness.

I still sometimes feel it when I tuck him in. It's residual fear, from when he was a baby, that this may be the last time I see him alive. I know how macabre that sounds, but those days still haunt me. The difference is that now I allow myself to *feel* rather than numb the sadness with drugs or alcohol.

It's not easy, but I've found a quiet dignity in acknowledging my feelings. To sit with pain and sadness, to be able to remind myself that what I'm feeling is not only normal, but also healthy and to have faith that the feelings will pass regardless of the outcome of the situation, takes true strength. I was raised to think of my emotions as weaknesses and because of that, I was afraid to feel. As I grew up and went through vicious bouts of depression related to my bi-polar disorder, I became terrified of my feelings. I was convinced that one day I would disappear into them and never be able to pull myself out, so it was easier to avoid feeling as much as possible.

This was, of course, impossible and the result was a cycle of futile desperation. I hated the way I felt, so I'd get high to numb myself, but like Novocain, the numbness wore off and not only did the pain return, but there was fresh sadness and hurt to add to it. So I'd smoke more and more meth, attempting to run away from myself, but at the end of every line I snorted or bowl I smoked, there I was, more wrecked and damaged than when I'd begun.

Like so much in my life at that time, I tried to keep everything separate, attempting to keep the drug world from tainting the purity of my life with Andy. But as I told my mother, "He has Down syndrome, he's not an idiot."

I knew that sometimes he would wake up in the middle of the night to find me gone. I'd come home and find him awake, watching movies or sometimes just standing outside my bedroom.

The first six months that I was sober, when we lived with my parents, Andy slept with me. He refused to sleep alone and at night, he always kept some part of him connected with me: his foot on my leg, an arm on my back, fingers on my cheek. His expressive language is limited, but I know what he was doing. He was making sure I stayed home all night.

He still needs to be sure of my presence, and if he's in bed and can't hear me, he'll call out, "Mom?"

"What, honey?"

"Um...innah bed."

"I know you are, Bug."

"Oh, nuffin, nevermind."

And these exchanges, which are diminishing with time, break my heart, because I know that I did this to him. I took away his security. I know my nightly absences made him feel insecure when he needed me and I wasn't there, and I hate myself for doing that to him.

Allan and I each had our own bedroom, but the only time he used his was when he had his son every other weekend. The rest of the time, we slept together in my room. We never discussed it, that's just the way it was.

In the beginning, I only left at night when when someone called about bail. I liked being home. When Andy was asleep, we'd go to bed, watch movies and eat Ben and Jerry's while he smoked pot and I got high. We had sex every night and most mornings. Great sex. Fabulous sex. Sometimes we watched porn, sometimes not. We were great in bed together. He never said, "I love you," and I didn't want to be the first. Somewhere deep inside, I knew that if I opened that door, I had to be prepared to deal with the consequences, and I didn't want to know what they would be.

For me, sex *was* love. I'd given myself up enough in the past to understand that on a cognitive level, but knowing didn't change anything. Love, to me, was all about the act of sex and physical contact. Even with the men I'd been with before who told me they loved me, I didn't believe it unless I was being constantly held and touched. Without that, nothing else they said or did mattered. To me, it wasn't love.

All of this, of course, was about self-worth. I wasn't a person unless someone loved me, and without physicality, there could be no love. *If no one wants me, I must not be worth wanting. If no one protects me, I must not be worth protecting.* Protecting and loving myself didn't make sense to me. Just the thought of providing myself with what I needed made me cringe. To do so felt selfish, narcissistic, greedy and wrong. I based my entire self as a person, woman and mother solely on the feedback I received from other people.

Even with Andy. Being a good mother was more important to me than anything else was, but I was never sure that I was good enough. Andy couldn't tell me how he felt and I rarely heard it from anyone else. The couple of times I heard my mother say it, I could feel myself sucking the words in, trying to savor them and store them away. At times like that, I wanted to beg her to repeat it again and again. The request would be right there, in the back of my throat and on my tongue: *please, please, please, tell me again.* I was so empty inside that I took all my cues about who I was from other people.

So the fact that Allan wanted to have sex with me - and often - was all I needed to feel wanted, needed and loved. The feedback I got from him was that I was a Goddess in bed. To me, that meant I was a *loved* Goddess and I sure as hell wasn't going to open a dialogue and risk hearing otherwise.

Chapter 12

Around the time we moved in with Allan, two significant things happened. The first was Garnett's release from jail. He'd been there nearly three months, but he was worse than when he went in. With nowhere to go, he was forced to live with his parents, whom he despised, and he was furious with Kilo and me for what he saw as cutting him out of business. Kilo would still sell to him, but Garnett no longer had any customers. All his friends, even those he'd known since high school, decided to stay with me rather than put up with his craziness. I met with him to give him the key to the storage unit where all his belongings were stored, and let him know when and how the monthly rent was to be paid. All the money I made from selling the meth he had at the time of his arrest, I'd put toward his expenses while he was in jail, so he had no money, but he told me he'd take care of the storage bill. Other than that, he wouldn't look at me and barely said a word. He never thanked me for anything I'd done for him, and as he walked away, I had an uneasy feeling.

About two months later, the storage company called to tell me I had five days to pay the past due rent or they were going to lock me out of the unit and sell my things. They were also pissed off that there was a chain and lock on the unit, which were expressly forbidden according to the contract. I told them I would be in to see them later that day, and went to find Garnett.

He wouldn't answer my calls, so I drove around until I saw his van parked in front of a friend's house. The friend was at work, but Garnett was there...in bed with the wife of a man he'd known since junior high.

I pounded on the door, yelling that I knew he was in there and I needed to talk to him, and he eventually opened it, pulling on his pants while the woman hopped up and down behind him putting her socks on.

He was smirking at me, which was the first thing that pissed me off. "The storage place called and said you haven't paid any rent."

He giggled. "So?"

"So? You need to pay that rent. They also said you put some kind of lock and chain on the unit. What's that about?" He pushed by me and headed for his van. I followed him. "Did you

hear me? You need to pay that or they'll auction off all your stuff."
I put a hand on his arm as he was opening the driver's side door.

He shook himself like a wet dog. "So fucking what? It's
your problem, Kiiiimberly. Not mine." He started giggling again.
"Did you forget whose name the unit is in? I'll get around to it
when I feel like it. IF I feel like it."

"But Gar..."

"Fuck you! Fuck you and all your monkey friends! I know
what you're doing." *Still with the monkeys?*

"And you and Aaallllllan better watch out. And that ugly
fucking retarded kid of yours, too!"

Sorry?

Now he was in the van with the door closed, sneering and
giggling at me. "That's right. Leave it to an ugly bitch like you to
fart out a stinking mongoloid piece of afterbirth and call it a kid.
Jesus Christ! How can you stand to look at the little fucker? He's so
fucking ugly." He let his tongue fall out of his mouth, rolled his
eyes up in his head and made moaning noises. "Way to go, Kimbo.
Why don't you go home to that UGLY FUCKING RETARD? HA
HA HA HA HA HA!" His tires screeched as he jerked his van
down the street. I could still hear him laughing and moaning.

I felt a cold calm wash over me and in that instant, I knew
what I was going to do. I took just a second to check for any
feelings of guilt I might have had, and found none. He could have
done anything. He could have *said* anything...except for what he did
say. I don't know if it was temporary insanity and he didn't know
what he was doing, or if he simply didn't see me as a threat. Either
way, it didn't matter.

I drove to the storage place, paid the past rent and
explained the situation: that I let a friend store his things there and
he was supposed to pay the bill. *So sorry for all this confusion. What's the
typical procedure if someone doesn't pay their bill? Oh, really? Well, how about
we just speed things up a little, what do you say?*

So I terminated my contract on the unit, and they used bolt
cutters to cut the lock and chain. Rather than waiting and selling the
contents at an auction, which is what they typically do, or donating
everything to Goodwill, which is another option, they took one
look, declared the contents to be junk and hauled everything to the
city dump the following morning.

Everything he owned: every book, yearbook, guitar, photograph and stick of furniture. All of it. Thirty-some-odd years of memories, gone.

When I told Allan, he was stunned. He couldn't believe what I'd done. "Holy shit, Kim! He's going to go nuts. You probably shouldn't have done that."

When word got around, people used words like, "gutsy," "ballsy" and even "crazy." Not one of them used the word "retarded."

The other major event that coincided with Andy and I moving in with Allan was Kilo's arrest.

He had just left my house and was going to make a drop to someone else when the police pulled him over. The reason for the stop was that he didn't wait until his rear wheel was completely across the line before turning off his signal when he switched lanes. The police had probable cause to search him because he had a warrant. They found a quarter pound of meth as well as marijuana.

The truth was Kilo was on their radar. The police already suspected him of dealing meth. He had connections to people who were already in the system on drug charges, and he had an outstanding warrant related to his previous criminal history. Once you catch the attention of the authorities, it's only a matter of time before you go down.

His arraignment was the following morning. Jill had to write the actual bond because of the amount: $125,000. For a bond that large, someone had to have property to put up as collateral, as well as $12,500 in cash. I arranged for his cousin to put up his house, and I came up with the down payment for the cash. Kilo paid me back when he was released, and paid off the balance to Jill sooner than she required. He was a model client, checking in with her weekly, as she required, and attending all his court dates. She was thrilled.

I hired an attorney I'd heard about over the years from different people. Word around the campfire was that Larry originally wanted to be a doctor before switching to law. In the era when Ken Kesey was forced to hide out in Mexico to escape prosecution for possession of two joints, Larry felt that the "heads" needed one of their own to represent them. Whether the legend was true or not, I admired the idea of a man with such integrity and idealism. I took Kilo to Larry.

I also hired Larry to handle Allan's case. He was sentenced to one year of probation, weekly drug classes and one hundred hours of picking up garbage on the side of the road. He didn't work for more than six months, and when he wasn't fulfilling his court ordered obligations, we spent our days together at home playing games on the computer and listening to music. He'd play his guitar for me and sometimes people would stop by, but mostly we got high. All day, every day, we would get high and have sex, and to me it felt like bonding. I didn't care that he wasn't working. In fact, I liked that he was home all the time with me. In my meth soaked mind, I thought I was living a dream. I was with the man I loved twenty-four hours a day, had all the drugs I wanted and didn't have to worry about money.

I didn't live like the drug dealers you see in movies like *Scarface* or *Blow*, but I was doing well and we wanted for nothing. I was bringing in six to eight thousand dollars a month, which was more money than I'd ever made in the legitimate world, and was spending it just as fast as it came in.

I didn't see an end. Part of me knew that it wouldn't last forever, but I didn't let myself think about that. Kilo sometimes talked about getting out - about saving some money and going legit - and had spoken of it more often since his arrest. But I honestly never thought much beyond the here and now.

It wasn't always that way. I planned on going to graduate school for applied behavior analysis. I wanted to do clinical work with people who had developmental disabilities. It was a dream I'd had since before Andy was born. But, his medical condition was serious and I was having flashbacks during classes. As I got older, my depression became harder to control and when I started self-medicating with drugs, all my dreams vanished in a cloud of smoke.

The jobs I had between my stints at school always ended in disaster. Keeping my depression a secret, my mood swings and meltdowns were unexplainable. I'd forget my meds and crash. The doctors would adjust my medication, but it would take time for them to work. I'd cry at work, excusing myself to the bathroom where I'd sob uncontrollably for too long, only to return with red, puffy eyes. Feeling like a freak, I'd become withdrawn and anti-social, and eventually, I'd lose the job.

When I started dealing meth, my moods didn't matter. There was no clocking in or out, no consequences for being late because I could barely function and no building in which I was trapped all day, hiding in the bathroom trying to stop my tears. I felt like my dreams were unattainable because of my mental illness, and I felt better excelling on the fringes of society rather than failing inside of it.

I thought about the future as far as knowing I wanted Andy to graduate from the local high school, which meant staying in the house for the next five years. Allan and I talked about it and that's what I thought was going to happen. We would stay in the house until Andy graduated and then...but we never talked about what would happen after that. If I were sober, I probably would have seen that as a warning sign, but I wasn't, and I didn't. We never talked about the future in any serious way. Allan always said that one day he'd pay me back. "Just keep track of everything," he told me. "It will all come back to you. Don't worry."

There are only two ways out of the drug life: prison or death. I've never known anyone who saved enough money to retire and live happily ever after. There's no gold watch at the end of this gig, no pension plan, no retirement party or 401K.

I would listen as Kilo and Craig talked about saving enough money to start a legitimate business. Josh envisioned himself as the Donald Trump of the Boise meth market. Shadoe was determined to keep on the way he was until the police tried to drag him out of his house, at which point he would, "go out with guns ablazin'."

Me? I say I never thought about it, but as I sit here reflecting, I realize that even if I didn't admit it to myself, I thought that my "out" was with Allan and the money he owed me. That's not something I'm comfortable admitting, but the more I think about it, the more valid it seems. The reason I never thought about the future was because I assumed that what he meant by paying me back was taking care of me once he became stable. Once Andy and I moved in with Allan, we were partners for life as far as I was concerned. From my point of view, we got along exceedingly well, bought a house together, paid our bills together and shared holidays at each other's parents' houses. We did everything a married couple would do.

Of course, my view was skewed because there was no "we." Not in his mind, anyway. I think Allan was as trapped in the situation as I was. At any point, either of us could have said, "Look, enough is enough. Let's cut our losses and go our separate ways." But we both stayed, pursuing our own agendas, and neither of us was honest with the other. My agenda was love; Allan's was financial. I often wonder how different things would have been had he not been pulled out of line at the airport that day.

Chapter 13

My brother, Chuck, moved into an apartment just a block away from us. He was driving cab at that time and had visitation with his two children every other weekend. It was nice having him so close because when my niece and nephew stayed there, Andy could visit them. The three of them adored each other and when Andy spent the night, it was like party central for kids: pizza, movies, video games and lots of time at the playground of the schoolyard that bordered Chuck's backyard.

My brother has his share of downfalls, but the one thing I will say for him is that he's great with kids. Especially his nephew. When Andy was born, Chuck was living on a beach in Hawaii with nothing but a knapsack in which he toted his few belongings. As soon as he heard that Andy had arrived, he somehow bummed an airplane ticket off a woman he didn't even know, and was home within forty-eight hours.

Jaden and Majel grew up with Andy as their older cousin, and there were never any questions about why he was different from other kids or why he talked so funny. They just accepted him as a surrogate big brother and loved him unconditionally.

Chuck worked nights, so our hours were similar. He was usually getting off work about the time Andy left for school. Allan started working again, and most mornings he left as soon as Andy's bus was gone.

For a while, Chuck's visitation schedule was opposite that of Allan's and his son, so Andy was able to spend time with his uncle and cousins one weekend, and with Allan and his son the next. My brother and I spent our time together on weekday mornings.

"Okay" I say, clicking the phone shut. "Any bets?"

"What? Who was it? Kelly? Man, that guy's a pain in your ass, isn't he?" My brother, Chuck, and I are in my living room getting high at 8:30 in the morning.

"Uh huh. What's your bet?"

"Mmmm...hole in the pocket. No wait! Left it in his other pants."

"Okay. I'll go with the hole in the pocket. Is that empty?" I take the glass pipe, reload and melt down the rock of meth in the bowl. "I told him to meet me at Lou's at eleven. You about ready?"

"Let's just finish this bowl and then I will be. The bet's the usual, right? Double Jager?" We finished what was in the pipe and headed for Lou's.

Lou's is one of a couple of bars in Boise that open at nine in the morning, serving only breakfast the first couple of hours, but no alcohol until eleven-thirty.

I'm sitting perched on a barstool in front of a video slot machine toward the back of the bar. Bars aren't built with daytime in mind, and a hard jag of sun spots me as if I'm a vaudeville act every time the back door opens. The vendors are crashing dollies bearing kegs into the back door and walk-in as they change out the empties. Liquor bottles clink and tinkle as the obscenely cheerful a.m. barkeep restocks vessels, some amber, some clear. The smell of soap steaming from the dishwasher chases the loitering stench of cigarettes and spilled beer, and the jukebox is still unconscious from last night.

It's jarring, this early morning scene, and it sets my teeth on edge. I feel wired, weird, wanky and uneasy with the mechanics of my own body, like an aardvark trying to gavotte. The back door closes a final time and I feel the delivery truck in my chest as it rumbles out of the back lot. The bar has turned its back on the sun and I ease into the shadows cast by the lights over the pool tables while the warm glow of neon signs speak to me in jingles from the walls.

Three or four sagging figures hunch over the bar with nicotine-tinged fingers and trembling hands, waiting for the alcohol to flow. I avoid eye contact because I feel their despair in the marrow of my bones, but I wonder what their lives must be like to bring them to this shadowy place every morning. I think that demons have chased them from the sunlight and better days, when tomorrow held more than the promise of drink. I think they come here to hide. They come here to forget about the sun.

The brotherhood I share with these men is utterly lost on me. The four yards that separate us are my moat of denial. I don't reflect these men directly, but I am their sister in a sideways world: a parallel existence where, while the details differ, we walk the same path. I am female, they are male. They are alcoholics, I'm an addict.

They appear closer to the end of their lives than I do, yet in this sideways place, the path simply is, and time is irrelevant.

As I settle into my morning routine, high on a stool in front of the machine, I feel a tug at the corner of my heart. Denial of what I've become allows me to feel pity for my brothers. I don't see myself as they are. I'm different. I am different. I am different. I am different. I'm a good person. Getting high is how I feel normal, and most importantly; if no one knows (my parents, society, law enforcement, my boss, my son's teachers, etc.) then there's no problem.

Shortly after eleven, a beam of light assaults the dim room, and out of the corner of my eye, I see Kelly coming through the back door.

"Hey," he sidles up to me. He always sidles, like a snake. I point to the cigarette box on the table to my left. "Thanks," he says slipping the box into his pocket. "Uh, listen, I only have half the money. I guess I must have left the rest in my other pants, but I can get it to you later today if that's okay."

"Chuck!" I yell. "You win! Go order yourself that drink and tell them to put it on my tab. And order me a Diet Coke, please. Extra cherries."

"What's that all about?"

"Nothing. Don't worry about it. And don't worry about later today. I don't want to see you more than I have to. Just bring the money next time." I'm still playing my machine, barely giving my attention.

"Oh, okay. Sorry about that. I guess I must have put on the wrong pants and..."

"Yeah. I know, Kelly. Look, I need to get going here pretty soon so..." I don't even look at him throughout the exchange. It's always the same with him. The only thing I can count on with Kelly in the three years he's been picking up from me is that he never has all the money with him. He's a weasel and a pain in the ass, but he's a consistent buyer and always ends up paying eventually.

"So dancer-boy left, huh?" Chuck says bringing the drinks to our table. He's missed Kelly's exit, so I go into my routine for him.

"Yeah," I say standing up. I start doing a little soft shoe. "Hey! Hey! Look over there. Don't look over here at what I'm doing. Hey! Hey! Look over there." My animated Kelly impression makes anyone who's ever met him laugh. It's the only other reason I keep him around: he provides great material for shtick.

William S. Burroughs said, "Junk is the ultimate merchandise. The junk merchant does not sell his product to the consumer, he sells the consumer to the product. He does not improve and simplify his merchandise; he degrades and simplifies the client."

Burroughs was writing about his days as a heroin addict, but I think the same is true for all drugs. I was a junk merchant. Simplifying and degrading my clients, if only to myself, helped solidify the "us and them" mentality that kept me trapped in my poison ivory tower.

"Well," I say half an hour later, "I have to go." Chuck is already nodding out at his machine and I'm starting to fade, too. I need to sleep.

At home, I bury myself in my down comforter. I'm so tired that I don't remember laying my head on the pillow. Sleep comes quickly and completely. It's hard, cold sleep that I imagine death to be - dreamless and dense. I sleep until I hear the van in the driveway dropping off Andy, and my instincts as a mother supersede those of self-preservation.

As I transfer the bail bond line to my phone, I listen to the voices outside my window exchanging goodbyes. I smile at the sound of little boy shoes running up the sidewalk in that funny cadence that's my symphony of delight.

It's difficult to explain, the way Andy runs, but any parent of a child with Down syndrome knows exactly what I mean. It's something in their gait that has to do with the hyper flexibility of their hips. It's one of a handful of things - folds at the eyes, square hands, stick-straight hair, speech - that unify people with Down's. You might not notice there's anything out of the ordinary unless you or someone in your family has Down's

When the front door opens, I tip my head back, close my eyes and smile at my favorite sound in the world. "Oh, hi Mom. It's me. I'm home."

Chapter 14

Despite Larry's best efforts, Kilo was sentenced to a year in prison. He asked me to take care of his dog, Puppet, until he got out. I owed him $2,500 dollars when he went in, so I sent him money periodically and gave some to his girlfriend whenever he asked me to. Occasionally he would ask me to send her flowers or order him a magazine. Once again, I broke all the rules by doing the right thing: I paid what I owed when not doing so was the custom.

That same loyalty led Kilo to pass me on to his connection, who turned out to be Craig. I knew he had connections in Mexico, but Craig was such an unassuming guy that I never guessed he was the man over Kilo. I was relieved, though. I knew him and we had a good relationship, so the transition went smoothly. It did not go as smooth with the boys or the Laotian community.

That Kilo turned his business over to a woman was bad enough. The fact that he had gone outside his own people only made things worse.

There's always debt in drugs. The logic is simple: when people owe, they have to keep working. The trick is to find the right balance, and it's different with everyone. Some people do well with high debt because they can pay quickly. Some do better with a lower balance and the privilege of having a little more time to pay. It varies from person to person, but that's why I was in debt to Garnett and especially with Kilo. Every time I brought my account current, he'd front me more product.

Before Kilo went to jail, he gave me the names of the people I'd be selling to, all of whom I already knew. He arranged for people I didn't know to buy from those I did, and he filled me in on everyone's quirks so I'd know what to expect.

In the beginning, everyone ripped me off. I extended to them the same conditions Kilo had, and they took advantage of it. I'd front someone an ounce and they would come back with no money asking for more. "Swear to God I'll have most of it for you next time, man." It pissed me off. I knew they would have been more respectful if I was a man, and they sure as hell would have been more respectful if I were an Asian man. But I was an outsider on both counts. I was the substitute teacher assigned to detention class. So I took away their hall passes and made them lie with their heads on their desks.

I didn't want to be their mother. I didn't want to be an outsider, but I had no choice. I cut everyone off unless they came to me with cash, and I jacked their prices up until they paid me off. After that, I slowly started fronting them again, keeping them on a short leash.

I went to visit Kilo in prison to let him know what was going on, and I talked to Craig, because putting my foot down meant things would slow down for a while.

And they did, for a couple of weeks. They said they were sorry. They tried to bargain and finally, they got pissed off and said, "Fuck you, bitch! We'll just go somewhere else to get our shit."

So I waited, and they all came back just as they always do, just as I knew they would. I had quality product, my prices were fair and consistent, and I either weighed the meth in front of them, or let them weigh the package themselves so they knew they were getting what they paid for. I was also discreet with no crazy bullshit. Those are rare qualities in a drug dealer and, from what I know of, nearly impossible to find in one person.

Of course they came back.

It wasn't as though I forgot that I was dealing meth, but the line between doing business and doing *illegal* business kept blurring. The deeper I got and the longer I did it, the easier it was for me to envision myself as an entrepreneur rather than a criminal. I often compared myself to a Tupperware sales woman, especially when people made comments about me carrying so much meth and paraphernalia with me at all times. "If I sold Tupperware," I'd say, "no one would say a thing about me carrying my products around with me. Why should this be any different?"

I was beginning to feel invincible.

In 2004, Andy was fourteen years old and settling in as an eighth grader at his new school. At first, I thought things were going well, although his teachers weren't doing much communicating in his daily notebook.

I got a call one morning, just before noon, from the school nurse telling me I needed to pick up Andy immediately because he'd had an accident. I didn't need her to explain. I knew what "accident" meant with Andy. He had diarrhea in his pants. This had happened before at school, though infrequently, but strangely, never at home. The thing I could never make anyone understand was that Andy didn't have diarrhea. He was constipated. To explain:

Since he was a baby, he's had terrible problems with constipation. I have all too vivid memories of he and I, both in tears, trying to get him to move his bowels. He was so tiny. So tiny that his surgical scars were still angry red slashes. I could put his whole foot in just the palm of my hand.

He'd try. He'd try so hard to go, but he couldn't and it hurt him, and that *killed* me. I could feel knots when I'd press on his tummy, massaging down his abdomen trying to get things moving. Jesus, the look on his face...he was terrified. He didn't know what was happening. All he knew was that it hurt and Mommy wasn't stopping it. His little face was red from crying so hard, and I'll tell you this: Andy rarely cried. The only other times I'd seen him cry was when he had to have IV's put in, or needed to be strapped to a flat board for a CAT scan or MRI. And the truly heartbreaking thing was that since he had almost no practice at it, he still cried like a newborn baby.

His eyes were full of terror and tears, and sweat beaded on his face soaking his baby-fine hair as he pleaded with me to help him. There was nothing I could do. I would put his feet in my palms, push them to his chest, let him wrap his fists around my thumbs and together we would sob our way through it.

There were times when I thought it would split him in two. It looked like the equivalent of giving birth, and most of the time the lower part of his mucosa - the inner lining of his colon - prolapsed, falling outside of his bottom. I would take a wet wipe and gently nudge it until it worked its way back into his rectum. Afterward, I would give him a sponge bath to clean away the hot sweat that covered him, then sit and rock him long after he was asleep.

His doctor and I tried everything to treat the constipation, but nothing ever worked. As Andy got older, I think he learned that going to the bathroom is (forgive me) a pretty shitty experience. So he would hold it as long as he could which, even in the best of circumstances, will lead to constipation that can manifest itself as diarrhea. His doctor compared it to a cork in a bottle. The cork is solid, but once it's released, well, you know.

So I knew Andy didn't have diarrhea, and he wasn't sick, but this was the first time he'd had an accident at his new school and I understood their concern. I explained the situation to the school nurse and his teacher, and I got the same look I'd grown accustomed to over the years: *You poor stupid woman. How can you be so cavalier about your son's health?* I'd seen it in the eyes of strangers as I shopped with Andy strapped to my chest, wheeling his oxygen tank with one hand and a grocery cart with the other. I'd seen it from people when he would cough, causing his trachea to collapse and make a wretched barking sound that I'd grown so accustomed to, I barely noticed it.

I'd seen the look from doctors, too.

When Andy was about eighteen months old, he began having what looked like seizures. He would suddenly go stiff, turn blue and lose consciousness. After a few trips to the emergency room, courtesy of Ada County paramedics, his pediatrician referred us to a neurologist who diagnosed Andy with epilepsy. "There are three choices of medication," he told me. "Take this literature home, read it and let me know what course of action you want to take. We'll need to start treatment immediately to prevent any permanent damage."

I spoke with his pediatrician, who agreed with the diagnosis.

"Yeah, but I don't think it's epilepsy."

"Let me explain it to you," he said. (Long explanation complete with sketches.)

"I'm sorry, but something just doesn't seem right. It sounds to me like diagnosis by default."

(Heavy sigh.) "Let's go over this again..."

But I knew Andy didn't have epilepsy. I didn't have to be a doctor, I didn't need to see the EKG results again, I just knew.

And I was right.

I called his surgeon and spoke with him about the situation, and after some discussion and an x-ray, he determined the cause of the problems. The surgery that connected Andy's esophagus to his stomach, allowing him to eat, was stricturing. Food was unable to pass normally, became backed up and the pressure from the esophagus against his lungs prevented sufficient oxygen. He would lose consciousness, which allowed the food to work its way into the stomach. Pressure against the lungs eased and consciousness regained.

His surgeon took care of the problem and I never put Andy on anti-seizure medication. It was never discussed again among the neurologist or the pediatrician and me.

So I was familiar with the look I saw in the nurse's eyes the day I picked Andy up from school. But familiarity does not equate comfort. I always felt people judged me about the decisions I made for him or the services and programs I fought for. I always knew in my heart that I what I was doing was right, but that knowledge was deep inside beneath stacks of insecurity. The looks, comments and resistance I faced from teachers, strangers, neighbors and other kids came without warning. In real life, there's no rehearsal - no time to access inner resources. Not for me. Not back then. It's like that stunned feeling you get when a person says something that blows your mind and you have the perfect comeback...four hours later.

He was in the nurse's office wearing the change of clothes I sent with him on his first day. Every year Andy's teachers requested that parents send a change of clothes to keep at school in case of emergencies.

The nurse came in looking quite serious and explaining to me that their policy was that children with diarrhea not return to school until they'd gone twenty-four hours after their last episode. I nodded and listened, as a good parent should, then asked where he was when it happened. She wasn't certain, so I talked to his teacher. Andy had the accident in his mainstream P.E. class.

All I wanted to do was get my son out of there as fast as possible. The incident was bad enough, but it happened in front of his typical peers. My worst nightmare for him, aside from his medical issues, was to see him shamed or humiliated in front of people, and especially other kids. It shredded the fiber that made me his mother to think of him in that situation, helpless and stinking while other kids laughed and made fun.

His teacher told me there was an aide with him and she got him out of there as quickly as possible. She didn't think anyone else was aware of what was going on.

I couldn't speak for the sobs in my throat, and I couldn't make eye contact with her because the tears were already betraying me. I just nodded, scooped up Andy's things and hurried him out of the office, through the front doors and into the parking lot.

I said nothing as I pulled out of the lot and parked on the side of the road less than a block away. My teeth were clenched to keep my jaw from quivering, but when the tears started pouring, the sobs lurched out in an, *uhhn* sound that made my chest hurt. Andy sat very still and quiet.

"God*damn* it, Andy! You can *not* do this. Do you understand?"

"I sorwy."

"You are a big boy. You do *not* poop in your underwear!"

"I sorwy." He sat, frozen while I shook and bawled like a child.

"Why didn't you ask to go to the bathroom?"

"I sorwy. Enna trwy again." I didn't say anything. I just sat there looking at him feeling helpless and hopeless. "Sorwy, Mom. Enna trwy again tomorrow, 'k? Enna trwy again."

And the thing is, I wasn't mad at him. I wasn't mad at all. I felt helpless and frustrated and I wished for the umpteenth time, not that he didn't have Down syndrome, but that things could just be *easier* for him. More normal. It was the way I felt when I saw boys his age skateboarding or riding bikes. I bought Andy a tricycle for his fifth birthday and tried to teach him to ride it. Other people, his grandparents and therapists, have tried over the years to teach him to ride a bike, but he doesn't get it.

I'd watch other kids do all the things kids are supposed to do, and I'd secretly resent them. I've never cared about the Down syndrome. I just wanted him to have a normal, happy childhood.

And he did. He had a normal childhood, Andy-style. He never rode a bike, not even with training wheels, but he rode a horse with a little help from his second cousin. He never ice or roller-skated, but he tried. He never played an instrument, but he was in honor choir every year in junior high and high school. (Okay, he's totally monotone, but one of his aides in grade school taught him to lip synch, and he looked great in the robes!) He never learned to read for pleasure, but he steals all my catalogues, Rolling Stones and Cosmos so he can look at scantily clad women. (Nuff said.)

He never learned a foreign language, unless you count Andowneese. (And I do.) And he'll never drive a car, but he drives me nuts every day and hopefully for the rest of my life. He went to his prom, graduated high school and started going to camp every summer where he goes white water rafting.

I can't speak for my son, but this is what I think: Andy has no idea he's different. Rather, he takes great pride in his extraordinary patience and tolerance for everyone else in the world that just doesn't get it. With enough time and repetition, one day they will. Until then, he'll wait.

"Enna trwy again. I sorwy."

"Sweetheart, I know." I stopped crying and wiped my face with my sleeve. "I'm not mad at you, punkin, I'm just sad about what happened."

"Oh essa not sad. Essa Mom's happy."

"Now that I'm with you, yes."

At home, I stripped his clothes, started the shower and threw all the damning evidence in the washing machine - with extra soap. I fixed him lunch and he spent the rest of the afternoon playing Mario Kart, waiting for Allan to come home so he could race against him.

Alone in my room, all the emotion flooded back, filling me with grief so deep that it felt like anger. I wanted to vent to someone, but there was no one I could talk to about it. I didn't want to hear what my mother would say:

Kimberly, stop it! There's no reason for you to be upset like this, and there's certainly no reason for tears. It's over. I'm worried about you letting things get to you this way. By the way, are you taking your medication?

Allan had a, "Sorry, man, you okay? Let's play Mario!" attitude. He didn't understand why I let things affect me the way I did. Nothing seemed to upset Allan. He just rode a kind of mid-level groove and let Mary Jane pay the fare.

That left nobody.

I knew from experience not to subject other people to anything but the pleasant parts of Andy's and my life. I've had friends encourage me to open up about his early years, only to never see them again. Experience taught me that people thought they wanted more information than they could handle. I didn't blame them. I mean, Christ, how would you react?

Hey, you okay? You seem upset.

I am, actually. My fourteen-year-old son shit his pants at school today. Excuse me?

Yeah, well the nurse says it's diarrhea, but he's actually constipated. See, when he was a baby...

Where was I supposed to start? Where was I supposed to stop? Most importantly: what gave me the right to lay all that on someone whether they asked for it or not? They had no idea what they were getting into. They were just being polite, and I couldn't blame them. I mean, what do you do when someone dumps unexpected heavy information on you?

When Andy went to his room to play Mario, I went to my room and got high. I smoked long and deep and pretty soon, I wasn't upset. A few minutes later, I was comfortably numb. The sadness and grief I'd felt faded like chalk wiped from a board. With a good eraser and little effort, the board comes clean a layer of chalk at a time. That's how it was with meth. Every bowl I smoked peeled away a layer: pain, sorrow, fear, self-doubt, shame, regret. None of it existed inside that high. It was just my drug and me, and the only thing that mattered was maintaining the numbness because what I would otherwise be feeling seemed unbearable.

That's how it happens. You start out wanting to get high, and you end up needing not to come down. Getting high - smoking meth - hadn't been *fun* for a long time. It was how I got through the day. It's what I did to keep from falling apart. I smoked meth to feel more social. I smoked as a way to relax. It made me feel normal. More importantly, it made me forget all my insecurities and pain, and it dampened my self-loathing for all the things I was and all the things I wasn't.

I had no coping skills and no boundaries. If I possessed the skills to handle things like Andy's accidents, the boundaries would be inherent. *Stop telling me how I should and shouldn't feel, Mom. I'm frustrated and sad about what's happening, and here's how I intend to handle it, so just back the fuck off.*

Just the thought of standing up for myself like that - of saying what I truly felt - terrified me because it was too risky. More than anything, I craved my parent's approval. They were all I had and I was afraid that if I ever did anything to disrupt the status quo, I would lose them. My fear wasn't unfounded.

In my family, love was conditional, based upon following rules and doing what was expected rather than simply for *being*, and God help you if you rocked the boat.

When I was in the third grade, I got the idea to throw my parents a surprise party for their anniversary. I was nine years old. I'd always wanted a surprise party and I assumed everyone else would, too.

Mom kept a list of phone numbers on a piece of cork above the telephone and though I didn't know most of the people on it, I called them all. Each person, or couple, was assigned to bring a main dish, side dish, dessert or booze. I told them gifts were welcome, though not necessary, and to please park on the surrounding streets to maintain the surprise.

Chuck went home with a friend after school to spend that Friday night, and my best friend's parents were picking me up at eight 'o clock, giving me time to play hostess.

Almost everyone from the list showed up and when Mom and Dad came home from work, the house was full of people yelling, "Surprise! Happy anniversary!"

I'd planned the party for weeks and was proud of myself for pulling it off so well.

When the doorbell rang at eight, I grabbed my little flowered vinyl suitcase and went to tell my parents goodbye. Mom grabbed my arm and asked through clenched teeth, "Where the hell do you think you're going?"

"I'm going to spend the night with Eve."

"You're not leaving here without doing these dishes, Kimberly! After all *this*, you think *I'm* going to do them?"

It simply never occurred to me. There were paper plates and plastic utensils. I wasn't thinking about things like glasses and serving spoons. I was a bad girl. I'd been thoughtless and inconsiderate, so I stayed and did the dishes while my friend and her dad waited in the driveway.

All these years later, my family still talks about that night and how stupid I was. According to my mother, the phone list was of people who were *acquaintances*, not friends. She barely knew most of them and was horrified to come home from work at the end of a long week to find virtual strangers in her house eating, drinking and generally making a mess. And to top it all off, I had the audacity to think I could get away with leaving her to clean up.

When I left Andy with Mom and Dad and lived in my van for a time, my father didn't speak to me for a year. When I called the house, he would set the phone down without a word and I'd wait for Mom to pick up the extension. When I was there, he wouldn't acknowledge my presence. He didn't get out of his chair, talk to me or speak to my mother about the fact that I was actually in the house. I never stayed long.

I asked Mom about it.

"He's hurt, Kimbo. He doesn't understand you, and you've hurt him."

"Is he ever going to talk to me again?"

She would change the subject

A year passed and Andy and I moved in with Allan when my mother called me on Valentine's Day to tell me my father wanted me to come to the house. He hugged me, gave me a card, and just like that I existed again. Nothing was ever discussed and hasn't been to this day, except for my mother to repeat what she'd said about me hurting his feelings.

In my family, we don't talk about the bad things, especially when the bad thing is me.

Which is why I think I never said anything about what happened to me in the sixth grade. I knew that what was happening wrong, but I wasn't sure that I was not to blame, and there was no way I was going to risk getting in trouble or losing the tenuous relationship I had with my parents by telling them my dirty secret. Keeping everything inside, living with pain, confusion and anger, even for the rest of my life, was worth the price of love.

As I grew up, I assumed that extended to people in general. You are the sum of what happens to you and the things you do. Tried and judged for your sins, the verdict determines your worth.

If moments of clarity and realization happened when they should be happening, maybe there would be no addiction.

Chapter 15

"Get out here, NOW!" It was a fall morning and I thought Allan was already gone, but something made him come back into the house to get me. I zipped a sweatshirt over my nightgown, slipped on my sandals and joined him in the front yard.

I was speechless. Hundreds of neon colored pieces of paper - green, pink and orange - littered our street from one end to the other. They covered the road, filled the gutters and flecked our neighbors' lawns, cars and porches. Allan handed me one of the five by seven homemade flyers. In large, bold, block letters it read, "Got meth?" with our address beneath the catchy phrase.

"Oh, fuck," was all I could say. I looked up and down the street, overwhelmed at what I was seeing.

"Come on," Allan said, and started picking them up as fast as he could.

It was shortly after seven in the morning. Andy's bus had already come and gone, but I doubted the driver could have read the flyers from his position. I hoped not.

We had no choice. I brought a garbage sack for each of us and we started grabbing. The lawns were set with early morning frost and our fingers quickly numbed. There may have been thousands of those damn flyers. They were everywhere: stuck to houses and the wheels of cars, tucked underneath windshield wipers, and wedged in bushes. The road looked as if it were painted in neon, and most of those papers had tire tracks on them where they'd been run over in the early morning hours.

A woman who lived a few houses down from us came out to help. Allan and I looked at each other, panicked, as she walked over to me.

"These have your address on them, don't they?"

"Yes," I said. "I'm so sorry for all this. We'll have it cleaned up as soon as we can."

"I'll help you. Is someone stalking you or something?"

Out of the corner of my eye, I saw Allan shake his head almost imperceptibly. I wasn't too surprised either. We looked like average middle class citizens. There was nothing about our house, our living habits or us to make anyone suspicious of any illegal activity. We were neighborly enough that people knew I was a bail bondsman, which explained my comings and goings at night. We did yard work and waved to our neighbors when Andy came home in the evenings. Allan's son rode his bike and skateboarded up and down the street on the weekends we had him, and the boys would play catch in the front yard. We decorated the house at Christmas and I took extra rhubarb from our yard to share with the neighbors. We were responsible for letting the irrigation water down to the rest of the block in the summertime.

"Something like that," I said. "An ex-boyfriend. You know how that can be." It was the only excuse I could come up with.

I knew exactly who was responsible: Garnett. There was no one else would would have or could have done something like that. He was back together with his ex-wife and apparently, I was his new hobby.

"Yes, I do! I'm so sorry for you."

"It's just that it's so embarrassing. You know. All our neighbors. You're so sweet to be helping us like this. You really don't have to. I just feel awful."

"It's not a problem. Let's get this taken care of before anyone else sees them."

We had the street cleaned within a half an hour.

The following Saturday, Andy and Allan were playing Mario Kart in Andy's room while I was locked in mine watching movies and getting high. I barely registered the faint knock on the front door, but I heard something in Allan's voice that I'd never heard before when he called for me. When I rounded the corner from the hallway to the living room and saw the two police officers standing in my house, I felt a surreal rush swarm through my body and for a moment, I thought I would lose consciousness.

"Can I help you?" I was relieved at the sound of my voice: conversational and relaxed. I sat on the sofa next to Andy who was sitting next to Allan.

"We've received some reports that there's a methamphetamine lab being run out of this home," the taller of two officers said. "We'd like to search the premises."

My face was frozen in a polite smile, but my brain was racing. In my room, on the table next to my bed, lay my loaded pipe and container holding three huge, clear crystals. There was also another quarter pound of meth sitting on the top shelf in my closet next to a half pound of pot.

"Do you have a warrant?"

"No, ma'am. All we have are these three calls, all saying the same thing." I waited for him to continue. He cleared his throat, asked his partner for the file he was holding and started flipping through it. "They all say that there's heavy evidence of a meth lab being run out of here." He looked at Andy, then back to me. "What we'd like is your cooperation. We can get a warrant if we need to, but if there's nothing to hide we can just clear this up now. Do you mind if we take a look around?"

Oh my God. Oh my God! That rat-bastard, Garnett. That stupid son-of-a-bitch. What the hell am I going to do? I can't let them search. I'd have to be out of my fucking mind to consent to a warrantless search, even if the house was clean. No, they can't search the house! For Christ's sake, what am I going to do? What am I going to say?

"I'm sorry, I can't let you search without a warrant." I was scared shitless and I was going to pieces in my head, but I held my façade. I sat with my legs crossed, looking, I hoped, like a polite, concerned, responsible citizen who was simply asserting her fourth amendment rights.

"Ma'am, we can get a warrant if we need to, but we'd rather take care of this now. Just get it out of the way so we can let the concerned party know that there's nothing to worry about. Will you let us take a quick look around?"

"I'm sorry, I really don't mean to be rude, but I can't, in good consciousness, allow you to search without a warrant."

The officers looked at one another, shifted their weight from foot to foot and cleared their throats.

"Ma'am," the taller officer started again, "if we can do a quick search, just have a look around, it'll only take a minute. We need to be able to let this party know that we checked out the situation and there's nothing to worry about."

Jesus, God! Get out! Get out of my house. I can't keep this calm front much longer. Does this look like a meth lab? Do you see any glass containers in here or outside? Any tubing? Do you smell an odor that makes you suspect that what Crazy-boy has told you is true? NO! So quit bugging me and go away!

"I'm sorry," I said, shaking my head, "I'm really not trying to make things difficult for you."

"Ma'am, there have been three different complaints about a lab being run out of this domicile. We need to know that this isn't the case."

"Officer, I think I know what's going on here. There's a man, someone I used to be friends with, who's been stalking me, and this is exactly something he would do. He was arrested last year for multiple counts of malicious stalking and harassment of his ex-wife, they got back together and now, apparently, I'm his new target. Can you tell me if all three reports were made by the same person?"

The second officer, who'd been quiet throughout the exchange, leafed through the papers in the file and said, in a low voice, to his partner, "It does look like all three of these..." I couldn't hear the rest of what he said.

The one I'd been speaking with pushed the file closed, pulled himself to his full height and spoke to me in his OFFICIAL POLICE OFFICER VOICE. "Ma'am, there have been several reports of suspicious drug activity and, specifically, reports of a meth lab being run out of these premises and we need to search your house."

I was terrified. Knowing you have rights is one thing. Asserting your rights is another. Asserting your rights when you are sitting in a house full of enough evidence for multiple felony convictions is an out of body experience. I felt as though I were watching myself on television. Shocked by what was happening and scared for the woman in the situation, I was in awe of her indignation. It was reality TV at its most base, and because it was happening to me I couldn't turn the channel.

"Will you give us permission to search?"

"Officer," *You stupid dumb-fuck! How many times do you want me to tell you no?* "Like I said, I'm really not trying to make things difficult." (Uncross and re-cross legs) "I know you're only doing your job, and you have no way of knowing who we are or what this is all about."

I can't breathe. I can't breathe! Jesus Christ, when the fuck are they going to leave? How long is this going to go on? What are they trying to do? Wear me down? Do you guys really think I'm going to change my mind?

It was then that Allan spoke up. "Kim, maybe we should let them..." and as I turned my head toward him, I knew from his abrupt silence that the expression on my face was the one I'd intended for him. I turned my attention back to the two policemen who were towering over Allan, my son and me as we sat on the couch in the living room. The sensation I had of slipping in and out of my own body/reality made me feel like I was going to vomit.

"Ma'am, you should listen to your husband. Just let us..."

"He's not my husband." *Quit calling me ma'am, asshole!* (Smile still in place? Check. Re-cross legs.) "I'm sorry. Unless you have a warrant, I can't allow you to search." *Leave, leave, leave! Don't you guys have any criminals to chase?*

"But if we had a warrant, you would allow us to search, right?"

What am I? New?

"I don't think I'd have a choice then, would I?"

They were there more then half an hour, rephrasing the question, trying to convince me to consent to a warrantless search. The more they pressed, the more indignant I felt. In my mind, the closet full of felonies no longer mattered. I was fighting the good fight. I was struggling to preserve my constitutional right as an American citizen to freedom from search and seizure. I was righteous.

If I was shaky when they were gone, Allan was epileptic. "Jesus, Kim! How did you do that? I can't believe that! I can't believe that happened. I can't believe you did that. How did you do that?"

"Allan, calm down. I'm as freaked out as you are."

"Yeah, but you stood up to them. Holy shit."

"Well? Fuck. How stupid would I have to be to allow a search without a warrant?"

"I don't think I could have done what you did."

"Yes," I said, "I noticed."

"Sorry."

After Andy was asleep, we talked about what happened and about the previous flyer incident.

"Kim, Garnett's not going to stop and this is getting dangerous."

"I know. I'm sorry about all this."

"Don't be sorry. I know it's not your fault he's crazy, but you have to do something. You have to stop." He looked at me. "Or find a way to be more careful. It's a good thing you didn't have anything here today. Well, other than probably your personal stash, right?" I didn't answer. "Right?" I gave him a look with my head cocked to one side that said, *don't be so naïve.* "What the fuck? What do you have? What's here?"

When I told him, he was pissed. "I don't know what you're so upset about, Allan. This isn't news to you."

"Yeah, but Kim, a quarter pound of meth? Why so much?"

"What are you talking about?"

"What the hell are you doing with that much meth?"

I shook my head, blinked and closed my gaping mouth before speaking again. "Allan, how much do you think I go through?"

"I don't know."

"Well, I guess now you have some idea."

"You're selling a quarter pound of meth a month?"

At first I though he was being deliberately obtuse, and it pissed me off, but I realized we hadn't discussed the technical aspects of my business since he'd quit using, and that was a while ago.

"A month? Allan, look around you. How do you think I pay for all this? The house, the utilities and groceries. How do you think I paid your back child support and your delinquent medical bills from that emergency you had in California when you were still driving? How do you think I paid your outstanding tickets in Oregon and California and the fees to reinstate your license? Where do you think the money came from to bail you out of jail and hire Larry to represent you?"

I fell silent. I hadn't meant to unleash on him like that, but once I started, it was hard to stop myself. He was quiet, too, but not because he felt bad, which is what I expected, but because he was mad.

"What the hell? How much do I owe you? Have you been keeping track?"

I wished I could take it all back. I didn't want to go into everything. Not then. Not ever, if I could avoid it. I wanted money to be a non-issue. I wanted to take care of the man I loved until he was able to take care of *us*, and as far as I was concerned, that was inherent in our relationship. At least it was in my sick, needy, addict mind. The truth was, I wanted him to depend on me so that he would need me, but I didn't want to be taken advantage of.

I don't know what I wanted.

"Yes. You told me to, remember?"

And I had been since that day back at my apartment when he told me to start keeping track of what I was sending with him on the road. And again, when I put up the earnest money for the house...and the bail...and the attorney...

He asked me to write it all down because he said that one day he'd pay me back for everything: MORTGAGE. ELECTRIC.

GAS. BONDS. LEGAL. MISC. MEDICAL. HOME
IMPROVEMENT. WATER/SEWER/TRASH. Everything was
listed by date in its specified column in a separate ledger.

"Yeah, I remember. So how much is it?"

*Oh, God. No, no. I don't want to go here now. Can't we just watch a
movie and have sex and not think about the money? Let's get high and
everything will be okay.*

"I don't know right off the top of my head."

"Well, go get your ledger."

"Allan, I don't want to do this right now. Let's just go to
bed, okay?"

"I'm not mad. I just want to know."

No, Allan. You don't.

But he said he did, so I told him. I was right. He didn't want
to know, because at that time, he owed me close to ten thousand
dollars.

"How the hell do I owe you ten grand?"

"Allan..."

"That's impossible. There's no way it's that much."

I felt like a greedy bitch. I felt guilty that he owed me so
much money. At the same time, I was mad at him for allowing the
whole thing to happen and then ignore it until I brought it up.
None of it made sense to me and I wished the subject had never
come up. More than that, I wished the whole money issue would
just go away. I was confused and hurt and mad.

"Here, look at the ledger. I kept track, just like you told me
to. If there's something you don't agree with, I have no problem..."

"I don't want to look at it."

He walked out of the room and didn't speak to me for the
rest of the night. The next day, he acted as if nothing had happened,
so I let it go.

He paid some of the money back. There were small
payments here and there, between fifty and two-fifty. Since we
moved in together, he'd paid sixteen hundred dollars toward his tab.
The problem was that the tab kept growing.

It was clear to me that something needed to change. Too
many things were happening and I was beginning to get nervous.
Allan and Kilo had both been arrested for drug charges, and
Garnett was involved in legal issues of his own. I knew enough to
know that when people start going down, others follow like

dominos. I was associated with all three men and one of them was playing a dangerous game using law enforcement to destroy his opponent: me.

Allan and I talked the day after the police came to the house and I decided that dramatic steps were needed to put an end to the crazy turn our lives were taking. There was only one thing I could think of to do. I had to get the drugs out of our home.

I needed an office.

Chapter 16

I found one downtown on the third floor of a lovely historic building. When the management asked what line of work I was in, I told them I was starting a gift basket business. I don't remember exactly why, other than I'd been passing time in craft stores and floral shops spending money on pretty things that I didn't need.

I had a theory that hiding in plain sight was the best way to go about the business of selling drugs, and in a building filled with four floors of offices for small businesses and lawyers, I felt safe. The Idaho A.C.L.U. was one door away from mine. Maintaining the appearance of a legitimate gift basket business was easy. With all the drug money coming in, I kept UPS busy delivering baskets, shredded paper, ribbon, dried flowers, greenery, bath products, gourmet chocolates and exotic foods from a dozen wholesale companies I set up accounts with. I hung a sign on the door beneath a hand-made wreath, lush with eucalyptus, cinnamon pinecones and dried roses.

One of my customers, a man who worked at Hewlett-Packard, had a three hundred dollar a week meth habit that he hid from his wife. After normal business hours, he brought me stacks of brand new ink cartridges that I listed and sold on E-Bay. That was how he covered his tab. Shipping out the cartridges put the finishing touch I was looking for on the gift basket business, so it worked out nicely for us both.

I had a state seller's permit and a tax I.D. number. I filed and paid taxes each month on nonexistent sales for the gift basket business. Paying *some* taxes made me feel more like a decent citizen. Again, there were times when the line between the legitimate and illegitimate would blur and I would forget that it was all a front for what I was really doing, which was selling meth. I did actually make some baskets for friends. I was good at it and enjoyed making them, but the money was nowhere near what I was already making. Once in awhile, I'd think how nice it would be if Allan were able to take care of us long enough for me to really give it a shot making baskets, but I knew that wasn't going to happen.

The office was five hundred square feet and housed my computer, a desk and two long tables laden with basket making supplies. Foam, paper shred, glue guns, basket sticks, glue dots, tags and ribbon were strewn about giving the place a busy and productive ambiance. The office smelled heavenly thanks to the flowers, candles, potpourri and cinnamon scented pine cones, so I had no worries about smoking meth there. But just in case, I had an air purifier that ran constantly, and I would blow the smoke into it so it wouldn't drift through the air ducts. The only windows I had in my third floor office were directly across from the elevator overlooking the arboretum in the center of the building. I kept the blinds partially open to maintain an appearance of normalcy; the worktables, boxes and baskets strategically placed to allow me the privacy I needed to smoke.

Sometimes, during the day, I would allow my boys to visit me there and pick up what they needed with the caveat that they be nicely dressed and didn't look all twacked out. Most of the time, if I wasn't visiting them at their home, as I did with Shadoe, I met them in bars. There was one bar in particular, different from the one my brother and I played the machines at, where I'd been spending more time. I knew the staff and most of the regulars so I felt safe there. They opened at eleven a.m., and had free pool until two 'o clock. Two or three days a week, I'd be there when they opened, playing pool by myself in the back corner, receiving visitors and trading cigarette packs for money, just as I'd done in Jackpot.

The downtown office became my home away from home. I was comfortable with the nightly cleaning service because I kept everything in the locked drawers of my desk: meth and sometimes pot, baggies for packaging, paraphernalia, my ledgers, a pocket scale for weighing up to an ounce and an electronic postal scale for everything else. I had everything I needed.

Craig called one afternoon from Mexico. I hadn't seen him or been able to get in touch with him for a few days, so I was relieved to hear his voice. Something happened, he told me, and he'd fled to where he had family deep in the heart of the country. He wasn't clear about the details of the situation except to say that I was safe. He hadn't mentioned anyone else and the police hadn't asked, so my name never came up. There was no link between Craig and myself.

He was calling, he said, because he always told me he'd take care of me if anything happened to him, and he intended to make good on that promise. He wanted to make certain that this was something I wanted to do before he set up the meeting.

"Of course," I said. "I trust you." He said he'd call back in a couple of days.

The meeting was arranged, and I met Craig's connection, Mario, at a Mexican restaurant. I didn't expect to be as nervous as I was, but as I approached the table, I could feel my pulse quicken. This was as big as it would ever get for me. I knew that at the time. Craig told me very little, but I knew enough to know how deep I was about to go. Mario's translator stood and motioned for me to slide into the booth next to him. He blocked my exit when he sat and it was as if the door between the rest of the world and me closed for good.

Until then, everyone I'd worked with, each step of the way was someone I knew. I didn't know either of these men and the one I would be dealing with spoke no English.

They were already eating and I declined their offer of lunch. I sipped water while they quietly finished their meal, conversing with each other in Spanish. When the plates were cleared, I watched Mario as he spoke to the man sitting next to me.

He was extremely handsome: smaller in stature than American men, as Mexicans tend to be, impeccably groomed, well dressed in a crew neck sweater and slacks. The only jewelry he wore was a simple gold chain of tasteful proportion. No rings, no bling, no flash. He was unassuming, polite and had devastating chocolate eyes. I thought he must be quite the ladies man.

The meeting was brief. Mario made little eye contact with me and his translator asked only a few generic conversational questions before bringing up the subject of the money I owed Craig.

"It's fifteen hundred. He and I talked about it and I'll be sending him money through Western Union whenever he asks me to until I've paid that balance."

He spoke with Mario and then to me. "We need you to pay money now. To Mario. He'll make sure Craig gets it."

I hesitated only a moment before asking how much they wanted. I assumed they were somehow testing me. Craig trusted Mario with his life, and I trusted Craig. He'd set up the meeting and I knew he'd take responsibility if anything went wrong.

They walked me to my car, I gave them three hundred and fifty dollars, the translator told me they would be in touch and that was it. I didn't know if I'd fucked up, if they'd ripped me off or if they simply didn't like me. I had no way of knowing what was going on until Craig called again from Mexico.

Andy's school called again. And again. And again. He began having accidents more than his usual couple of times per school year, and before long, they were happening at least once a week. I talked to his teacher who said she had no clue what was going on. On the off chance that the accidents were intentional so he could stay home and watch movies or play Mario, I grounded Andy from those on the days I had to pick him up. His teacher and I set up a schedule for him to go to the bathroom every two hours. Nothing helped.

The scariest thing for me about Andy is that he can't tell me what's going on with him. When he's sick, he can't tell me where he hurts. Sometimes, since I've been sober, he'll bring his pillow and crawl into my bed in the middle of the night, wriggling himself close and tucking his head into the curve of my neck before drifting away. I've been sober four years now, and he's done this only a handful of times. My instincts tell me he's having bad dreams, but there's no way to be sure. I ask him, but it's moot. He can't tell me. He doesn't understand.

Andy talks in his sleep and sometimes I can understand the dreamy non-sense, but most of the time the Andowneese is too garbled for even me to understand. He laughs in his sleep, too. Funny, raspy giggles and full belly laughs. I watch him sometimes. I have since he was tiny. I watch as his eyeballs move in R.E.M. beneath his lids, and I wonder what his dreams are made of, but I'll never know because he can't tell me.

That's why I've adamantly refused to hire outside babysitters or use the respite care available to me through Medicaid. If something happened to Andy, I would never know, and I will not take that chance.

I knew something was going on, but I had no way of knowing what. Frustrated and feeling helpless, I pulled him out of school and made an appointment with the director of special education for the district to discuss our options.

Frustration and helplessness are inadequate words to describe what I felt. I was enraged, and I had nowhere to put that anger because my rage was toward something I couldn't identify. By all accounts, nothing out of the ordinary was happening at school. Those accounts, of course, did not include Andy's, so they were incomplete as far as I was concerned, but there was nothing I could do.

Something was wrong at school. Something was happening or had happened to my son, and not only will I never know what it was, but there wasn't a Goddamn thing I could do about it.

I remember picking him up from school the last day he went. I wanted to destroy the classroom. I wanted to scream until I had no voice. I wanted to smack those looks of pity off the teacher's face. Instead, I collected his things and left quietly, ignoring their polite goodbyes.

At home, I was exhausted and angry - not at Andy, but at the situation - and I didn't want to feel that way. I wanted to be numb.

While Andy was in the shower, I smoked frantically, trying to make the feelings go away before he was finished. It's hard to get high when you're crying.

When he was in his jams, I sat on his bed and pulled him up to my lap. "Are you okay, Andy?"

"Oh, yeah."

"Okay, well, you don't have to go back to that school again."

"I sowry. No, no, no poop in annunderware. Enna trwy again tomorrow."

"No, honey, I know you didn't mean to poop in your underwear, but you don't have to go back there."

"Enna trwy again. I sowry."

I sighed. "Sweetheart, it's okay. We'll find you a new school."

He wrapped his skinny arms around my neck, kissed me on the mouth and whispered, "Enna twry again."

"Andy!" I pulled him away so I could look at him. "I'm not mad at you." *Then why am I raising my voice?* "You're all done at that school, okay? You don't have to go anymore. All done." I searched his eyes. "Understand?"

"Enna watch *Star Wars*, essa Jedi." He started pointing to the posters on the walls of his room. "Essa Wook (Luke) enna Vader, enna spookies (storm troopers.)"

I felt beaten. "Sure, bug. Go ahead."

"Essa little pizza?"

"It's not dinner time yet," I said closing the door. "Wait until Allan's home."

I stood there in the hallway for a minute, listening to my son talk to the characters in his movies, acting out his favorite parts and growling like Chewbacca, and I felt utterly alone and not nearly numb enough.

I didn't want to call Mom yet. Everything was too close to the surface and I knew I'd start crying immediately, turning the subject from Andy to my inability to cope with everyday life. I'd wait until I got high. Until I was numb. The meth wouldn't take away all the emotion, but it might be enough to get through explaining to my mother why I'd removed Andy from school.

I couldn't wait too long, though. She would want to know immediately and if not, *why* not. I sat on my bed, rocking back and forth, smoking, smoking and trying not to cry. Trying desperately to block out the anger and helplessness I was feeling, I made a macabre game of refusing to let the tears that brimmed in my lower lids fall. If they did, I thought, I would come apart. I thought of them as a watery, fragile dam. Everything inside me was shaking loose: my bones, my organs, my veins and muscles. It wasn't visible on the surface, but inside I felt like a house of cards and if those tears fell, the wind would blow. I couldn't let them fall, and I wouldn't allow myself to wipe them. They had to recede themselves.

So I smoked. For two hours, I did nothing but rock and smoke, and eventually, the tears receded and I felt calm. I transferred the bail bond line and when Allan came home I fixed dinner, moving through the evening like a robot. I felt cold and empty - a huge improvement. I'd rather feel nothing than too much.

Craig arranged things between Mario and I and we began doing business together. He brought his translator the first few times, but after that, he started meeting me alone. He was picking up English fast, and I knew a little Spanish. I bought an English/Spanish dictionary for us to use when we needed to.

When Craig needed money, I sent payments via Western Union to some little town in Mexico I'd never heard of. I paid him everything I owed.

Mario and I got along well and I felt comfortable doing business with him. In the beginning, the exchanges were made in public.

"Keem? You ready?" Mario's English was much better than my Spanish was, but Mexicans always have problems pronouncing my name.

"Sure. Forty-five minutes? Same place?"

"Okay. You call me."

Right on time, I called Mario as I pulled into the furthest spot I could find at the Wal-Mart parking lot in Caldwell. Five minutes later, a small blue pickup truck drove by with Mario behind the wheel, and I pulled in after him, seamless and smooth. We didn't acknowledge each other. It wasn't necessary. I fell in behind him and we drove until he found a place where he felt comfortable - usually some rural stretch of road or around an industrial area. He pulled over and I did the same. He walked back to my car and dropped a plastic-wrapped package through the driver's side window, picking up the roll of bills I'd already set on the outside armrest. Then he walked back to his vehicle and drove away. The whole thing from the time we pulled over took less than a minute. We never spoke during those meetings. It was all business: short, sweet and efficient. Then I'd drive to my office to double-check the weight and start making calls.

I met with the district supervisor of special education. There were two programs she suggested that would be good placements for Andy, and invited me to visit each of them to determine which would be the most appropriate for his needs.

The school I chose had a strong program and the teacher was an advocate for her students participating as much as they possibly could with their typical peers.

So again, I went through all the I.E.P., assessments and paperwork required to transfer him, and Andy went back to school. There were a couple of accidents in the beginning, but by the end of the first month, he was back to normal. I took it as a sign that he was happy. His new teacher was outstanding at communicating with me, not only with the notebook, but also with phone calls. She was upbeat and positive. There was a male aide - a rare thing in special education - who Andy seemed to especially like, and best of all, for my son at least, was that every Thursday, they went swimming at the YMCA, and to the B.S.U. student union building to eat lunch. Swimming is one of his favorite things to do...especially if there's a chance he might see a blonde chick in a bikini.

Chapter 17

Allan started working full-time installing rain gutters. He enjoyed his job and the people he worked with and it soon became apparent that he'd found a place he intended to stay. He was taking pride in himself again and that seemed to give him a sense of independence.

Then, one night, he went to brush his teeth and I did the same. I waited in bed, listening as he let Puppet out for the last time. I arranged our pillows and turned off all but the little light on my side of the bed. And I waited. And waited.

The house was quiet and the hallway dark. I sat listening to stillness and heard nothing else. I got up and looked out into the hallway. All the lights in the house were off and there was no sign of Allan or Puppet. I walked through the kitchen and checked the backyard. Nothing.

Coming back through the house, I noticed the door to his bedroom was closed. Sick, blue light from his television set showed through the crack beneath the door. I stood there, not knowing what to do, when I heard him saying something in a low voice. Then I heard a bark. That was the night Allan stopped sleeping with me and started sleeping with the dog.

When Kilo went to prison and asked us to take care of his dog, I was honored. I had known Puppet since she was first born. The runt of a litter of pit bulls, she was so small that Kilo carried her in his pocket. She was his baby and he was her Asian, as he would say. I adored Puppet. As she got bigger, I would play with her, getting down on the floor with a towel between my teeth and growling; she would catch the other end and we would play like canine mother and child. Of course, she could stay with us and we would take good care of her until she and Kilo were able to reunite.

My affection toward her soon faded, though, as Allan showered all his attention on her. She was the one he played with and cuddled with on the couch at night. She went everywhere with him on the weekends - even just to the store to buy cigarettes - while I stayed behind, uninvited. He bought her pretty collars and toys and took her for grooming.

In the evenings, Allan sprawled out on the couch, dozing in front of the television, with that damn dog's head in his crotch. I hated that lazy-eyed bitch, and every morning after he affectionately told her goodbye, throwing me a "see ya'" over his shoulder as an afterthought, I threw her outside for the day. Dog shit filled the backyard because Allan never bothered to pick it up in all the time she was with us, and I did not intend to clean up after his whore. I wasn't able to enjoy my own backyard due to the stench. I couldn't stand looking at her. I knew how irrational and immature I was being, but I couldn't help it.

I was hurt and humiliated, but I couldn't talk to Allan about it. What was I going to say? We'd never defined our relationship before and had never spoken about sleeping together. Before that night, it never crossed my mind that he would want to stop sleeping with me. I was so determined that this would work, that we were right for each other. If I could only find the right combination of doing and giving what he needed, everything would work out. As awful as it to felt to be dumped, knowing I'd been dumped for a dog was fucking humiliating.

Every night after work, Allan lay on the couch absorbed in some television show, smoking pot and caressing the dog. When Andy was in bed for the night, I'd go back to my empty room where I would sit smoking meth and listening obsessively for any sign that Allan might come back to me. Around eleven, he'd take Puppet outside one last time before they'd retire to his room, closing the door behind them.

Even if I'd had the guts to confront him, what the hell would I say? Why her and not me? What does she have that I don't have? The whole thing seemed so bizarre to me, yet it still hurt. Worse than that, it was embarrassing.

The unbearable weight of my heart in my throat brought tears to my eyes, and the only remedy I had for the pain was to get high and stay high. Meth's ethereal smoke snaking its way into my lungs and brain eased the pain that clenched me at my core. It was all I had.

I started playing poker online in 2004, when Internet gambling was still legal. It became my new obsession and I bought every book I could get my hands on, subscribed to poker magazines and studied the pros. I played at my office, mostly in the middle of the night while Andy and Allan slept, or during the day when they were at work and school. As empty and dark as that room was, it was far less lonely than being at home.

Any game I could find in Vegas, I could play online twenty-four hours a day, and I lost hundreds of thousands of dollars in the dark years of addiction. Not because I'm a bad poker player or unlucky at slots, but because I'm an addict and gambling had the same effect on me as meth. It took me out of myself for long periods and disconnected me from the world.

The thing about being an addict, though, is that it never mattered how much meth I had or how much money I won. It was never enough. I always wanted more, more, and more. For me, there was no reason to quit and every reason to keep going. The drugs and the money flowed like the ocean tide: no matter how much went out, it always came back. There was no foreseeable end and as with the ocean, it was easy to get lost in the vast emptiness.

I was incessantly buying things I didn't need, filling my office with pretty things for gift baskets I never made. I gambled like a fiend and smoked meth constantly. I was running out of ways to run away from myself.

I was on call most nights and never knew when I would have to go to the jail to write a bond. I spent many of those nights downtown in my office getting high and gambling. It was better than being at home where I would stay up all night listening for Allan. Listening for him to get up and come to me, tell me he loved me and sleep in my bed again as he had when Andy and I first moved in with him. I obsessed about Allan and with nothing but movies for distraction, my thoughts consumed me, threatening my sanity. In the morning, I would hear him get up, play with the dog and get in the shower. I felt stupid being jealous of a dog, longing for attention that never came, and my sadness would turn to rage for which there was no release. Away from the house, alone in my office, gambling away money for hours, getting high all night, allowed me temporary relief from the sorrow and rage bottled inside me. Gambling and meth swallowed me whole and in that space, I had no thoughts, no pain and no sadness. For a little while, I was free.

One night I started playing seven-card stud at a three hundred dollar-minimum table. The poker Gods were on my side that night. I had never been on such a winning streak, and within five hours, I had turned three hundred dollars into just under twenty grand. The high I experienced at the virtual table that night far surpassed any high I ever experienced with drugs. In the early morning hours, in a room where the only light was the sick glow of the computer monitor, I played standing up. I smoked less than usual, as the elation of winning was powerfully intoxicating. I couldn't lose. I knew what everyone was holding, and my body rocked back and forth in rhythm to the falling cards. I was invincible that night. I felt electric.

Three hours later, it was gone: not just the excitement, but also all the money, plus another five hundred in bets I made attempting to win it all back. Chasing the dragon. Gambling was just like meth for me. No matter how much there was, it was never enough, and I wouldn't stop until it was all gone, and with it the numbness. Just like that, I'd be back inside myself again, and I was such a mess that I didn't fit anymore.

Everything I'd been originally running from was buried far beneath all that I'd piled on top. It wasn't even that I thought I would fix my life at some point in the future. My intention was to keep running because I was afraid to stop. I knew how bad I hurt inside and I did all I could to avoid feeling that pain because I didn't know what to do with it.

I could take care of everyone. Except me. In my mind, I wasn't worthy of what I gave to others. If I had deserved love and attention, I wouldn't have had to ask for it, or hope for it in vain. I wasn't taking care of myself, and I was disappearing. I didn't know I was slipping away until it was too late, and by that time I was so far gone, taking care of myself wasn't even an option.

If Proust was right, and happiness exists only so we can experience unhappiness, causing grief that develops the powers of the mind, I should have been the smartest motherfucker alive. If that were true, though, I wouldn't have decided to take Allan on vacation to Mexico.

It was October of 2005 and he was selling his timeshare because I was tired of making the payments and he couldn't afford them, but he had a balance so we used the points to reserve a condo in Cabo San Lucas. Now, I'm sure I'm not the only person who's ever smuggled drugs *into* Mexico, but I knew Allan still liked coke once in a while, so I brought half an ounce as a surprise for him.

When I emerged from the bathroom to give him his present, his jaw dropped and he let out a *hunh* sound. "You crazy bitch!"

"I am not a bitch," I said, and he hugged me and we started railing up lines.

I daydreamed of Mexico for weeks before we went. I had visions of us swimming in the ocean, dancing in clubs and walking on the beach at night. As pathetic as it sounds, I actually thought that once he was away from his lazy-eyed whore for a while and we could spend some time together with no other distractions, things might be different. But it was pathetic. And stupid. Mexico sucked. We went parasailing and I chartered a private boat for deep sea fishing one day, but other than that, we pretty much hung around the condo and did coke while Allan smoked pot he bought from a local.

Actually, it was fine with me. I didn't bring any meth because I only liked to smoke it and didn't want the hassle of smuggling paraphernalia. I did a lot of coke that trip, but the high is nothing compared to meth and I ended up sleeping most of the time.

There were two bedrooms and we slept in separate beds. The first morning, I woke up very early and slipped into bed with Allan. He rolled over and fucked me. We didn't have sex. He just fucked me, and that was that: a chore he wanted done and out of the way. I stayed in my own room the rest of the trip.

When we got back, the Garnett situation began to escalate. I started getting pulled over for no reason. One officer would stand at my window asking me questions about where I was going and where I was coming from while another shined his flashlight around the inside of my car. Twice, there was a K-9 unit present, and they would walk the dog around the perimeter of my car. The staff at the bar I spent so much time in told me that the men's room was plastered with papers similar to the ones that were scattered on our street that day. They were also getting calls from what was obviously a man disguising his voice as a crazy woman asking for me and saying he needed to buy meth.

I met with Larry, the attorney I'd hired for Allan and Kilo, explained what was going on and asked what it would take to have him on retainer. "Don't worry about it," he said. "When and if the time comes, I'm your lawyer."

All the trouble Garnett was causing should have been enough to scare me. Multiple run-ins with the police should have scared the hell out of me, but they didn't. This is how sick I was:

I saw myself as a righteous woman being attacked by a deranged psycho. I knew that I was too smart to get caught with anything, and his efforts to bring me down were annoying at best. He was a thorn in my side, but I never saw him as a threat. He was so crazy and his claims so outrageous, that I thought I had nothing to worry about. Eventually, the police would grow tired of harassing me and, finding nothing, would see Garnett for what he was - someone who desperately needed psychiatric care.

As for Allan...I did every dumb-ass thing in the Desperate Woman's Handbook. I sent myself lavish bouquets with notes saying I missed me. I stayed out all night even when I wasn't on call, or when Andy was spending the night with Chuck. On these nights, I rented hotel rooms. I spent a lot of nights in hotel rooms during the last year we were living together. I went through his wallet when he was asleep, not looking for anything, but just to touch the things that he touched. I wrote long letters, on more than one occasion, that make me want to claw my eyes out today when I look at the words. I did all those things, trying to make him jealous, I suppose, but jealousy only exists when there are feelings involved. So I spent a lot of time slamming my head into a wall.

Dear Allan,

I've been waiting for the right time to talk to you. I've been patient, understanding, and supportive while kids, families, jobs, friends, bills, your legal issues and everything else under the sun has taken precedence in our lives. I have tried many times to talk to you and started more letters than I can count. I've walked the streets alone at night and cried more tears than you can imagine. I don't know what to do anymore, but I feel like I'm dying inside. I don't like the way I feel and the more time I let pass, the more things happen to further confuse and break me. I've come to dread being at home at night because of the emptiness that fills the house. I would rather be here in this dark, quiet office than at home where I feel invisible and isolated.

There are so many things I want to discuss with you....so many conflicting emotions I'm struggling with. I'm mad as hell at you. I'm hurt, sad, enraged, embarrassed, uncomfortable and confused. If I could turn these feelings off, there's nothing I wouldn't give to do so. I envy you men and the way you seem to be able to just move through everything seemingly unscathed and with no residual anything.

I can no longer tolerate our ambiguity. I need definition. I need clarity between us in order to be able to go on from wherever we are now. I can't continue to pour everything I have into a situation where I feel I get nothing in return. I feel like I'm living in a vacuum-like I'm being sucked dry and soon there will be nothing left of me.

I want to ask you a million questions...I want to tell you a million things...I want to yell at you...scream at you...make you understand...make you want to understand. I want to feel like if I disappeared from your life tomorrow, you would notice. I want to be appreciated for who I am, not grudgingly tolerated for financial security. I don't want to be anyone's "sugar mamma," "roommate and best bud," or "roommate with benefits." I try very hard to express what you mean to me... to show, as well as tell you, that you are important to me.

If that's what I am to you, then nothing else that's bothering me matters because...

Either I have been living in a convoluted reality-horribly misinterpreting the past year and a half-or you have been thoughtless and cavalier in your actions and words...

and you mutter a few words that trail off. You don't touch me, or hug me. You shower the dog with all your attention, physically and otherwise.

We don't do anything, we don't go anywhere. You seem not to want me around at all...

So I'm embarrassed and angry and hurt and lonely. I feel weak and pathetic saying all this, but I miss you, Allan, and I need for you to talk to me about all of this. I've written you before and said that I really needed you to respond and asked you to PLEASE not just blow me off. You did exactly that. You ignored the whole thing. After everything I've written here, don't you think I know how difficult it is to face uncomfortable situations? All I'm asking is that you respect me enough not to take the easy way out and continue to ignore me.

I don't know what else to say right now, so I'm going to print this out, pick up my son and go home. I'm going to get him ready for bed, give this to you and take a long bath.

Kim

The letter was and is embarrassing. The whining, bitching and moaning went on for ten solid pages, but I gave it to him anyway.

I set the letter on top of the entertainment center where I knew he would find it. The only reason I know he read it is because it was gone while he was in the bathroom that morning. When he came out, he set it back where he'd found it, and that was that.

Except it wasn't.

After he left for work and Andy had gone to school, I spent half an hour getting high and cutting the letter into a thousand tiny pieces. When I was done, I went to Allan's room, pulled down the covers and scattered the remnants all over his dog-hair covered sheets. Then I pulled the blankets back into place. I knew how childish I was being, but I couldn't help it. I was furious, embarrassed and heartbroken.

That was the day I decided to get rid of the dog.

I didn't have the heart to drive the bitch out to the country and leave her there. I didn't want that on my conscience. I knew if I took her to the pound Allan would find her and bring her back. I had to find a home for her. A good home where I knew someone would take care of her. After all, she was Kilo's dog and I had much respect for him. I didn't want to give her to some tweaker, although most of them wanted her. She was a pit-bull and tweakers just love pit bulls. They're like a status symbol because, of course, every nickel bag meth-head thinks that everyone - especially the police - is *just around the next corner*, waiting for them with beady eyes and malicious intent. It took me a long time to find the right family and work up the courage to send the bitch packing. When the day finally came, I sent her with the collar she was wearing and nothing more. All her stupid toys and pretty leashes stayed because I didn't want Allan to know what I'd done. I was hoping he would think someone stole her out of the backyard. He never locked the fence. I thought the plan was genius but I was nervous the whole day, waiting for Allan to come home.

When he did, he went straight to the back door like always and whistled for her. I went to my room and started playing poker because my heart was racing and I wanted to appear as normal as possible. A few minutes later, I heard him coming down the hall.

"Where's Puppet?"

"In the back yard where she always is." I couldn't look at him so I busied myself counting and bundling a shoebox full of money in preparation for my meeting with Mario later that evening.

"She's not there."

"What do you mean she's not there?"

"I called for her like five times. She's not there."

"Allan," I said as if this were the most ridiculous thing I'd ever heard, "she has to be there. Did you look in the barn? Or on the other side of the house?"

He went to look. *Shit. This was even harder than I thought.* I'm a terrible liar and the whole situation was making me very uncomfortable.

"She's not there." He sounded upset and I felt a little twinge of guilt but I was sure it would pass with time. "Were you here all day?"

"No." *Yes.* "I was at the office most of the day and then I had to see Shadoe. Oh no!" I feigned shock. "Do you think someone stole her?"

"No. The gate's still closed." Oops. I hadn't thought about that.

"Well if someone did steal her, they would probably shut the gate so we wouldn't notice right away." I didn't want to talk about this anymore. Just let it go, Allan, I thought. Just accept that she's been dognapped and forget about it. He was ruining my high.

"I don't think so," he mumbled, walking away. "I'm going to look for her. See ya' in a while."

As soon as he left, I got my pipe out, loaded it and started smoking. I felt guilty and pissed off knowing I had done something to hurt him. That's when I realized the full impact of my actions. I'd given him more reason to obsess about her, which is exactly what he did.

He spent the next few weeks making signs, checking the animal shelters in three different cities and generally being glum. Part of me, a very big part, was thrilled that his lazy-eyed whore was gone. Sometimes I would walk by the couch where Allan was lying, watching T.V. and looking like he was going to cry. After a few weeks, I had kind of forgotten about the whole thing and would ask him why he looked so sad. "I miss Puppet," he would say. Oh, puke. I felt like slapping him. I wished we had never taken the stupid dog in the first place. But I also knew that if it weren't Puppet, it would have been something else he paid attention to and showered with affection. Anything else. Just not me.

Chapter 18

On a cold Thursday night in 2006, two policemen came to see me at the bar where I spent so much time. I wasn't on call that night, so I was drinking and playing pool by myself at my usual back corner table when I heard my full name over the intercom. I knew before I looked. Who the hell else would use my full name?

They asked to speak with me outside and we stepped out the back door.

"Ma'am, we've had a report that you're selling methamphetamine out of the bathroom of this establishment."

I said nothing.

"The person reporting tells us that you use these premises to conduct the business of selling meth on a regular basis, and that you always carry everything with you."

I remained silent. There was nothing to say. No one had asked me a question.

"Ma'am, is this true?"

"No." I was telling the truth. I had not made any deals in the bathroom that night.

The officers looked at each other. "Then why would someone make a report saying that you are? They gave us your full name and told us exactly what you're wearing tonight, so there must be something to this."

I relaxed my posture. "Okay, here's what's happening. There's a guy who's stalking me. He keeps making reports like this. I've had police at my house, he's littered my street with flyers, he's been doing this for two years, now."

The officers looked doubtful.

"Did the caller give their name?"

"Actually, it was someone who flagged us down."

"What did he look like? Wait, no," I gave them Garnett's full name and proceeded to describe him, complete with impersonation of his mannerisms. I told them what kind of car he drove and gave them his license plate.

They looked surprised. "That's him alright. In fact, he's driven by twice since we've been out here talking."

They kept glancing at my purse, so I decided to do something I felt strongly against. "Look," I said, "I never consent to warrantless searches. Never. But I'll let you search me and my purse right now if it will put an end to this." I shoved my purse at one of the officers. I was angry and my voice reflected it. They hadn't asked to search and it went against everything I believed in, but I thought if it would help them see Garnett for the crackpot he was, it was worth it. Also, everything I had was in my bag in the trunk of my car.

The officer took it and tentatively opened it. "It's okay with you if we look in here?"

"Yes," I said. "I'm giving you permission. But I'm warning you, there are tampons in there."

He laughed. "That, I can handle."

"You know," I said to the other officer, "Garnett has felony stalking charges against his ex-wife. This isn't new for him."

"You should file a complaint." He handed my purse back to me.

"Yeah," I said, "I know. I guess I'm kind of hoping he'll just go away, but it doesn't look like that's going to happen."

We regarded each other for a moment before I said, "Are we finished here?"

"Yes, ma'am. Thank you for your cooperation. You have a good evening."

I didn't start shaking until I was back at my table in the corner. Of course, everyone saw them come in and heard me paged, so there was a lot of curiosity about what I was doing chatting with the police. Most of the regulars and all the staff knew about the situation with Garnett, and were very sympathetic. (The bartenders who did drugs knew what I did and bought from me. The ones who didn't do drugs knew nothing, but they all loved me because I tipped astronomically.)

It took two double shots of Jagermeister to calm me down. The thing that bothered me most was that I hadn't seen Garnett. I prided myself on being aware of my surroundings, not only because of the drugs, but because I was a woman and a bail bondsman who spent a lot of time alone in places women weren't normally alone. He knew what I was wearing, but I never saw him. *That's* what bothered me the most.

I still felt righteous and with each encounter with the law, I felt more invincible. I was beating the system. I was smarter than they were.

When you do as much meth as I did on a regular basis, alcohol has little to no effect, so if it weren't for my chat with the police that evening, I would have driven my car to my downtown office when the bar closed. I didn't want to take any chances, though, so I called a cab and figured I'd go back and pick up my car in time to get home and get Andy ready for school.

Mine was the only car left in the lot. I paid the cabbie and he drove away as I slid in behind the wheel. I'd just pulled out of the lot when I realized I had a flat tire. *Shit.* I called another cab. I'd have to wait until Allan had time to help me with the tire.

He was busy all day with no breaks and I forgot he was going skiing with his friends for the weekend. He planned to leave right after work. No problem. I rented a car and he promised he'd help me as soon as he got back.

His truck was in the driveway when I got home that afternoon. I knew he planned on taking a quick shower and throwing some things together before hitting the road. When I opened the front door, I nearly vomited. There on the floor sat a brand new snowboard, boots, pants, gloves...everything you'd need to go boarding. I couldn't move. I just stood there, staring at his shiny new toy (accessories sold separately) listening to the shower run. I was still standing there when he came out wrapped in a towel.

I don't remember what was said. What I do remember is feeling as if I'd been punched in the chest, and Allan leaving in a hurry telling me he'd help me with my car when he got home. And then he was gone.

I was still standing there twenty minutes later when Andy got home, and I remember feeling a numbness that was comparable to what I got from meth, except I still had a strange feeling, like my bones were too heavy and my chest might implode.

I'd like to think I said something like, "What the fuck, Allan! You went out and bought this when you owe me so much money? Did you even think about paying me back? Even a little? What the hell is wrong with you, you selfish prick? Take this shit back and bring me the cash!"

I'd like to think I said those things, but I didn't. I just stood there with my mouth hanging open, looking like an idiot.

Allan got home late Sunday night, exhausted from his ski weekend, so we went to my car on his lunch break the next day. He was going to change the tire, but that wasn't the problem. Someone had pulled my valve stem.

Allan did whatever was needed to take care of the problem. He drove me to drop off the rental and back to my own car which I drove home at around two 'o clock. A couple of people dropped by in the afternoon before Andy got home. Other than that, it was a quiet day.

I was home until just before nine, when I got a call from someone who needed to make a payment on a bond. I arranged to meet him in an hour, and started gathering my things. All my dope was at my office downtown. All of it, that is, except for my personal stash: three pea-sized rocks, a pipe and my pocket scale. I kept these in a small, black zippered case and it went everywhere with me, tucked inside my rolling briefcase. That night, though, I sat on my bed looking at it, debating whether I should take it with me or not. The only reason I did was that I intended to go to my office from the jail and I would need my pipe.

The people who'd visited me earlier that day told me later that when they left my house, the surrounding streets were swarming with cops. They both assumed they were the ones being watched and never made the connection to me. It wouldn't have mattered if they'd called to tell me. I was invincible.

There was a convenience store/gas station two blocks from our house. It was February, and definitely dark at nine 'o clock, but there were bright lights over the pumps and I was on empty. I used a credit card to fill my tank, then walked into the store, filled my mug with Diet Coke, and bought a lottery ticket. There was a man at the pay phone just outside the entrance. He held the receiver to his ear, but he wasn't talking. He was doing the same when I left and seemed to be watching me. *Odd.* I got back into my car and pulled out of the lot. Almost immediately, there was a cop behind me. No lights on, just following me. In my side mirror, I saw another pull in behind him. That's when the lights went on.

It started out as the same thing that I was used to: cop number one chit-chats with me, telling me he's got a report of me making a drug deal, while cop number two shines his flashlight around the inside of my car. This time was different, though.

"We just got a report that you made a methamphetamine deal at the convenience store back there." *Well that's pretty damn specific, isn't it?* "You know anything about that?"

"No."

"Did you stop at that store?"

"Yes."

"Why?"

"I needed gas, and I filled my mug."

"You didn't talk to anyone?"

"Other than the clerk, no."

"Did you sell anyone meth?" Something was wrong. This guy was being a complete asshole, and this wasn't the usual harassment stop I was used to.

"No."

"Well, why did we get a report that..."

"I got it!" The cop with the flashlight was excited about something.

"Got it?"

"We got it."

And that's when the testosterone kicked in full force.

"Get out of the car!"

"Put your hands where we can see them!"

"Get the fuck out of the vehicle, ma'am!"

Both officers on either side of my car were jerking on the door handles, but they were locked. They automatically locked when I reached a certain speed. It wasn't as if I'd hit a lock button. Everything was going on at once. I had no idea what they were talking about "getting," I didn't know how to put my hands where they could see them, unlock the doors and get out of the car all at the same time, so I just sat there until they quit yelling over each other.

"Unlock this door, ma'am," the officer who'd been speaking to me said. I hit the button, unlocking both doors. "Get out!" I got out. "Go stand on the sidewalk." I did.

They stood together on the driver's side of the car with the door open, shining the light on the floor and they were laughing. They were having quite a good laugh, and I found out much later why. It wasn't until my preliminary hearing when the prosecution had to present its evidence that I learned what started the chain of events that led to my arrest. The officers found a piece of popcorn on the floor on my car, and used that as probable cause to search my vehicle which, of course, led them to find my little black zippered bag inside my big black bail bond bag.

I heard all the tapes later, including the 911 call that Garnett made, and the recording of him talking to his handler. I'd misjudged him in thinking he was simply being a nuisance. He was actually a police informant.

But all of this is window dressing. The way the police treated me during the arrest is window dressing. One way or another, I would have gone down. We all do, unless we end up dead. There are only two ways out of the life.

Chapter 19

Mario and I talked after my arrest. He'd been in the business a long time and he knew that I couldn't afford to stop working. He asked me if I wanted Garnett taken care of.

A couple of days after my arrest, my parents received an envelope with the return address simply, "A. Friend," in Garnett's handwriting. Inside, was an enlarged picture of my mug shot, and nothing else.

The next morning I was driving home from the jail after writing a bond. It was early enough that I had to use my headlights, but light enough to see the row of reality signs along the side of the main street leading to our house. Each held my enlarged mug shot with the caption, "Got Meth?" in bold letters beneath my face.

As I collected all fifteen of those signs, I thought about Mario's offer. Craig told me about the men who came from Mexico to handle situations. No one knew their names. A call would be made, details arranged down South and three men would come, staying just long enough to clean up a mess, then they were gone. Sometimes, they left nothing behind.

Mario and I had grown close in the time we'd been working together and although he never spoke too much about business on the other side, I did know that he was part of a cartel and that he knew the men Craig spoke of. I didn't ask beyond that. I assumed I was better off not knowing too much.

So when Mario asked if I wanted Garnett taken care of, I knew he could make it happen.

"I don't know," I told him. "I've thought about it and this is what I'd like done: I want him kidnapped, taken out to the desert, and stripped naked with his hands and feet duct taped. Then..."

"Keem," he said, "no, no." He'd learned English well since we began working together. My Spanish, to my disgrace, remained about the same. "We don't do that. That's...that would..." He searched for the right word.

"Be beneath you, right?"

"Yes."

"So it's all or nothing."

"Yes. These men, I pay much money. Not to come all the way here for..." He shook his head. "They come, this man will go away. Forever. No one can find him. You understand?"

I understood as much as I needed to. "How much?"

He shook his head. "No, Keem, no. I do this for you. You no worry, okay?"

And I thought about it, but not for long. In my mind, giving the okay would be the same thing as pulling the trigger. I don't believe in God, but on the off chance that there is a hell, I know that my penance for that action would be to be chained to Garnett for eternity. There was no way I was going to risk that.

I was getting tired. Tired of people, tired of running around and tired of me. Proust said, "No exile at the South Pole or on the summit of Mont Blanc separates us more effectively from others than the practice of a hidden vice."

It seemed like everything happened so fast: moving up the way I did, and everything with Allany. I didn't know how to stop. I couldn't imagine giving everything up and living a normal life, whatever that might look like. What would I do? A regular job wouldn't pay all the bills. My lifestyle was far from extravagant, but I couldn't just give everything up and start from scratch. I had nothing saved. With the money always rolling in, I never worried about tomorrow. I never thought seriously about what would happen if it all ended. I spent thousands on gambling every month and more buying things I didn't need. My meth addiction, compulsive shopping and gambling; all of it was me trying desperately to run. Away from myself, away from my demons, away from all the pain and hurt I'd kept inside for so long, but was afraid to feel.

I was running out of ways to run away from myself.

But there was something else. Something more insidious. I loved meth and couldn't imagine living without it. I'd been using for so long that even if I could, I wasn't sure I wanted to go back to life before meth.

I was in my car one day, driving home from doing a deal with Kelly, and I popped in a CD that I hadn't listened to in a while. K's Choice, I'm Not an Addict was the first song and it was like a slap in the face. I'd heard it dozens of times, belting out the lyrics as I drove around with the top down.

I'd sung the song a capella while in the shower and doing yard work. But on that particular day, it was as if I were hearing the song for the first time. And as Sarah Bettens smoky voice grew more intense, I felt like maybe there was a reason I'd put that particular CD in the player after having not listened to it for so long. As cliché as it sounds, the lyrics that day felt like needles trying to tattoo themselves into my skin.

It was a short drive home, and when I got there, I sat in my car listening to the song again. I must have played it four or five times before I finally went into the house. That was the first time the word "addict" floated through my mind in close proximity to the image I had of myself. I wouldn't allow them to connect, but they shared the same space.

It would be nice if recovery were as simple as that. You hear a song, make a connection, have an epiphany, get sober and live happily ever after. Recovery is not that simple, but I remember that day vividly as being one of the many beginnings of finding my way back home.

I knew on some level then, and certainly now, that my drug use was, at the very least, fueling all my problems, but it was the only thing that made me feel good. When I smoked, all my troubles evaporated and I felt smarter, prettier, funnier and invincible. I think that's why anti-meth campaigns say, "Not even once." There's a saying in recovery that once is too many and a thousand is never enough. That's definitely true with meth. Aside from the physiological effects, meth is almost indescribably good. I don't know anyone who's tried it and not wanted more immediately.

The truth is, nothing is this world will ever make me feel that good, and nothing will ever rip my life to shreds the way meth did. There's a high price to pay for seduction. These days, I'll settle for serene happiness and an even keel. I've been on the ride, and if anyone had told me what was waiting for me at the last drop, I'd have never bought the ticket.

Some people call meth the Devil, the Devil's drug or evil incarnate. Everyone is entitled to his or her opinion, of course, and this is mine:

To vilify anything is to shun responsibility, and responsibility is power. To hold the belief that meth is anything other than what it is - a man-made drug - is to give it power while robbing you of your own. I believe that meth is the most vicious, addictive drug known to man, but that's all it is: a drug. The only "evil" involved, if that's what you want to call it, lies in our own ego. We wage the war against ourselves.

Getting sober is hard. It hurts, mentally and physically.

Staying sober takes true courage. The courage to heal not only the pain caused by addiction, but also all the pain that led to addiction. It's a process and it takes years. I was sober for a year before I realized I actually *wanted* to be sober.

Dismissing meth as "The Devil's Drug" lessens the addict's responsibility and robs her of the opportunity to find courage in herself she never dreamed existed.

Chapter 20

When facing drug or alcohol charges, the defendant is required to undergo two different evaluations to help the court determine sentencing. The first is a drug and alcohol evaluation. The second is a P.S.I., or pre-sentence investigation. The evaluation is exactly what it sounds like. You meet with a certified drug and alcohol counselor who assesses your proclivity for addiction and sends the results to the court.

The P.S.I. is more involved and is only required for felony cases. The interview is like a condensed autobiography. They want to know about your childhood, how you were disciplined, and family history with substance use/abuse. They ask about the socio-economic status of your family of origin, extended family ties and how you feel about an array of subjects. The interview takes a couple of hours. Prior to that, you have to have at least three people write a letter to the court about your character. They want to know if you, soon-to-be-convicted-on-a-felony-drug-charge, have any redeeming qualities.

Both of these evaluations required me to take an inventory of my history of drug use. Later, I would have to repeat the exercise in rehab, as part of working the twelve steps of A.A., and as part of a requirement of probation.

The first time I huffed gas I was twelve. I started drinking at thirteen and smoking at fourteen, the same year I first took speed. The first time I smoked pot I was fifteen. I took my first hit of acid in my junior year of high school during a ten-minute break between morning classes. I didn't take shrooms until my senior year. After that, I drank my way through three semesters at the University of Idaho. I tried crank a few times when I was nineteen and became an almost daily user when I was twenty-seven. At twenty-six, I started using cocaine on a daily basis. When my coke dealer suddenly left town and I was without other resources, I quit drugs by default and stayed clean for four years.

My chemical history, in black ink against stark white paper, stripped of all excuses and glorification did seem excessive. The first time I had to write it all down, I may have missed a few shots here and a hit or two there and as detailed as the inventory was, it still wasn't accurate. I hadn't left anything out, but when I wrote "alcohol four or five times per week," for instance, I was speaking of days, not actual drinks. If I were to break it down that minutely, I don't know that I would or could ever finish the inventory. Do I count a bottle of Jagermeister as one drink or two? Is it different if I drink it straight out of the bottle as opposed to my usual six or seven double shots when I'm at a bar? What if my brother and I are passing the bottle back and forth? Does each swig count as one drink? It's the same with Crown Royal. If I make my own drink and fill the glass three quarters of the way with booze and just a splash of mixer, it's technically a drink, right? What if I'm so coked up that I keep ordering shots with beer chasers and forget to drink them and just keep ordering more? It was a dilemma.

For the five years prior, my drug of choice was meth and my preferred method of ingestion was smoking. I didn't just smoke it; I consumed it with every fiber of my being. And it consumed me. We were lovers intertwined from the core and meshed together like strands of DNA.

The evaluation was first.

I remember feeling defiant about having to do everything the court was requiring me to do, but there was something else, too. I hoped that the evaluator would *do* something. I wasn't sure what I thought they might do, but I was secretly hoping for rescue. Part of me wished they would see how broken I was and not let me leave, but somehow help me instead. I was still sure my drug use was ancillary to my bi-polar disorder, but I felt certain that a professional would recognize that. I would have been pissed off and indignant on the outside, but secretly relieved, even if the outcome of the evaluation was commitment to a psych hospital. I felt so alone, so broken and so lost. What I truly wanted was for someone to notice me. To that end, I decided to be as forthcoming as possible during the evaluation.

I think the drug and alcohol counselor thought I was being evasive and trying to minimize the quantity of meth I was using.

"When was the last time you used?"

"What time is it?"

"It's 10:15, why?"

"About twenty minutes ago."

"You used just before coming to this evaluation?"

"Yes." I have always considered myself an honest person.

"How often do you use?"

"Every day, all day long."

"And how much would you say you use in a week?"

"I have no idea."

"You have no idea. Mmm hmm. Well, what about in a day? How much do you use in a day?"

"I really don't know."

"Come on, you must have some idea. You don't seem like a stupid person. You know what you're buying and how much of that you're using in a day, right?"

"No."

"No?"

"No." I was uncomfortable with this. Not because I wanted to hide anything, but because I knew what I was going to say next was not what she was expecting. Not by a long shot. I tried to come up with a way to explain it to her so she would understand. I was trying to figure out a way to soften the blow.

"Okay, here's how it is. I always have as much as I want of the very best there is. Always. So I always get the best of the best. I don't weigh it. I just take out what I need when my pipe is empty and reload."

"But you know how much you've bought and even if you're selling some of it, you should have some idea of how much you're using, Kim. Would you say a gram? A teener?"

Some of it?

She didn't understand what I was saying. She was so professional looking sitting with her notepad and pen, glasses perched on the end of her nose, and her legs crossed. She was petite with a kind of Kathryn Hepburn thing going on: charcoal gray slacks, tailored white blouse and tasteful, low-heeled burgundy mules with a matching burgundy sweater casually tied around her shoulders. Blonde hair pulled back into a neat French twist. Pearl earrings and a wedding band were her only adornments. She was studiously beautiful, clean and pure. I felt like I was going to somehow taint her - as if I were about to spray liquid shit all over her.

My intention wasn't to shock her, but rather to be as honest as possible because while a small part of me thought I might actually need help, I also thought she would be impressed at how well I function considering my daily chemical intake. I thought she would agree with me that my main problem was actually depression and that meth was simply my way of self-medicating.

I had to talk to her and I couldn't tell her the whole story because I was being evaluated for a felony possession charge and I wasn't about to volunteer to make my situation worse by confessing to one of the collective "them."

I sighed. "My best guess would be somewhere around an eight-ball a day." Roughly three-and-a-half grams. She jotted this down in her notebook.

"Do you think you have a problem with alcohol?"

I paused. "No. I mean I have...at times...drunk a lot, but I'm not an alcoholic."

She set her pad and pen down. "Do you think you have a problem with drug abuse?"

I answered immediately. "Yeah, because normal people don't do this. I know I'm self-medicating my depression."

She just looked at me.

The whole assessment took about an hour and then I was dismissed. In my car, I started crying. I wanted someone to notice me, and I thought if it were to happen, this would be the time and place. I was hoping she would just commit me to Intermountain Hospital, the psychiatric hospital in the city, and someone would finally take care of my depression and me. But she didn't. She just jotted everything down in her little notebook and sent me on my way. It's not illegal to *be* high. It's only illegal to posses drugs or be under the influence while creating a public nuisance.

I don't know what I would do to change the system. What I do know is that people fall through the cracks all the time, and unless the addict is ready and asks for help, forced intervention won't work. Even if she had somehow intervened that day, then what? I wasn't ready. I wanted to be taken care of, not necessarily quit using meth. I was in denial, thinking my only real problem was depression. I wasn't ready for sobriety yet. The professionals in the system know how addiction works. I felt betrayed that day, leaving the evaluation. I felt like the system let me down and was allowing me to slip through the cracks, but the reality was, it would have been a waste of time and money for them to step in at that point. I had to come to sobriety on my own. Ask any addict/alcoholic or their family. It doesn't work any other way.

I cried all the way home, and I cried while I loaded my pipe. When I took that first hit and held it deep in my lungs, I stopped crying. I started to get pissed off. The more I smoked the angrier I became. At what, I don't know. Everything seemed so pointless.

A couple of days later, I received the results of the evaluation in the mail: *"From the information made available during this evaluation, it is clearly evident that Kim has a significant drug abuse problem. Her assessment test scores were all very high and she reported drug use had affected at least three of the six major life areas. Kim reported she was using methamphetamine daily and had been for four years...It is imperative that she becomes involved in an inpatient program as soon as possible so she can get off the drugs. It has been affecting her health, employment, and now she is in the legal system. I recommend that Kim attend a very intensive inpatient substance abuse treatment program as soon as possible. The program should include a yearlong aftercare and relapse component."*

The prosecution received the same results from the P.S.I.

Nothing changed after the arrest, except that I began deteriorating, mentally. I'd been taking my medication sporadically for a few months, but hadn't bothered going back to my doctor when the prescriptions ran out. A common problem with people who have bi-polar disorder is that once we start feeling good, we decide we no longer need our medicine. We'll stop taking it and by the time we realize we've made a mistake, we're so far down in the spiral we can barely function, and even making a doctor's appointment seems overwhelming.

That's what happened. My meth use increased with my depression and I began shutting down. It's a strange feeling when copious amounts of speed leave you nearly catatonic, but that's what was happening.

I cried until the tears wouldn't come anymore. I'd come home in the middle of the night and curl myself around Andy, feeling his warmth radiate, feeling his *alive*ness, and I'd envy him.

Allan and I barely spoke anymore. He would come home from work, fall asleep on the couch watching TV, then wake up and go to bed.

I lost interest in gift baskets and shopping, so I closed the office and moved everything to the house where it stayed, stacked in boxes. I even lost interest in gambling.

I didn't want to see people; I didn't want to talk to anyone. All I wanted to do was smoke meth and sleep. At night, I would go to my bar and play pool in the back corner by myself until closing time. I started renting hotel rooms more often so I didn't have to be in the house alone with Allan there. Being alone is unbearable when people are present.

I felt more alienated from Andy, too. He was growing up and wanting to spend more time by himself with his games and movies. He loved going places with Allan on the weekends, but never wanted to go anywhere with me. I know now, and I probably did then, too, that he was being a normal adolescent boy, but at the time, it felt like everyone I cared about was rejecting me. Feeling helpless and lost, I did the one thing I've always been able to do, regardless of how dark I feel. I wrote.

Journal entry - October 2006

This isn't my home. This is a place where I'm waiting to die. I've lived here almost four years and I've never even completely unpacked. My sentencing is in December and I don't care what happens. I don't know if I'll get sentenced to prison or if I'll receive probation, and I just don't care. I don't know that I'll be around long enough to find out. I want to die.

I've lived with depression all my life and nothing I've felt before has ever come close to this. I'm in a dark, dark place inside myself where everything's still. Usually my mind races with thoughts, ideas and the constant chatter of my inner dialogue, but all that has stopped. My head is filled with thick, clotted, black ink as dark as the inside of a coffin. Nothing moves inside me. I can't even cry. All I do is sit and stare stupidly at movies most of the day. Sometimes I stare at the wall.

I sleep so much. It's the only thing that gives me relief. The meth isn't working anymore, although I keep smoking it whenever I'm not sleeping. It seems to be the only thing I do when I'm awake - smoke meth and stare stupidly. I don't know what to do, so I do nothing.

My sleep is dreamless - like the sleep of the dead. All I can think about lately with any kind of concentration is killing myself. I'm so lonely and wish someone would come save me, but no one does. I miss my mom and dad, but there's no way I can talk to them. If I could, I would say to them, "Please take me in. Please take Andy and me away from everything. I'm dying inside, Momma, and I don't think I'm going to make it. Daddy, please come get us and don't hate me. Just let me sit on your lap and rock me until everything's okay. Please don't leave me alone, because I'm dying and I don't know what to do."

But there's no way I can do that. No way I can tell them what's happened to me and why I stay away from them. How can I possibly tell them what I've been doing to myself all these years? How can I let them see how broken I am? I can't. I can't do that to them and more important, I can't risk them hating me. And they would hate me if they knew how I am...what I am. I know they would because I hate myself and I know they'd never forgive me because I can't forgive myself. If I want things to be all better, I'll have to do it alone. But I've been alone so long, living with only me, and I'm sick of me. I'm sick of thinking about me and I don't know how to make everything better.

I thought about Intermountain Hospital, the psych hospital in Boise. I spent hours researching electroshock therapy on-line. It's not what it used to be in the 50s and 60s. It's much more humane now. I thought it would be nice to check myself in and undergo a series of shock treatments. I read about the effects of ECT on depression - how it can often jar the brain into resetting itself after a few sessions. With no insurance, I tried to figure out how to finance a couple month's stay in a mental hospital complete with E.C.T. This is what I fantasized about: committing myself to a mental hospital.

I was so sick. I thought of meth as medicine that I had to have. Without it, I reasoned, I wouldn't be able to function at all. It was all I had until I could figure out how to fix the depression. Once I had the depression under control, I would stop doing meth. I didn't think it would be a problem. All I wanted was to feel better.

Committing myself was never really an option, though. Money aside, what about Andy? What about Allan and the house? If I went away for a couple of months, we'd lose the house and where would that leave Andy and me?

I began to think about killing myself. I spent days rolling the idea around in my head and the more I thought about it, the better I felt. The fog surrounding me began to lighten as I considered methods. I didn't want to use a gun for two reasons. The first was because someone would have the unseemly job of cleaning up one hell of a mess. Second, if I got jumpy at the end and didn't make a clean shot, I could end up paralyzed for the rest of my life. If that happened, I'd never had a second chance.

That's the same reason that a car crash or jumping off a building was no good: too much risk of permanent injury rather than death. If it were possible to overdose and die from meth, it would have happened long ago and as for pills and booze, the risk of regurgitation was too high. Either that, or a trip to the ER for a quick stomach pump.

I was still searching for a foolproof way of killing myself, when I was watching the movie <u>Magnolia</u> again. I was at the part where Julianne Moore's character is sitting in her car in the garage with the motor still running when it hit me like an adrenaline shot to the heart: the perfect way to kill myself was asphyxiation. I didn't know of anyone, off the top of my head, whose garage I could use uninterrupted, but I definitely had my method. The logistics would come.

One day, as I was drifting in and out of sleep with a loaded pipe in my hand, I realized that I knew exactly how to do it. Jill, the woman who owned the bail bond company I worked for, has a condo in McCall, a little resort town in the mountains, that is private and has a tiny, one-car garage. She let Andy and me stay there one weekend, and I was sure if I asked, she'd let me use it again. I pictured the garage: small with solid walls all around and no windows. Everything had clicked into its proper place, and I became serene, like an early morning lake.

I felt guilty involving Jill, but I didn't think there would be much of a mess. I felt at peace for the first time in months.

Then I thought about Andy.

I knew my parents would take him, but what would they tell him? Would he ask for me the rest of his life, not understanding where Mom was and always thinking I could be back any day? I couldn't do that to him. I couldn't leave him, possibly missing me for the rest of his life and never comprehending what happened.

But I couldn't live anymore, either. I'd already decided that. I felt torn apart. I was Olivia de Havilland in *The Snake Pit* when the lightning splits her in two just before she drowns.

A thought began to creep into my mind like a sneak thief pulling aside a curtain in my mind. Just a finger at first, then a toe, then a foot, until the rat-bastard was just *there*. When I began to entertain the thought seriously, it seemed like the only logical thing to do. The only *humane* thing to do. I couldn't leave my son behind. I had to take him with me.

I did not come to the decision lightly. Thinking of what I was going to do hurt me physically - like something was wrong with my skeletal structure - but at that time, in my sick mind, I couldn't see any other way.

I began to play the scenario through in my mind. *He'll be okay, getting in the car with me. I'll tell him we're going to get pizza. By the time he starts to get tired of waiting, he should start to get drowsy and then I'll sing to him. I'll sing the "I Love You" song I used to sing to him as a baby when he was spending so much time in the hospital. I'll talk to him the way I did when he was in N.I.C.U. and I couldn't hold him-when he was unconscious and I just wanted him to hear the sound of my voice. I'll tell him how much I love him and how perfect he is. I'll tell him that the best thing I ever did in my whole fucked-up life was give birth to him. My bug in a boy suit. My perfect person. The best human I've ever known. I'll hold him on my lap and kiss his face as I tell him again and again how much I love him and we'll slip into sleep together.*

There could be no mistakes. I had to make sure we both went. That was the most important thing. If I went and he didn't, who would find him and take care of him? I didn't want him trapped in the garage, scared and needing me, not being able to wake me. What about the alternative? What if I survived but he didn't? I couldn't bear to think about that

For the next two weeks, the thought of following through with my plan consumed me. I obsessed about it in my mind until sometimes I felt it was already done.

Chapter 21

The more I rehearsed the suicide in my head, the sicker I felt. How could I possibly do this to Andy after everything we've gone through? All the surgeries, all the doctors, the diagnoses (both correct and incorrect,) the oxygen, the feeding tube, the assessments, ambulance rides, bowel movements nearly ripping him in two, the flashbacks, the poop in the underwear and cleaning liquid shit off a fifteen year old's hairy ass...and that laugh. My, God that raspy, trachea slamming unique-only-to-Andy laugh that makes my heart pitter-patter...and the way he talks...the Andowneese that only I can translate...skinny arms around my neck and kisses on my mouth that he won't release until I do the *muha* thing...the way he feels in the morning when I have to wake him up: warm and soft and yummy...how deep my love for him is and has been since conception...how proud I am of who he is and how I tell him every day, without exception, that he's the smartest, funniest, most handsome boy in the world: he's a perfect person.

I didn't feel like I deserved to live, but he didn't deserve to die and since I couldn't leave him I was back where I started, staring into the abyss.

I had to do something, though. I couldn't go on the way I was. All I wanted was to feel better, but I felt so far gone that even if I were to go back on my prescription medication, I didn't feel it wouldn't be enough.

All of this made sense at the time. I remember feeling very rational about the decisions I was making, or trying to make. It blows my mind to look back and remember the window of time I'm describing here, because now, in my right mind, I see that there's nothing rational about any of it.

I believe everything happens for a reason. Most people believe that, though depending on their faith or philosophy, they may use another term. However you want to look at it, the events that took place after I gave up the idea of suicide took place almost immediately and happened as rapidly as I'll relay them to you here.

I started searching on-line for someplace to get help for my depression. I was looking for dual-diagnosis treatment centers: programs that provide help for two or more disorders, like depression and drug addiction. The more I read, the more I began to think about my drug use, although I still considered depression to be my main problem.

The treatment facilities that popped up first were for places like Malibu that cost upwards of ten thousand dollars a week. The pictures are mouth-watering: lavishly appointed rooms (private, of course,) swimming pools, oceanfront and or view, spa treatments...everything you would want for a lovely vacation getaway.

Most of the places I found were in California, so I did a specific search for programs in Idaho. The only inpatient treatment center I could find was the Walker Center in Gooding, Idaho. I spent over an hour on the modest web site pouring over every paragraph and picture. It bore no resemblance to the splendor and elegance of its upper-class cousins, but the bone structure seemed similar. It looked plain, but nice. I read about their dual-diagnosis program. There was a medical doctor on staff who made assessments and provided help with depression and other mental illness while the patient received individual and group therapy for drug addiction.

The typical stay was thirty days and the cost was around ten thousand dollars. The most appealing thing to me was the thought of going to a place where someone would finally take care of me. That thought appealed to me very much. They didn't offer payment plans, though, and there was no way I'd be able to afford it.

Then I got a rare e-mail from my mother:

"Kimbo, I haven't heard from you in a while and you never answer your phone. I'm worried about you. Please let us know you're okay. Remember, I'm always here if you want to talk. Love you, Mom."

I re-read it three times before deciding I had nothing to lose, so I hit reply:

"Mom, I'm sorry I've been out of touch, and I'm not okay. Take a look at this web site, and please, please don't hate me. Love, Kimbo."

I included the link to the Walker Center site, hit send and shut off my computer. I was scared to death of what my parents would say. I knew they'd probably hate me, and I started to panic. *What the hell did I do that for? Fuck! There's no turning back now. I've essentially just told them I have a drug problem and there are no do-overs on this one. I'm terrified of what will happen. They'll be disgusted. They won't even respond. They'll never want to see me again. I feel like an idiot. What the hell am I expecting?*

I felt like a caged animal that's too frightened to escape when the door's ajar. I wanted to run, but I had nowhere to go, so I sat on my bed, smoking meth and nodding off and on until morning.

I didn't turn on my computer until later that day. I was afraid of what I will find. When I finally did, I was stunned by Mom's reply:

"Kimbo, I think this is a good idea. Call the Walker Center today and ask them about the program. Find out how much it costs and when you can go. I could never hate you, Kimbo. Love Mom."

Just like that.

I sat there, staring at the monitor for a long time. I spent most of the day getting high and avoiding my phone. Around four o'clock I made the call. The woman who answered asked me a series of questions about my drug use, and although I'd been through it all before, I found myself crying, barely able to choke out the words. There would be a bed available on Tuesday, she said. I was calling on a Friday. I told her I would talk to my parents about it and call her back. I e-mailed Mom again, but she wanted to talk to me. I bawled through the entire phone conversation, which, as I remember it, was brief:

Was I using meth?

Yes.

Did I think I needed help?

Yes.

Did I think this place could help me?

Yes, and they'll help me with my depression, too.

Then call and reserve the bed.

I was shocked. My parents *didn't* hate me, at least my mother didn't, and maybe they even understood a little, although she never mentioned the word addiction. The conversation was as I'm relaying it to you here. Yes, they looked at the web site. Make the call. When can you get in? Make the reservation.

That was it.

I quit crying and realized I felt better - emotionally exhausted but hopeful.

I called Jill the next day to tell her I was going away for a month. I didn't know what I should tell her. Dad suggested I tell her I was checking into Intermountain Hospital to save myself the humiliation of letting her know I was going to rehab, but I wanted to finally admit everything to her - what really happened during the arrest, that I thought maybe I had a drug problem and I was going to rehab. I didn't want to do it, but I felt bad about keeping everything from her. I was tired of hiding and tired of secrets. I just wanted to be honest.

"Jill," I said. My voice was shaking. I was scared of what she would think of me. "I need to take the next month off. I'm going away for a little while."

"Kim," she says in a sharp voice that reminds me of my mother. "Do *not* tell me what I think you're going to." I knew she thought I was about to tell her I'd been lying about my arrest. What else would give her cause to react the way she did? But she's not stupid. There's no way she could really think I was innocent. She knew the police found drugs in my bag, not just supposedly on the floor of my car. Her denial infuriated me even though I'd encouraged her ignorance. Just as with my parents, though, people believe what they want to. No one wanted to believe that I was meth addict, and they sure as hell didn't want to believe I was *dealing* meth. I don't blame them. It's a tough situation to be in on either side. I don't know that I wouldn't have acted any differently, but it suddenly felt like a very bad time to come clean with Jill.

"No, no," I said quickly. "I'm checking myself into Intermountain Hospital. I've just been under so much stress lately with my court date coming up and Allan and everything."

She sounded relieved. "Oh, Kim. I think that's great! It will give you some time to relax. Hey! You'll be just like Mariah Carey. Just taking a thirty day break to re-energize."

Yep. Just like Mariah.

I felt awful letting her believe it, but I didn't feel as though I had a choice. I didn't want her to hate me and I knew from the beginning of the call what her reaction to the truth would have been.

By that time in my life, I assumed that anyone who knew the truth about me would hate me. It made perfect sense, considering I knew the whole truth, and I hated myself.

Chapter 22

The car is idling out front with the passenger-side door open. Andy and my parents are waiting to take me to the Walker Center and I can't stop getting high. I've been up all night frantically getting rid of the last pound of meth. My plan is to get rid of everything - scale, paraphernalia, dope - so when I come home there will be no temptation. I've fronted most of it out, but collected enough to pay off Mario, so I know there will be money for me when I get home.

I'm not smoking the last of my meth, I'm breathing it. I've loaded the bowl with the biggest of the three rocks I've saved for myself. It's almost full and I have to be careful not to let the liquid spill. There's at least a teener in it and I'm smoking - breathing it in as fast as I can. The only breaths I take are filled with my last high. I want to finish the bowl and my last two rocks before I leave so the house will be clean for my return from rehab.

It's seven-thirty and Allan isn't up yet, or at least I haven't seen him.

My dungeon-room is a mess - papers and books across the floor and desk, clothes strewn all over the unmade bed that I haven't laid in for days. It reeks of cigarettes and that indescribable biting chemical smell that only comes from burning pure meth, even though my window is open. My suitcase is already in the car, which is still idling with the door open. I don't know if they know I'm in here having my last hurrah. If they do, they won't say anything. They'll tell themselves I'm just late - as usual. I've been late for family dinners, holidays, parent-teacher conferences, licensing exams, classes, finals, interviews, jobs, dates, awards ceremonies (where I was the recipient), airplanes, time changes, you name it. I was late for my grandmother's funeral where I was to read the eulogy I had written. They couldn't start without me.

I'm still inhaling the smoke with mad desperation like gasping for last breaths on my deathbed. I'm trying to get high enough to go to rehab, but I can never get high enough. I feel like I'm going to pass out because I'm hyperventilating the smoke. Dad's impatiently honking and I know I have to leave, but the bowl's not empty yet and there are two rocks left. It doesn't occur to me to get rid of them. The thought honestly never enters my mind. I stash them in the nightstand thinking I'll just sell them when I get home. I still haven't seen Allan, but I hear him in the shower. He knows what time I'm leaving and he hasn't come say goodbye. I walk out the front door, slamming it as hard as I can (a ridiculously childish, "fuck you,") and climb in the back seat next to Andy.

"Sorry, sorry," I say. "I just had to clean up a few things."

"You nervous?" asks mom.

"Yeah, but I'm okay." Sure I am. I'm always okay. I'm so high it hurts to breathe and I'm still not high enough for this trip.

"I'm proud of you, Kimbo. You're doing the right thing."

This is what makes them proud of me - going to rehab. Never mind everything it took to get me to this point. Never mind anything else I've ever done in my life. This is what makes them proud. At first, I'm touched. They're proud of me. Then, irritation sets in, and I'm thinking, "Fuck you. You've never been proud of me for anything else, why start now?"

I'm so happy to see Andy. He's been staying with my parents for the past three days so I could prepare myself for rehab. It was their idea, but I was grateful. I didn't want him to feel the energy of desperation in the house.

"Hey, bug!"

"Oh, essa Mom. Yes!" and he wiggles next to me in the backseat.

"I love you so much, I'll sing you a song, that says: I love you, I love you, and I guess I'll always love you . . .

"Essa mom, inna hospital?"

"Yep. But just for a while. I'll be home pretty soon and Mamma will be all better, okay?"

"Oh. Inna stay gamma pappas?"

"Yeah. Is that okay?"

"Awight. Enna Allan, enna bus?"

"Allan will stay home and Grandma will bring you here every morning for the bus."

"Allan stay gamma, pappa's too."

"Allan's staying at home, Andy," my mom says. "You can see him in the morning when we go to the bus." My parents have no idea what Allan and my relationship is like. They're happy I have a man, and they're impressed with how good he is with Andy. They also know that he's close with his own family because of the split holidays we've done since we've moved in together, and Andy's birthday parties where Allan's whole family comes.

I lean over, put my head in his lap and Andy softly pats my head as I drift off to sleep after smoking enough meth to kill a horse.

Southern Idaho is desolate. Nothing but sagebrush for miles. The hour and a half to Gooding is one long, drawn out stretch of freeway. It's November so the landscape is dead and brown, although it doesn't matter what time of year it is. Other than when it's snowing, it always looks the same. I've driven this road hundreds of times running drugs from Boise to Twin Falls, Jerome, Kimberly and Jackpot. As we pass Mountain Home, about forty-five minutes out of Boise, I try to pinpoint the spot where I totaled my car.

Riding in the car with my family on my way to rehab, I see the area where the accident happened and a shiver runs down my spine as I think about how I could have died that night - not just from the crash, but alone in the black, cold nowhere searching for that fucking pipe. Something about that scares the shit out of me, but I'm high enough to shake the thought from my head.

During the drive, I'm drifting in and out of sleep until the turnoff at Bliss onto the rural highway leading to the Walker Center. I'm getting nervous. When I get nervous, I play with my hands, twisting my interlaced fingers grossly. I'm in the backseat wringing my hands and bouncing my knees up and down and I know I must look exactly like what I am: a twacked out meth-head.

Thirty miles to go. My heart starts racing, which kick starts the latent chemicals in my body, and I'm high all over again. I'm nervous and amped and it's getting worse the closer we get.

"Almoss 'ere?"

"Yeah, bug. We're almost there."

"Essa mom, essa hospital."

"Yep." I'm jumpy and agitated as we pull into the parking lot of the Walker Center. I don't want to get out of the car.

"You ready?" my dad asks. The three of them are already out, waiting for me.

"No. Shit!" It takes me a minute before I work up the nerve to put my feet on the ground and stand.

Dad has my suitcase and I'm carrying my down-filled pillow and blanket, and my purse hangs from my elbow as we're buzzed in the doors. Near the front desk is a little sitting area with a couch, a loveseat and coffee table scattered with pamphlets about the dangers of various drugs. It's a pleasant place - kind of homey, and it makes me want to scream. I want to run. This is a mistake. What the hell have I done? What have I gotten myself into? My voice is trembling as I give the lady behind the desk my name. "Have a seat," she says. "Someone will be right with you."

I can't sit down. I'm way too antsy. "I need a cigarette."

She looks at my parents. "We'll go with her," Mom says. Outside, I'm having trouble breathing. I think I'm hyper-ventilating. My hands shake as I light my cigarette. Mom moves toward me to put an arm around my shoulder, but I jerk away. I think if someone touches me now, I'll unravel.

I pace the sidewalk in front of the center rapidly up the long sidewalk and back, walking as fast as I can. I finish my cigarette and immediately light another. Dad's standing by the front door keeping an eye on me while Mom is inside reading anti-drug pamphlets to Andy like they're storybooks. I go back inside. I'm shaking all over and it's still hard to breathe. For no reason at all, I'm suddenly pissed off at my dad and decide to ignore him.

I sit next to my mother and whisper, "Mom, I can't do this. This is wrong. I can't be here. I'll be okay. I just want to leave, okay?"

"Kimbo, you're doing the right thing."

"Mom's right," my dad says. "You're very brave to do this. We're proud of you. You can do this, Kimbo. Just calm down and try to relax."

My brain is screaming, "Fuck you! Fuck! Can't you see I'm not alright? I feel like I'm going to lose my mind. I'm going mad right here in this stupid waiting room in front of my son. You can't leave me here," I'm thinking. "Jesus, I can't do this! Please don't leave me here, Mamma. I'll be good. I'll be a good girl, Daddy. Just don't leave me here. I want to go home."

Hot tears are burning my eyes, threatening to fall. Oh, God! What have I done? This was a mistake - a bad idea. I go to Andy and put my arms around him, soaking his shoulder with my tears.

Mom puts a hand on my shoulder. "Kimbo, you're scaring him. Stop."

You fucking bitch, leave me alone! I shake like a wet dog, trying to get her hand away, because I can't say these things to her. I don't want to hurt her feelings.

The intake woman comes out and takes me to the back office to fill out my admission papers while a counselor takes my family to tour the facility. I'm answering questions and signing papers and my fear has turned to rage. I'm pissed off and giving mono-syllabic answers to the same fucking questions I've been asked by everyone. I won't look this woman, Laura, in the eyes. Fuck her. She's a fat bitch with ugly flowers on her smocked shirt. I hate the way I'm acting right now, but I can't help it. I'm in fight or flight mode and flight is not an option.

I'm pissed off at my behavior. I'm acting like a spoiled brat who's been brought here to be locked up against her will and forced into unwanted treatment. I know this isn't the case. I know I have no reason to be acting the way I am, but I seem powerless to stop. I feel like I'm outside myself watching everything happen, and I'm looking at myself thinking, "What a bitch! Would someone please put her in time out?"

My intake complete, I'm back in the sitting area saying goodbye to my family. I'm still pissed off and give my parents the briefest of hugs as if this were all their fault - as if this whole rehab thing was their idea and I have no choice. The Walker Center is an unlocked facility. Admission is voluntary, meaning I can always leave but if I do, I can't come back. It would mean leaving AMA – against medical advice.

I soften when I hug Andy and tell him to be a good boy. "Mom will be home soon, okay? I love you, honey."

"Ayu you."

I grab my suitcase and other things and follow the woman down the hall to my room. The building is long with the men's side separated from the women's by a section of counselors' offices.

I have no idea what to expect. The website mentioned drug education, a rope course, counseling and mental health care all wrapped up in a twelve step program. I can't imagine what this place can possible teach me about drugs that I don't already know, and the only thing I know about the rope course is that there will be physical activities designed to help me overcome my deepest fears. Whatever. What I know is that I need help with my depression, since I feel that this is the core of my problem, and I'm looking forward to one-on-one therapy with a counselor.

"This is your room."

There are two beds, a bathroom and long desk on each side of a big room divided in the middle by a half-wall. Two women are lying on their beds; one is sleeping, the other keeps pushing up her glasses while writing in a little notebook. A matronly woman is sitting at one of the desks taking notes from a book. County music is playing from a radio/alarm clock. I hate country music. The room is too bright. It hurts my eyes.

"Okay, Kimberly, this is your bed. Go ahead and open your suitcase for me."

"Why?"

"So I can search it." No one looks at us. It's business as usual.

She goes through everything: every pocket, sock, nook and cranny. "You think I'd bring drugs to rehab?" It suddenly occurs to me that this isn't a bad idea. I've smuggled drugs on every plane trip I've ever been on. Why not rehab?

"Some people do," she says, still rummaging through my things. "We also have to check for mouthwash, perfume, aerosol sprays, that kind of thing. You would be amazed at what some people will do to get high." No, I wouldn't.

When she's finished, she points to the closet and dresser next to my bed. "You can put your things away. If you don't have hangers, ask the others. I'm glad you're here."

I start putting my things away when the woman with the little notebook notices my carton of cigarettes. "Hey, you smoke? You wanna go outside?" She walks me out to the smoking area and we both light up. "So, Kimberly, I'm glad you're here. I'm Betsy. What's your drug of choice?" She has dishwater blonde hair and glasses. She doesn't look like an addict but more like someone who might work here.

"Uh, meth," I tell her, "and my name's Kim. I mean it is Kimberly, but I go by Kim. What about you?"

She blows smoke out of the side of her mouth. "I'm an alcoholic."

Other women join us and one of them notices the emblem on my coat. "Are you a bail-bondsman?"

"Yeah. In Boise."

"Whoa! What's your drug of choice?" I decide that this is the rehab equivalent of saying hello.

"Meth."

They look me up and down. "Shit. You don't look like a tweaker. Have you detoxed?"

"No," I say like this is the stupidest question I've heard.

"Oh, no. Do they know that?"

"I don't think so. They never asked, or if they did, I don't remember. It's okay, though. I've been doing it so long it's no big deal. I can sleep on this stuff, eat...I've been doing it for years. I don't need to detox."

A couple of them roll their eyes. One woman is all jittery and twitching. She's the epitome of a meth addict. "Oh man. You're gonna crash big time. When did you last use?"

"Seven-thirty this morning, and I won't crash. It'll be nice to get a good night's sleep, though." They look at me like I'm insane. Of course I won't crash. I'm used to sleeping only a few hours and then not again for a day or more. A whole eight hours, and I'll be just like new. (What I'm not thinking of at the moment, though, is that my pipe won't be there the second I wake up. The number of hours I sleep aren't going to matter if I don't start getting high the minute I'm awake.)

Back inside, someone walks past my room ringing a bell saying, "Lunch time! Ten minutes. Kimberly, your counselor, Dorothy wants to see you. Her office is the third one on the left in the counselor hall. You can eat when you're done."

Fine with me. I have no desire to eat.

"Come on in!" Dorothy is an older woman, maybe in her late fifties. She looks like a shorter, grayer version of Marion Cunningham. "Have a seat." She thumbs through my intake papers. "Well, Kimberly, I'm Dorothy. I'm glad you're here." Jesus, what is this? Some kind of mantra?

We go through the rules and what she expects of me while I'm here: I have to attend all classes and participate fully in the recovery process. No one can do this for me; I have to want it. I listen and nod with a forced little smile on my face. I don't want her to think I have a real drug problem like the other people here. I want her to understand that I'm different - I'm mostly here for my depression.

We go over my history of drug use and she gives me a packet of worksheets she wants me to finish as soon as possible. "This way, we can design your recovery plan. You and I will both know where you are now and how best to help you."

"Okay, no problem." I smile and nod.

"So. Your drug of choice is meth. Do you think that when you get done here you'll be able to drink alcohol?"

This is a little out of left field, I think, but I tell her yes. I'm not an alcoholic. She smiles and scribbles on the legal pad she's been taking notes on.

"The first couple of days you're here, we give you a lot of latitude. You don't have to go to classes or attend A.A. meetings unless you feel up to it. After that, though, I expect full participation. I'm strict with my people. I expect you to be showered and dressed with your bed made by seven-thirty every morning. I expect you to turn in your daily journal on your way to breakfast and I expect you to eat complete meals – especially at breakfast. You do that, follow the rules and participate in your recovery and you'll do just fine." She stands up to dismiss me. "I'm glad you're here!" I'm going to puke if I hear that one more time. I try to remember reading anything about Jim Jones having a mantra. I'm almost certain the Moonies did.

The rules don't seem too difficult. I'm not sure I like being told how to eat, but I assume that's a rule that can probably be bent. I've always been a "good girl," up until recently, that is, and have never had problems with authority figures. In my experience, those of us who complete our homework on time and don't cause problems, so to speak, are allowed to bend the rules a little.

After the others are finished with lunch, Angie, a meth addict she tells me, takes me on a tour of the building and grounds. She doesn't need to tell me her thing is meth. I can tell by looking at her. Her face is covered in sores and she's twitchy in both speech and mannerisms. In other words, she's nothing like me.

Back in my room, I start working on the papers Dorothy gave me. She expects these to be done by tomorrow afternoon and I have to write a journal entry, which is due in the morning. I want to get all of this done and out of the way so I can just relax tonight. I have no intention of going to the A.A. meeting with the other women at some church in town.

After dinner, when everyone else is gone, I get back to work. I'm in my nightgown and robe and I need to hurry and get my homework done because I'm starting to fade. I stand up and walk around the room a lot trying to keep myself awake. I want to get this done before I go to sleep. I want to be the alpha rehabber. A couple of times a counselor comes in and asks me if I'm okay. Of course, I tell them. I just want to get this done before morning. I want to do a good job. I want people to think I'm a good girl. I write my first journal entry.

"I know you explained to me that there is a specific format you want me to use for journal writing, but after filling out the other forms, I don't recall exactly what you want, so I'm going to punt.

This has been a very long and emotional day for me. I've never been to any kind of treatment before and have only in the past few weeks even admitted to anyone - including myself - that I have a problem. This - coming to inpatient rehab - was solely my idea. Frankly, I never thought it could actually happen. I didn't have the money. I am still shocked that my parents are paying for it and were even willing, apparently, to pay for other programs I looked into that were three or four times the cost of treatment here.

When they dropped me off today, they told me they are proud of me for doing this. I feel so guilty - like I am selfish to have even looked into something I can't afford, let alone burden them with the truth about my drug use.

When I look back, though, I remember a couple of times over many years I've lived with this huge secret, wishing and wanting more than anything for someone to take me away and take care of me. I never thought it would actually happen.

Now I'm afraid to hope that this is that wish coming true and I'm ashamed of being weak enough to have ever wanted it in the first place. Why did I have to go and shatter the illusion? What if this doesn't work? Right now I can think of so many better ways to spend ten thousand dollars. I feel like a bad girl. I feel weak and needy and pathetic. I wish I were strong. I wish I could just disappear."

I can't keep my eyes open and I barely finish the packet of work when I fall into bed. It's Tuesday night. My first night in rehab.

I don't wake up until Saturday morning.

Chapter 23

I have flashes of someone taking my vital signs and waking me to drink water or tea. I remember going to the bathroom a couple of times, but the images are hazy. I sit up in my bed. It's almost nine in the morning so I've missed breakfast and meditation. The dorm is silent so I guess everyone must be in some group session.

I found out later that several things contributed to my hibernation. I was sleeping hard and no one could wake me, so Dorothy gave permission for me to sleep all day Wednesday with the condition that I begin participating on Thursday morning. Her days off happen to be Thursday and Friday, so she assumed that's what happened. When she got back to work on Saturday to find me still sleeping, she wasn't happy. I don't know what went on between her and the staff, but what I interpreted as anger was her being tough with me. I needed to start participating and following the rules. She wanted me to know I wasn't on vacation. Sleep time was over. It was time to work.

According to the other women who shared the room with me, the dorm staff tried to wake me several times, but I was so incoherent and lethargic there wasn't much they could do. Betsy, my alcoholic roommate and a nurse in the real world, was the one who insisted on taking my vitals. It frightened her how deep I was sleeping. She couldn't tell if I was breathing. She's also the one who made sure I took liquids during my little hiatus. So the staff were trying to do the best they could with this lump of a person, and all I could do was sleep, so there was certainly no effort on my part. Regardless, Dorothy was pissed, probably because I'd missed so many classes, lectures and activities meant to help me get sober. In other words, I was wasting precious time.

I feel awful. I'm weak and it's like there's some kind of thin film on my eyeballs, so it's difficult to focus. I get up to go to the bathroom and I feel like a slug dragging itself through primordial ooze. When I come out, Dorothy is standing by my bed, and she's pissed. I'm trying to look at her, but my eyes hurt when I try to focus. The morning sun stabbing through the blinds doesn't help.

"What are you doing, Kimberly? I'm told you've been sleeping for four days."

What does she mean what am I doing? This isn't my fault. Besides, she's just answered her own question. I hate rhetorical questions and I hate the name Kimberly. It was my "in trouble" name when I was a little girl.

"When I left Wednesday night for my two days off, I told the day managers to make sure you were up and participating on Thursday morning. Now I come back to work to find you've been sleeping all this time."

I stare at the carpet and concentrate on standing. I feel like I'm going to crumple to the floor at any second, not only because I'm so weak, but because I'm embarrassed. I'm in trouble and I'm a bad girl.

Alcoholics and addicts get stuck, emotionally, at the age they were when they started using. I heard this at rehab and I've heard it from my therapists. It makes sense to me, and it explains a lot of my behavior at this time in my life. I started smoking pot and drinking when I was fourteen and that's where my emotional growth stopped. I think about the foster daughters I had who were at that age and how they drove me nuts. (No one understands me. Why me? Why can't I? It's not fair. You can't make me. WHATever!) Then I think of myself during my meth addiction and early sobriety. Yep. That was me: a fourteen year old in a thirty-eight year old woman's body. I'm glad I wasn't my counselor.

"I want you to get showered and dressed, and I expect you to be at the 10:00 group." Her voice is edgy. I know she's mad at me and when she leaves, I can't keep the tears from spilling down my face, soaking my nightgown. I feel stupid and humiliated. I am not the alpha rehabber and this embarrasses me.

I get ready, but I'm so disoriented and shaky that it takes me the full hour to do the bare minimum: shower and dress, hair barely blown dry and no makeup. Fuck it, I figure. I'll just cry it all off anyway.

The next group, my first, is about forgiving ourselves. We're sitting, twelve other women and I, in a circle of chairs with a counselor. I can barely keep my eyes open and I'm nodding toward sleep. The room is fluorescent bright, the chairs unforgiving, and in spite of that, it's a struggle to stay awake. I'm still having trouble focusing my eyes. All I can think is, "I don't want to be here. Run! Run away!" I look at the carpet, worn and frayed from years of absorbing the pain and sorrow of addicts, to avoid eye contact with anyone.

"Part of recovery," the counselor begins, "is forgiving yourself. It's a huge part, in fact, and today we're going to work on that." She pulls out a hand mirror. "I want you to share something with the group that you feel you can't forgive yourself for, and when you're done, I want you to look in the mirror and say, 'I love and forgive myself.'"

What the hell is this? I'm panicking because there's no way I can do this. Tell myself these things? I don't love myself. The concept is completely foreign. As for looking in the mirror, that's something I try to avoid. I think I'm ugly. On a good day, when I don't think I'm quite ugly, but plain, I feel stupid allowing myself that concession. No one's ever told me I'm pretty or even cute. The two times someone called me beautiful were during sex, so I don't count those. In fact, if someone were to call me beautiful now, I would probably be pissed off because it's so obviously bullshit. Even when I get my hair cut I have the stylist turn my chair around so I don't have to see myself.

Amy starts the exercise. She's a meth addict, too. She's been here three weeks, she's gained some weight, and her face is clearing up. She has shoulder length, light brown hair and doesn't look like a tweaker. She looks bookish with her glasses on. The only thing that gives her away, really, is her healing face. She looks at the group as she speaks. "I'm Amy and I'm an addict."

"Hi, Amy," everyone says in unison. One of the rules is that anytime we talk, we have to say our name and identify our addiction.

"The thing that I'm most ashamed of is that I haven't been there, haven't been present I mean, for my daughter. She's three years old and so beautiful and I've just spent so much time using, that I've ignored her a lot." She starts crying. "I wasn't mean to her or anything, but I would spend so much time in the bathroom getting high when I should have been playing with her." Amy is sobbing now and I feel tightness in my chest. "I remember little fingers under the door, you know that space between the bottom of the door and the floor, wiggling, and her outside saying, 'Mommy, what are you doing?' And I would just keep telling her to go play and I'd be out in a minute. But it was never a minute. I'd spend hours in there getting high while she was in her room playing by herself." She's crying so hard now her words come out in loud, choking sobs and I start sobbing loudly - snot running, tears streaming, and I know my face is red because it feels so hot. I can't stand this. I can't stand this because I know exactly what she's talking about, and I get this memory of…

"Andy." He was sitting on his bed flapping his book as usual. "Do you want to go to PoJo's?" He loves the video games at the arcade. Especially the Star Wars game.

"Yeah!" He scooted off his bed and turned off his television.

"Then run in and go to the bathroom, brush your teeth and get your shoes on. Mom will be ready in a minute." He rarely wanted to do anything unless it was with Allan, who he adored, so I was delighted he said yes.

As always I couldn't leave the house without getting high, so while Andy was getting ready, I did the same. I sat on my bed smoking as fast as I could - so fast I wasn't really breathing other than when inhaling and exhaling the smoke. After a few minutes, he was standing in the doorway so I hid the pipe behind my back. "Awight. Et's go! Yeah! Yeah!" He was smiling and jabbing the air with his fists.

"Okay, honey, just a minute. Go wash your glasses and I'll be right there."

A few minutes later, "Okay, Mom. I weady!"

"Okay, bug. I'll be right there." I could never get high enough, but I promised him, and I wanted to go play with him. Just one more bowl. That should do it.

Twenty minutes passed. "MOM! Are doing?"

"Honey, I'll be right there! Just a minute!" I was yelling, pissed off, but not at him, at me. Jesus. What was wrong with me? Just one more bowl. He's such a good boy. He waited for me.

Forty-five minutes and two bowls later, I wasn't any higher so I bit the bullet, put everything away, and went out to the living room. There he was, sound asleep curled up in the rocking chair sucking his thumb.

I felt sick. What was wrong with me? I told myself I was a shitty mother, and I felt so ashamed, which made me sad, which, of course, made me need to get high. Instead of waking my son and taking him to play video games, I retreated to my room and continued smoking meth. "I should just go wake him up," I thought. "Do this! Do this and don't be a bad mom." I was so filled with guilt and shame I couldn't stand myself and I was actually glad that he had Down syndrome because I never had to deal with the questions of a typical, angry, hurt child. Having those thoughts made me feel even guiltier and I knew the only thing that would numb what I was feeling in my soul was to get high. An hour passed as I smoked two more bowls and then woke Andy. He was still excited and wanted to go and I was so angry with myself. I felt like scum. He forgave me. He always forgave me because I was his mom. I loved him so much, and I didn't deserve him. I thought of other mothers who abandoned or abused or used in front of their children and I knew I wasn't them. Deep down, though, very deep down, I knew I had abandoned my son. I didn't spend enough time with him. He was so independent, and I knew I'd made him that way by not being with him as much as I should have been. Guilt and shame consumed me and I knew I could never tell anyone about how I felt or what I was doing because people would be appalled at what a shitty person I was. I was alone with the horror of being me.

Two more women take their turn with the "I love myself, mirror" thing, and I'm next. I'm still crying, my body heaving with sobs. I'm a mess and all this crying is making my eyes puffy. There's dried snot on both sleeves and the front of my shirt. I'm so embarrassed to be doing this in front of these strangers, but I can't help it. I want to slide down the chair and into the floor. I want to disappear.

"Kim, can you tell us why you're crying?" a counselor asks. I'm starting to hyperventilate and now this touchy-feely woman wants me to talk? I shake my head. "Maybe this is too much for her on her first day," she tells the others. "We'll move on."

I spend the rest of the group doubled over in embarrassment, exhausted as my tears quit coming. I fade out a couple of times, nodding in and out of sleep, and then the group is finally over. I head for the door but a counselor stops me. "We need to close group," she says. Everyone stands in a tight circle with their arms around each other's shoulders or waists and puts their right foot in front of them. I have no idea what they're doing so I just follow along. My skin is crawling. I don't want to be touched, and here I am in this tight circle of camaraderie that I want nothing to do with.

"The right foot represents," they begin chanting, "the alcoholic and addict that still suffers and will die today. The circle represents what I cannot do alone, we can do together. God, grant me the serenity to accept the things I cannot change, the courage to change the things I can, and the wisdom to know the difference."

I head for my room and flop on my bed, asleep instantly. Someone is ringing a bell outside in the hallway and yelling, "Five minutes 'till group!" I drag myself off my bed and follow the others to another room. Betsy, the alcoholic nurse, walks with me. She's artificially cheery.

"It will get better. You've missed a lot, but we're glad you're here." I want to claw her eyes out. I hate this place. I hate the other women who are obviously so fake, walking around, smiling, being glad I'm here. Shut the fuck up! You don't even know me. If you knew what I'm thinking right now, you might not be so happy I'm here. Idiots.

In the classroom, one of the patients, Cheryl, is jumpy and talking a mile a minute. She's pretty in a plain sort of way and has the thickest, longest brown hair I've ever seen. It hangs halfway down her back. I think she must be a meth addict the way she's acting but I later learn she's a late stage alcoholic. She's forty, but looks like she's barely thirty, which is the opposite of what I've seen in most addicts and alcoholics. They usually age prematurely. Cheryl gave up custody of her daughter and lives with her parents. She does nothing but sit in her childhood bedroom and drink all day. She's been in the hospital numerous times for alcohol-induced seizures. If I met her on a street somewhere, I would never guess she's an alcoholic.

Rene, tall and skinny with short, naturally curly hair is talking to a couple of other women. She's almost as amped as Cheryl. She's also an alcoholic and came here just a couple of days before me. This is her second time at the Walker Center. She's back now just two weeks after her release because she immediately relapsed and nearly killed herself drinking. The day before she came back, a friend found her passed out in her living room. She smashed her head on a coffee table while she was having an alcohol-induced seizure. If no one had found her, she would be dead.

I look at all these women and it's difficult imagining them wasted. The all seem normal to me aside from their nervous and neurotic tics. The tweakers are easiest to spot. Meth addicts find it hard to sit still. They're always shaking their leg up and down, rocking back and forth, or chewing on their fingers or nails. The pill poppers and opiate addicts, users of heroin, Oxycontin, Vicadin, and all their candy colored sisters and cousins, are more difficult to identify. Unless they are initially detoxing, they seem normal. A little sad, maybe, but we all look sad. The party kids whose tastes run toward designer drugs like Ecstasy, GHB and MDMA are easy to spot. They're young, usually in their twenties, and carry remnants of their "clubbing" with them: dyed hair cut at odd angles, colorful tattoos, tongue rings. They all look like they've just exited the thumping bass and psychedelic lights of last night's rave, and the early morning sky has reached down and smacked them right in their multi-pierced faces.

The alcoholics span the generations, and even the ones in the late stages don't have any obvious give away, unless their liver is on its way out and then their skin and the whites of their eyes have turned yellow.

"Okay, ladies," a counselor says. "Let's get started. Everyone sit on the floor, back against that wall." We go down the line saying our names and identifying our addictions, then the facilitator begins.

"This group is a little different. It's called 'desensitization.' Many of you, at one time or another, will come into contact with your drug of choice. It can happen when you least expect it. A party, maybe. Or on a date. Certainly those of you who are alcoholics will encounter alcohol every time you go to a store. There are triggers besides the actual drug, too. Paraphernalia, like glass, baggies, syringes, medication bottles and wine glasses can all trigger cravings. You need to anticipate triggers so you can avoid them or, if that's not possible, think about what you will do before it happens so you're not blindsided."

Another counselor wheels in a metal cart with a white cloth that hides whatever is under it. "On this cart are actual drugs, alcohol and paraphernalia. Each of you will come up here to touch and hold the things related to your addiction." She whips away the cloth, and sure as hell, there's a smorgasbord of temptation. "What the hell is wrong with these people?" I think and I stand up and walk out of the classroom.

Outside, I'm pacing around the gazebo that's the designated smoking area. This is wrong, all wrong. I don't need to see a bag of meth and a glass pipe right now. I need help with my depression. I walk in circles around the little gazebo, pissed off and confused.

At lunch, my first meal here, I go through the cafeteria-style line. I'm surprised at how good the food is. Everything is homemade and there are always two or three choices of entrée and a big fresh salad bar. The cooks are friendly and quick to customize an order if they can. While I'm eating, Dorothy comes to my table and says she wants to see me as soon as I'm finished.

I knock softly on the open door to her office. "Come on in, Kimberly and close the door." I sit down in the chair next to her desk.

"It's Kim," I tell her.

"All right, Kim, let's talk about today. You are required to attend all the groups and meetings. You can't just leave in the middle. If you're here just to avoid your legal problems, we don't want you here. Maybe you should go to jail. You can sleep all you want there. The Walker Center is for people who take their recovery seriously and from I've seen and heard, all you want to do is sleep." I start to cry and I'm angry at myself because I don't want her to see she's gotten to me. "And I think your crying all the time is because it's your way of avoiding anything you find unpleasant. I think you use it as a way to control people."

Fuck you! You don't know a Goddamn thing about me, bitch. How is my crying a way to control people? I hate crying all the time. I hate you, sitting there with your perfect hair and perfect clothes, judging me. Treating me like a child. I hate you, and I hate this place!

"What do you think? Do you want to leave?"

I'm crying and I feel embarrassed, ashamed and pissed off. "Dorothy, maybe this isn't the place for me. I chose this program specifically because it teats dual-diagnosis but no one is helping me with my depression at all." I've conveniently forgotten that I've only been awake here for half a day, so I'm feeling self-righteous. "And I'm not here to avoid my legal problems either! I'm the one who sought treatment. I don't even have sentencing until a week after I get out of here."

"Do you know how much money your parents have paid for you to be here?"

Goddamn it, how fucking old am I? Stop it. Stop treating me like a child.

"Yes." All I can think is that I want to leave her office and go to bed. I'm so angry and as usual, I have nowhere to put that anger. I have to sit there and take it. My head hurts and I'm doing that wringing thing with my hands - interlacing my fingers and twisting them grotesquely. I feel so hot - like my insides are boiling, creating steam that's oozing out my pores.

"Well, why don't you give it some thought today and let me know what you decide by tomorrow. In the meantime, you are to attend and fully participate in all meetings and activities." She picks up a pen and opens a file that's not mine. She's dismissed me.

That bitch! That fucking June Cleaver, prim and proper, stupid, gray-haired bitch. How can she talk to me like that? Maybe I don't belong here. What I really need is someone to help me with my depression. Maybe I belong in a mental hospital.

I'm sullen the rest of the day, and although I participate in all the groups, I'm stoic and aloof. That evening, I write my journal entry:

"Ok. I tried to tell you that I'm concerned that this is not the appropriate place for me. Your only response was that if I'm only doing this to avoid my legal problems then maybe I should just go to jail because I can sleep all I want there.

I'll give you the benefit of the doubt and say that it's possible I didn't explain well enough. I am not here because I have to be. I am not here to avoid ANYTHING, and yes, I know exactly how much this is costing my parents.

I – ME – MYSELF - ALONE (as usual) am the one who decided to seek treatment. I am the one who made the decision to expose myself by asking for help.

Until about three or four weeks ago, no one knew about my meth use and it was easy to downplay my arrest because of the circumstances of it. If I had continued to keep everything to myself, I most likely would have received probation, which is probably what I'll get when I'm done here.

I want help. I have been saying all along that I'm terrified that if I don't get help - the right kind of help - that I do not want to continue to live. That's why I specifically searched for a program that would treat dual diagnosis. I understand that I became addicted to meth and that I need treatment for this. I was under the impression, however, that my depression would be addressed here as well.

When I question the appropriateness of this program for me at this time, it is not that I'm trying to take the easy way out. It's that I'm desperately crying out for help while I can still cry. I'm thirty-eight years old, and I'm so tired of feeling the way I do. I'm just wondering if this is the best use of my parents' money. Maybe I should be in a psychiatric hospital.

I'm not sleeping because I'm lazy. I'm not crying because I'm trying to get out of doing things. I CAN'T HELP IT AND I'M ASKING FOR HELP I CAN'T HELP IT AND I'M ASKING FOR HELP I'M ASKING FOR HELP PLEASE HELP ME PLEASE HELP ME PLEASE HELP ME PLEASE HELP ME HELP ME HELP ME HELP ME HELP ME HELP ME HELP ME PLEASE PLEASE PLEASE please."

I'm crying, as usual, while I write, and I'm just so damn tired. I put my journal in Dorothy's box outside her office and am in bed, asleep, at 8:30.

After Sunday breakfast (bacon and eggs cooked to order, French toast, homemade biscuits, hash browns,) I return to my room to find my journal on my bed. Dorothy has written:

"I am here to help you. But I won't work harder than you do. I have been where you are. It would be a blessing for me to guide you through the darkness to the light."

I read those sentences again, then sit and stare at them for a few minutes, trying to figure out how I feel. Part of me wonders if the scene in her office yesterday was real. Did she say those things to piss me off intentionally? Did she want me to get mad at her as some kind of confrontational therapy thing? I decide that I don't know, and I'm too tired to try to sort out head games, if that's what's going on.

I reread the last line of her comment, "It would be a blessing for me to guide you through the darkness to the light." I feel deflated. All the emotion that went into my journal entry and what I get back is rhetoric? She should have written, "We're glad you're here." It would have saved her some ink.

I remember feeling numb reading her comments. I was hoping for more. I was hoping she would take the time to honestly respond to what I wrote, but I felt exactly the way I did when I wrote the letter to Allan and got no reaction. In both cases, I spent time figuring out exactly what I wanted to say. I felt like I took a risk letting each of them see inside me a little bit, and in both cases, I was ignored.

Chapter 24

Sundays are visitation days, but I haven't been here long enough even to have phone privileges, so I'm shocked when I hear my name on the loudspeaker. For a second I hope it's Allan, but I'm thrilled to see my parents and Andy. "Mom!" he yells, running down the hall toward me in his funny little Down syndrome way. I catch him in my arms just as he gets close, and he wraps his arms around me tight.

"Hey, bug! How are you? I've missed you so much." We hug for a minute, then he backs away, smiling at me. His beautiful blue eyes are alive with his excitement.

"Essah Mom, ennah hospital?"

"Yep. I'm so happy to see you, sweetheart."

Mom and Dad both have tears in their eyes and take turns hugging me.

"Okay, Mom," Andy says, taking my hand. "Ess go home."

"Oh honey, I can't yet. Mom has to get better first."

I take them on a short tour showing them the cafeteria, lounges, auditorium and the smoking area outside. Visitors aren't allowed in our rooms. Not even spouses. At the gazebo, we smoke and talk a little and I introduce my family to a couple of the women. Visitation is three hours long. We're half an hour into it; we've done the pleasant chitchat thing and now there's just awkwardness. We don't know what to do. I take them into one of the empty lounges, and we sit down.

"I don't know if this is the right place for me," I begin. "No one's even addressed my depression yet and that's one of the reasons I specifically chose this place." I can NOT tell my mother about sleeping for four days. All hell will break loose. They don't know about detox and I think they'll be disgusted if they know how bad my meth problem really is.

"Have you talked to your counselor about it?" Mom asks.

"No. She doesn't even have time for me. I've only seen her twice. Once on the first day just to go over the rules, and then yesterday for a few minutes, but she didn't even ask about my depression. Maybe I should be in a mental hospital."

"Kimbo, you need to talk to her and ask to see the doctor," my dad says. "You need to get as much out of this place as you can, right?"

"I know, I know, but..." the door opens and Dorothy comes in all smiles and graciousness, introducing herself to my family.

"I'm Dorothy, Kim's counselor," she says, extending her hand to my father. "It's so nice to meet you all. Has Kim been telling you what's going on?"

"She's been telling us she hasn't spoken with anyone yet about her depression," Mom says. "We were under the impression that she would get help for that."

Dorothy looks at me with a 'gotcha' look. I know what's coming and I feel nauseated. Why did she have to show up? Go away! I think. No one asked you to come in here.

"We haven't had a chance to talk about her depression or do much of anything," Dorothy tells them. "Kim's been sleeping all week."

"I have not been sleeping all week." My parents are both looking at me with shocked expressions. I'm starting to feel that hot feeling in my stomach.

"When did you get up?" Dorothy asks me.

"Yesterday morning."

"What?" my mom says sounding shocked. "What do you mean you've been sleeping all this time?" I don't say anything. I cross my arms in front of me and stare at the floor. I was right. My parents don't understand. They don't know about detox. I decide I'm mad at them for this.

"Kim and I had a little talk yesterday, and I'm not sure this is the right place for her. I told her that if all she wants to do is sleep, she should just go to jail." She's saying this in a cheery, condescending voice - the way people talk around little kids.

"Dorothy, I think Kim has been using sleep to avoid life for a long time now," Mom says.

She knows I've been sleeping a lot lately, because that's what I've told her. I spent the last few weeks lying in bed, getting high and dozing. Also, when I did sleep, it was in the daytime because I worked at night writing bonds. That's why I was always asleep when she called. Or was it? I couldn't remember what I'd told her when. Things are getting confusing.

"I agree," says Dorothy. "It seems to me that she's used sleep as an escape - much like a drug - and that her excessive crying has been her way of manipulating people."

I stand up. "I told you! I'm not trying to manipulate anyone.

I can't help my crying. Do you think I want to be like this? I hate it that I cry all the time. It's embarrassing!" I'm angry that they're talking about me in front of me as if I were a child. This woman doesn't even know me. How the hell does she know what I'm like? I'm angry about everything and I just want to be left alone.

"Why don't you take some time as a family," Dorothy says sweetly, "and discuss whether or not Kim should stay here. Meet me in my office in half an hour."

I'm livid. Not wanting to be here is one thing, but someone telling me I can't be is another. I feel like a child who isn't allowed to make decisions for herself. What the hell have I done that's so bad it warrants me being kicked out of rehab?

We go the cafeteria. Everyone's quiet for a few minutes. I feel my parent's sorrow and disappointment, and I know I'm the source.

"Kimbo," my father says, "you need to be here. What the hell are you doing? Do you want to go to jail?"

Why does everyone keep talking about jail? No one ordered me to come here. It's not as if my sentencing is contingent upon my success or failure at rehab. The judge may look favorably on my decision, but I wasn't thinking about that when I started this. Now, everyone's talking like it's either rehab or prison, and that's not the case.

"No! I can't help sleeping. I'm tired all the time. If you weren't tired could you make yourself sleep? Jesus! Dorothy just hates me and no one's doing anything to help me." I know I'm acting like a spoiled brat, but I don't care. I feel cornered and desperate, like an animal in a cage. I have no control, and it's pissing me off.

My mom looks at my dad and then at me. "I think that if you want to stay here, it's up to you, Kimberly. But if you're going to stay here, you need to get with the program and start participating. Dorothy doesn't hate you. The people here are trying to help you, but you need to try to help yourself, too. This isn't a one way street."

I'm staring at the Formica table, seething because I feel ganged up on. I don't want to be here. I don't want to have to do the work involved with getting sober. I think about how much easier it would be just to get high and stay high forever. Fuck everyone else. None of them understands how shitty I feel.

Then I look at Andy sitting there drinking his juice. "Come

here, bug." He sits on my lap and wraps his arms around my neck. I rest my head on his chest and close my eyes. I miss him so much, and I want to be there for him. I want to be the mother he deserves. I concede.

"Fine. I'll try harder," I say, my eyes still closed. All I care about is my son who doesn't deserve any of this. He shouldn't have to be driven two hours to a hospital to visit his mother.

Thirty minutes later, we're all sitting in Dorothy's office. "Did you have some time to talk?" she asks us. I'm sitting there with my arms crossed and head down fuming with rage and embarrassment and trying not to jiggle my leg up and down.

"We have," says Mom. "Kim has agreed to have a better attitude and to participate in her recovery."

"Dorothy, we want what's best for her," says Dad. "We think this is the best place if she can put the past week behind her and get to work here."

"Well," says Dorothy, "I think that if Kim can tell us what's expected of her...Kim, can you tell us?"

Everyone's looking at me and there's no way out. I have to talk. I have to answer her stupid question if I want to stay here. I take a deep breath and begin.

"I need to attend all the classes and lectures," I say through clenched teeth. "I have to be up showered and dressed with my bed made by 7:30 every morning, and I have to eat breakfast. I have to participate and I can't leave any sessions."

Dorothy looks at my parents, smiling that high and mighty smile of hers. "Well, I think she's clear about what's expected and as long as she can live up to these rules, I think she'll do just fine here."

They're still talking about me in front of me; treating me like a baby, and when Dorothy is finished with us, Mom, Dad, Andy and I sit in the cafeteria again for a few minutes. Other than seeing Andy, I wish they hadn't come. It's been an afternoon of humiliation. I just want everyone to leave me alone.

My parents tell me they're not mad at me. They tell me they know how hard this is for me and they're proud of me. They're proud of me. Of course they are. I've decided to be a good girl.

The only time I soften is when I tell Andy goodbye and sing him our song. I stand at the window and watch them drive away. I feel empty. I take a nap for the remainder of visitation. It's okay to sleep if you don't have visitors so I take advantage of this luxury. When I wake up just before dinner, I'm calm. I've resolved to do whatever it takes to excel at rehab. I'm going to shake off the past few days and give myself do-overs. I will make everyone proud of me.

I write in my journal:

"I'm so grateful for my parents. I'm the luckiest mommy in the world to have my son. Today's visit was exactly what I needed even though I didn't know it. My mother told me that she told my grandmother and my aunt that I'm here. This is the first that anyone outside of my immediate family has been told anything about my drug use. It was a good feeling. That may sound strange, but it made me feel less ashamed, or rather, that my parents were less ashamed of me. I don't know...maybe they just didn't have a choice as to how to explain my absence.

I want to address something here. I know I was pretty much a wreck today, and I know that I've been sleeping a lot etc., but I felt very uncomfortable around you (Dorothy) today. I feel like you were condescending in the way you spoke to me today, especially when my parents and I came to your office at the end of visitation and you had me repeat what was expected of me if I wanted to stay here. I know that you wanted everyone to know that I am clear about what's expected of me, but I felt like you were treating me and speaking to me like a child. That made me feel angry and resentful. I hope this doesn't make you mad at me, but I remembered you said on the first day we spoke that I should let you know things like this."

And the next morning:

"Otherwise, I feel really good today. I'm still hesitant and a little uncertain, but I'm here...so here I go.

Last night we read a chapter in the Big Book about figuring out our higher power. It was good because it sort of answered questions I had been having. Basically it was saying that I need to turn my life over to God or Buddha or whatever I can accept turning my life over to because I obviously can't do this sobriety thing on my own. Not that I necessarily need to even name whatever it is right now. Not having to name it made it a little easier. Right now my higher power is the universe. At least it's a start."

I spend time writing the entry. I want it to reflect my new outlook and show Dorothy that I'm "thinking recovery." I addressed how I felt, only stating facts and leaving emotion out of it. I think this shows I'm working on my boundaries. I mentioned

A.A. and the Big Book, the A.A. handbook, and let her know I'm working on finding my higher power. I am onboard. I'm part of the team. I'm playing ball. I'm in it to win it. I'm going to make Dorothy and my parents proud.

And I'm not trying to be flippant. I really did feel charged up and ready to tackle and conquer. I felt like I was part of a team, along with my parents and Dorothy. I was going to give rehab my best effort and get all I could out of it. The problem was, I was no longer there for myself. I did all the activities, worked all the steps, became involved with the other women and truly felt as though I were immersed in the experience.

Looking back, the signs were there. When my parents came to visit, I couldn't wait to show them the drawings I'd done in art therapy. When my group won first place in the skit contest based on my idea, I almost knocked them over at the front door to show them my little paper "ribbon." When the other women voted me to lead morning meditation for a week, I called them almost every night to talk about the songs I chose or the passages I read from a daily meditation book. I did the same with Dorothy.

"Look at me. Look at what a good girl I am. I'm not causing problems; I'm getting so much out of this experience. I AM the alpha rehabber."

Chapter 25

"I don't get it." Rene's sucking on a hard candy, as usual. She used to weigh over three hundred pounds but her gastric bypass surgery and chronic alcoholism, has turned her into a rail. She's exactly my height. Five ten. I envy her slim frame, but she's always getting dizzy because of her low blood pressure or blood sugar, so she's constantly sucking on hard candy. "You're so smart, Kim. Why would you let that happen to you?"

We're sitting in the "co-dependency" group with the other women, and the topic is Allan and me.

"What do you mean?" I ask. Inside, I'm cringing the way I always do when someone talks about me being smart. I hate it. I don't know why, but it always makes me uncomfortable - as if I'm a fraud and everyone's going to find out that I'm not smart, but stupid.

It's not just about being smart or not. I feel the same way about all compliments. My gut reaction is to think, "Bullshit," and become suspicious of the motives of the person involved. I think they're secretly making fun of me. It's a knee jerk reaction that stems from what happened to me in grade school. It's sad how much of my life was determined by the events of one year, and it pisses me off to think that I've wasted four decades vehemently rejecting and mistrusting people. I wish I absorbed people's kindness instead of deflecting it.

"I don't understand why you're still with this guy, and supporting him. You're smart, pretty and funny as hell!" You're so full of shit, Rene, I think. I'm not pretty, I'm ugly. I start wringing my hands. "You've got a great personality," she continued. "I would think you could have any man you want, but you're with this jackass who doesn't love you, treats you like shit and owes you - how much did you say? Twenty grand?"

The room is quiet and everyone is looking at me. This is the first time I've really talked about Allan and me. Now that it's come out, everyone is horrified at my situation.

"Yes," I say, "a little over twenty thousand dollars." I feel stupid and pathetic admitting this out loud to anyone, let alone twelve other alcoholics and addicts. It's bad enough when I let myself think about it, but saying it out loud is embarrassing. More than that, it feels crippling and I don't want to feel this way. Now I'm jiggling my leg up and down. Between that and my hand-wringing, I probably look autistic, but at least I'm not rocking. Yet. "It's hard to understand, I know," I say, "but it's not like Allan's a bad person. He's not mean or malicious, he just..."

"He just decided to sleep with a dog instead of you after everything you've done for him, huh?" I wish Rene would shut up. I hate it when people put me on the spot like this. "My God, woman, look at everything you've done for him: you've paid his back child support, paid off traffic tickets in other states and then paid for him to keep his license so he could continue to drive long haul. You supported him for almost a year when he lost his job and you're still paying most of the bills, right?" I'm frowning and looking at my jiggling knee, wishing I hadn't said a thing about any of this.

"Okay," I say. "But it's not like I'm a saint. This summer I got his checking account number. I don't remember how, exactly. I think maybe he played poker on my computer one night and I got it then. I don't know. Anyway, I used it to gamble. Just fifty dollars at first. I don't even know why. Maybe it was because I was mad at him. When I started playing, I was in kind of a daze and when I lost the money, I snapped out of it. I couldn't believe I had done that. I felt really shitty, you know? I don't steal, but I did from him, and I panicked. I didn't want him to know what I'd done so I figured I would win and then deposit the winnings into his account and he wouldn't be mad. I don't know what was wrong with me."

"You were high," the counselor reminded me.

"Well, yeah, but my God! That's no excuse. Anyway, I kept going. Fifty more, a hundred more, and I just panicked because it wasn't working. I wasn't winning. I ended up taking him for eighteen hundred dollars. I felt sick. I mean, what kind of person does that to someone? Especially a friend?"

"What happened when he found out?" asked Betsy.

"He came home from work one day with a three-page printout from the bank and just handed it to me without saying a word." My hands are starting to hurt from wringing them so hard and I'm staring at my lap. I'm so ashamed. I still can't believe I did that to him. I want to cry. "I owned up to it. It was the hardest thing I've ever done. I mean, he could have had me arrested! I tried to explain what happened, but it sounded just as stupid as it does now, telling you guys."

"So what happened?" Betsy asked.

"I paid him back."

"What?"

"I paid him back. I was grateful I was able to. I was completely humiliated."

"Shit, you're still paying most of the mortgage on his house and all the bills and you paid him what you owed him when he owes you all that money?" Betsy says.

"What else was I supposed to do? He couldn't afford to...I mean, he needed that money. I stole it from him and I paid it back. It's different from what he owes me. Anyway, I told you, we refinanced in March so my name's on the house now."

"Why the hell did you do that?" I don't want to answer this because the answer makes me feel sick. Also because I don't want these women to think badly of Allan. I guess I don't want them to know that I'm so desperate not to lose this relationship that I'll do anything, and have done anything, to keep it going. I am sick and twisted. I am an addict and my addiction is to more than just meth.

"Well, remember when I said that last December I got tired of everything and decided I wasn't paying the bills anymore?" They all nod. "So I told Allan that starting in January of this year, he was going to start paying the mortgage and utilities because that's the only way I can see that he'll ever even begin to pay me back. So he had the money for that month's house payment, but he had an idea. There was an auto dealership that had gone out of business and was selling all these accessories. I don't know what they were, like fins for the backs of cars, weather shield strips...I don't know. Anyway, he bought them with the money that was for the house payment. He said he thought he could go around to other dealerships and sell the accessories at a profit. It didn't work. He sold a few things, but most of it's still in our garage. When our second foreclosure notice..."

"His second foreclosure notice, you mean," says Rene.

"Okay, fine. His second foreclosure notice. When it came, he didn't know what to do. There was no way to come up with the money we...he owed. Even I couldn't put that much out at one time. It was like six grand. So he started to talk about selling the house and I...I don't know, I couldn't imagine being without him. I didn't want us to go our separate ways. So it was my idea to refinance with me as the co-owner. He was all for it. He said it was the only way he was ever going to be able to get me any of what he owed me. So we refi'd. It was a pain in the ass, too. I had to come up with all these records to prove that I'd been working at least the past two years. They wanted W-2's, paystubs...I had to look legit, on paper anyway. I had to have a valid way to explain where the money was coming from. The finance lady knew I was self-employed. I told her I wrote bail bonds and had a gift basket business, but I still had to have a way to show where the money was coming from.

"Bail bond records were easy. Jill had me fill out this sheet every night that I worked showing which bonds I'd written, how much money I'd collected and my commission. Thank God I had the gift basket business registered legitimately. I had to show my books for the company, which I didn't have. So I created a ledger and backdated entries so they showed I made enough money to qualify to buy a house. Which I did. Make enough money, I mean, but it had to be clean."

"So did Allan know where the money was coming from?" asks Cheryl.

"Of course he did. He knew everything. He used to use meth, too, but he quit after our first year living together. Just quit one day. He said it was easy for him because he knew I always had it and he could have it anytime, so he didn't have to jones," I shrugged. "I don't know. I don't get it, but that's what he said, and I know he's never touched it again.

"So anyway, we refinanced but our payments went up instead of down. Allan had gotten some kind of special financing where the payments were fairly low the first year or two but then went up. So even though we refi'd, the payment was thirteen hundred dollars a month. Now that my name's on the house..."

"You're trapped," Rene said. I'm starting to cry a little and I know my face is flushed because it feels so hot.

"Well, I don't know if that's the right word. Let's just say that I have too much invested to just walk away. Even if that's what I wanted to do."

"Let's just say you're trapped, okay?" says Betsy. She's irritated. "Call it what it is. You're stuck." Now I'm really crying and I've gone from wringing my hands to wiping my tears.

"Let's hear from someone else now," the counselor says. I'm relieved to be out of the spotlight. I don't really hear anything for the rest of the session. I'm thinking about Allan...and the house...and that stupid fucking dog.

It was unnerving, having a group of women nail my situation the way they did. I never talked about my relationship with Allan to anyone, and in my head it was easy to rationalize or find ways to excuse his behavior, or mine for that matter. Speaking it out loud, though, made it real. To hear Rene and the others pissed off about what was going on validated my feelings. I should be mad. I had a right to be mad. I had a right to be furious.

Chapter 26

The part of rehab that creates the most tension for all of us is family week. It's actually only three days but I guess they call it "week" because that's what it feels like. Our families attend lectures and receive education about addiction. Then there are sessions guided by our counselors where we're supposed to talk to each other about how addiction has affected the whole family. It means that when one member is an addict, there are problems with the whole. The intention is not to imply that our families are just as sick as we are, or that they've somehow caused our addiction, but to have us look at the roles each of us assumes and how they have affected us all.

The day before family week starts, the counselors tell us there will be no medication allowed other than our prescriptions: no aspirin, no Tums or Rolaids, nothing extra for anxiety. We are to experience everything we feel with no chemical relief whatsoever. "Yikes," I think. "What the hell do they have in store for us?"

I start to get nervous about my parents coming. I'll be thrilled to see Andy for three days in a row, but I'm scared of what will happen to Mom, Dad, and me. I'm afraid they'll hate me and think I'm disgusting. My addiction is definitely disgusting. I'm hoping they can separate the two.

The first speaker is Mike. He's been a counselor at the Walker Center for years. The contrast between the man who's speaking and the person the story is about is almost incomprehensible. Mike started using heroin when he was nine years old. His cousins thought it was funny to see him shoot up and that was the beginning of decades of drug use. He's been in and out of jail and done prison time. Hearing him tell his story tears at the mother part of me. I want to take the child he's speaking of and protect him from what's to come. Strange how my maternal instincts kick in when I come across someone hurt or wounded, but they never kick in for me.

The next speaker is Dorothy. Prim and proper, she takes the stage in the small auditorium - the same place we exercise and sometimes have lectures. She's prepared, complete with an easel and a large pad of paper with major points bulleted and neatly printed on consecutive pages. She even has a pointer. I always figured she was either a tee totaling, book educated do-gooder, or a garden variety alcoholic whose biggest transgression was being too hung over to host a Tupperware party. I was wrong.

Dorothy spends the next hour sharing her story about the pill-popping, booze-drinking, NyQuil-swilling housewife she'd once been. She speaks like a master storyteller with a sense of humor that reminds me of Erma Bombeck. She talks about her children, who are themselves addicts and alcoholics, and recalls scenes of staggering up from the basement, where she'd been chugging NyQuil, and stumbling over the unconscious bodies of her grown children and their friends. "You know that little plastic cup on top of a bottle of NyQuil?" she asks. "I didn't know what the hell that was for. It was too small to be a shot glass."

She has the audience in the palm of her hand and my mother in tears, doubled over with laughter along with the rest of the room. She talks about her grown children struggling with their addictions and bad decisions, moving back home, and how she finally came to terms with her co-dependency. She warns our families not to pay our bills or give us money, telling them they'd only be enabling us. "If you absolutely must give your addicted children something," she says, flipping the last page over the back of the easel, revealing the words as she speaks them, "buy 'em underwear."

It's her big finish and the crowd loves her. It's like a George Carlin concert when he uses satire to get a point across while the audience laugh their asses off. I gain a new respect for Dorothy that afternoon. She reminds me of myself: an ordinary, average looking woman whose packaging was the perfect disguise for a life of debauchery.

The next two days are the family sessions. Most people have their significant others with them but some, like me, have their family of origin, or some part of it, attending. We're in the group with Dorothy along with the others in her caseload. As we sit in uncomfortable chairs in a large circle of strangers, she explains the ground rules.

On the first day, the family members will talk and ask questions while we, the drug addled and afflicted, face them. We cannot respond in any way, but must listen to what each person has to say. When that person is finished, they have to tell what they are most proud of about us and why. On the second day, we will again sit in front of each loved one, answer any questions from the day before and explain what our addiction has been like for us. Then we must say one thing we are most proud of in the other. If anyone needs a tissue, he or she must get it themselves. No co-dependent behavior is tolerated during family sessions.

One by one, the mothers, fathers, children and significant others of the patients tell personal stories of how addiction has affected their lives. Anger, sorrow and grief hang over our small circle like slow moving storm clouds on a cold winter day. Children ask their parents why they were so mean sometimes and why didn't they play with them anymore. Parents wonder out loud what they've done to cause their children's addiction. Spouses ask their partners about suspected infidelities, and speak of loneliness and abandonment.

My parents and son are the last to speak. Dorothy tells Andy what a good boy he's been throughout the long day. "Is there something you would like to say to your mom, Andy?"

"Oh, ess okay."

"Are you sad that Mom used drugs and didn't spend time with you?"

"Oh, yeah." He's smiling at everyone and flirting a little with the women. My son's always been a ladies' man and he loves being on stage. "Essa circle."

Dorothy presses on, unaware that Andy isn't comprehending what she's saying. I can't tell if she doesn't understand his disability, or if she's just trying to make him feel like part of the group or what, but I can't say anything. Those are the rules. "Can you tell your mom how her drug use has affected you?"

"Oh, yeah."

"What would you like to tell her?"

"Uhhmm," he says, pushing up his glasses and straightening in his chair. "Essa hospital, enna Mom. Allan, uh, Star Wars, movies, pizza." He's smiling so big and his grin pulls my heartstrings. He's proud of himself right now and I want to tell him how proud I am of him of him, too but I'm not allowed to talk, so I just smile at him and hope he knows how I feel.

"Okay," says Dorothy. "Let's move on. Ed? How are you feeling right now?" My dad's head is bowed because he's crying a little and is embarrassed by his emotions.

"I just...I just feel so sad for everyone here," he sniffs, wiping his eyes on his shirt sleeve. My mother reaches for the box of tissues.

"Chris," Dorothy says gently, "let him get his own."

My dad continues. "It makes me feel just awful for everything these families have gone through. Especially the kids." He smiles at Betsy's son and daughter across the circle from him.

"Ed, can you tell Kim how her addiction has affected you? He's looking at me with such love in his eyes and such sadness. "We've missed you, Kimbo."

"Speak about how you feel," says Dorothy.

"I've missed you. You've been away from us for so long and we don't spend time together the way we used to. Your mom and I...I mean we...I mean I had no idea what was going on with you. I knew something was wrong, but w...I thought it was that you weren't taking your medication. I had no idea you were using drugs. I never thought you would use drugs. I love you so much, Kimbo and I want you back. I want us to be a real family again. You've really hurt your mother. She cries almost every night and blames herself for how you and your brother turned out."

I've heard my mother say this for years: "I must have been a terrible mother because look at how my children turned out." And that was before she knew I was using drugs. Chuck sort of floated through life in his bohemian way, and I never finished college, had emotional problems and trouble holding a job. I never knew what to say. I mean, how do you respond to something like that?

He pauses and clears his throat. "I would like to know how much you've been using...and for how long." He stares at me. I look back at him, hoping he can feel that I know how hard this is for him. He keeps staring expectantly. I look at Dorothy as she waits for him to continue, but he just keeps looking at me. Finally, he leans a little closer and says, "It's now or never."

I look at Dorothy again. I don't think she'll mind if I break the rules just a little bit because I know my dad has forgotten them. "I'm not supposed to talk today," I whisper. The group chuckles some, relieved, I suppose, for a bit of levity.

"Oh," he says. "Right. Sorry. I guess I'm supposed to tell her what I'm most proud of about her. I'm proud of you for being a foster mother and taking such good care of those kids. I don't know how you did it, but I'm real proud of you for that. I was also proud of you when you lost all that weight a few years ago and were working out all the time." He smiles at me and mouths I love you, as he wipes the last tear from the corner of his eye.

I move my chair over to sit in front of my mother. If this is difficult for my dad, she's dying inside. Of the two, my mother has always been the more stoic one. She's always been the main breadwinner and handled all the family's finances. My dad has a playful side to him, but my mother is all business all the time. Sharing feelings and actually communicating have never been encouraged in my family and now here she is in front of total strangers, expected to be open and honest. I know my mother and I know she would give almost anything not to be here with these people. This is at least as bad as how she felt at her surprise anniversary party. Probably worse.

I also know that she's putting herself through this agony for me, and I love her for that. I look at her, smiling. She looks at me the way she did when she used to ground me when I was a teenager. She's all business. Instinctively, I lose the smile and lower my head. This is no time for being happy. I've been a bad girl and now I am going to hear about it.

"Kimberly," she starts and I immediately know what's coming. Shit. "I don't know what to say. I'm disappointed and I'm hurt. I never in a million years thought you would use drugs. Like your dad said, we knew something was wrong but we didn't know what. I knew you weren't taking your medication but I didn't know why. All I knew is that there was something very, very wrong and you wouldn't talk to us. I miss you and want to see you. I want you to come to the house like you used to and not just send Andy to spend the night when you want to go out doing whatever you feel like doing." Her voice is starting to break, adding to her suppressed anger. "I don't think you know how much you've hurt me. I guess I was a bad mother. Look at how both my kids turned out." I close my eyes. My mother, the martyr.

My parents leave and I go outside to smoke. I'm angry. I'm livid. "What a bunch of bullshit!" I say to Betsy as she joins me.

"What?"

"All that Goddamn shit my dad was saying about how he felt so sorry for all the families and especially the kids and yadda, yadda, yadda. What'd he do? Have his fucking memory erased?" I'm walking in fast, tight circles around the smoking area. "Jesus, they act like nothing ever happened. Like they're just shocked that other people's lives are so sad. What the hell? Did they forget what they were like when we were growing up? They used to take a cooler full of beer anytime we went somewhere out of the city and drink the

whole way to wherever the hell we were going." I turn to Betsy.
"The son of a bitch used to disappear for days at a time." I know
I'm yelling but I'm so furious I can't help it.

"They seemed real nice. I know they love you a lot. You can
tell how much they care about you."

"Bullshit! I don't give a shit what you think you saw! What
the hell's wrong with them?" I leave Betsy, who looks confused and
a little scared, and go to my room. I want to break something. I
want to hit something. I want to scream. I do not want to feel this
way any longer. I pull out my journal and write in fast, hard strokes
that bear little resemblance to my handwriting:

"I'm mad today. I'm not exactly sure why. I know my
Effexor is working because, while I felt very agitated, I didn't feel
out of control during the session. I'm mad at my parents, I think,
for their naiveté and for what I know they want. They want to not
have to acknowledge that there's anything wrong, because it's all
about appearances and we never talk about the ugly things and
certainly not if those things are their things either partially or
completely.

I don't want to hurt them. I know this isn't about blame or
attacking. I will not, however, continue to pretend that the pile of
elephant shit in the middle of the room isn't there.

Andy will be easy: I'll tell him what I tell him every day. I'll
tell him he's my hero, because he is. I'll tell him he's the best human
I've ever known, because he is. I'll tell him how proud of him I am
and that the best thing I ever did was bring him into this world, and
that the best thing I ever did for the world was bring him into it. I'll
tell my parents that I love them very much and I'm sorry for
everything, but I'm going to address how things really were. I'm
going to tell them that if we can't start being honest and open with
each other, they can't be part of my recovery."

I drop the journal off at Dorothy's office and go back to my
room. I feel better having written down my feelings, but I'm
exhausted and my head is throbbing and all I want to do is sleep.

We're back in the circle and it's our turn, today. I take Andy
on my lap and put my arms around him. "Hey, bug," I say.

"Oh, hey." He kisses me on my nose.

"I love you so much."

"Ayu you."

"Okay. I want to tell you something. When you were first

born, I woke up without you. I didn't know where you were and I was all alone in a room. Grandma brought me a picture of you and told me you had Down syndrome and I said, 'I'll have him with me forever.' I loved you even while you were still in my tummy and I wanted you so much. The first time I got to hold you was just before your first surgery when you were three days old. You were so yummy! I wanted to slip you under my skin so I could get you close enough to me.

"You were very brave and very strong. They said you would be in N.I.C.U. for maybe a year, but you came home just a little over a month later. I had to feed you through a tube in your tummy. That's why you have your tummy scar."

"Essa wight here?" He points to his stomach.

"Yep. You had fourteen more surgeries after that. One time you got really sick and were in the hospital for a long, long time. You don't remember because you were still a baby, but you had to have an operation even though you were sick." I take a deep breath. My words are coming out shaky. "The doctor told me I was going to lose you, bug. So that night, I went to the hospital and talked to you. I told you how much I wanted you, but that if it was too much for you, if you couldn't fight anymore, it was okay for you to go if that's what you needed to do. I told you I would be okay and that I hoped you would stick around, but I knew how weak you were after everything you'd been through. I was so sad that night."

"No, essa mom's happy."

I wiped a tear away from my eye. "Yeah, honey. Mom's happy now, because you decided to stay and fight. And you got better. And you've never been sick since then. When they called me the next day and told me you were awake, I was so happy. I came to the hospital and there you were, sitting up in your bed. You were so skinny and you smelled so bad."

"Ohhh...go on!" he says laughing.

"You did! You smelled blechy. But I crawled up into your bed and held you. You were just like a baby monkey. You wrapped your arms and legs around me and just clung to me." He wipes a tear from my cheek and kisses me. "I want you to know, Andy, that you're my hero. You're so strong and brave and I'm so happy to be your mommy. Thank you for being who you are. I love you so much, bug, and I'm so sorry I haven't been there for you like I should have been. I'm sorry for all the times I left you and for all the times I did drugs instead of playing with you." I'm really crying now. Everyone in the room is crying now. "I want you to know that I'll be a better mommy, okay? You deserve better than...you deserve everything, Andy. I love you."

"Ohhh, go on." He always makes me smile, this son of mine. I hug him and kiss him on the forehead. I feel such shame for not being all he deserves and such sadness for the time I've lost with him. I promise myself I'll be the best mother I can be from now on.

I move my chair to sit in front of my father. He looks at me with sorrow and pity. Like he's so happy to be here for me yet so sad for all the heartache in this room. My dad has always reminded me a little of Fred Flintstone, although at sixty, his hair is more salt than pepper. He's so sweet and I know he cares about me, but I'm conflicted. I love him so much and am grateful to him for paying for rehab, but I feel rage at his hypocrisy and denial, which have followed me my whole life. I don't want to hurt him, so I'm scared to say what I want to because I don't want either of my parents to be mad at me. I'm thirty-eight years old and I still can't stand for people to be mad at me, especially my parents. I'll do anything to avoid conflict, but I feel like if I don't take this opportunity to say what I'm feeling, it will be a waste of my time here. I'm scared, but I also feel safe knowing that, because of the rules, he can't say anything and I'm safe from immediate aftermath here in my thirty day womb.

"I love you," I begin. "I'm so sorry for hurting you. I want you to know how much I appreciate everything you've done for me, especially helping me get to rehab." I take a deep breath. I can't believe I'm going to say the things I have planned. I can't believe I'm going to be so honest with him, with them, about my life. "You said yesterday that you want to know about my drug use. Okay. I've smoked pot, done speed, dropped acid, eaten mushrooms and taken downers, although not much because I didn't like them. I've used cocaine and crank and I've been smoking meth for about five years. Every single day." His eyes get big. "I started using drugs when I was twelve, if you count alcohol, and I've pretty much used drugs since then. I was sober for almost four years when my coke dealer left town. That's when I had the foster kids. I've never used needles and I've never used heroin." I know that heroin is the big one to him. He thinks it's the drug of all drugs. At least he used to. He may have changed his mind recently.

He's shaking his head like this is all so unbelievable and I want to scream at him for his stupidity. "I was high a lot at home, especially in high school. The first time I dropped acid was in the middle of the day at school and I was still blazing at home that night." He looks utterly defeated. "I want you to understand, Dad, that this isn't your fault. I don't blame you guys for my addiction, okay?" I reach over and hold his hand for a second.

"I'm sorry, Dad, but I have to call bullshit on you about yesterday." My voice is starting to shake. "You were so sad about what these poor families and kids have gone through and you sat there acting like this is all new to you, but it's not." I start jiggling my knee up and down and put my hands on it to make it stop.

"You seem to forget what it was like when we were little and you would get drunk. I remember, Dad. I remember you disappearing for whole weekends sometimes and how pissed Mom was. I remember you getting so drunk that time at Thanksgiving that you threw up and passed out in Uncle Tim's bathroom. Don't you remember that? I was mortified but we went ahead and ate anyway. Do you remember being in the backseat of the car while Mom drove down Fairview, and she was pissed as hell because you were back there with the door open, puking all the way home? I remember every road trip or vacation we ever went on, you guys had a cooler of beer in the front seat and drank the whole time. So when you sit here and act shocked at everything these families have been through, it makes me mad. Nothing you've heard here should shock you. Either you're in denial or you have a very bad memory."

He's crying a little and looking down at his hands. I feel like shit for saying these things to him and for embarrassing him in front of these people, but I also feel better - lighter somehow. I feel empowered and this makes me feel guilty. Seeing his shame makes me want to take it all back. "Daddy, I love you so much and I'm not trying to embarrass you, okay?" He looks at me and nods.

"Ed," Dorothy says gently. "I think you might be one of us." He nods a little at that.

"Now," I say, "for the good things." I lower my head so I can catch his eye. "You want to know what I'm most proud of you for? Andyy Barr. You taught yourself how to use a computer back when PCs first came out. You had that little Franklin 286 and back then, everything was DOS. You had no idea what you were doing, but computers interested you. Teaching yourself something that complicated requires focus. You told me that you found you couldn't have a drink and still concentrate on what you were doing and that's when you stopped drinking. You taught yourself everything you know about computers. You've told me you were a bad student in school, that you got Ds and barely graduated. I know you think you're not smart but I think you're amazing. You went from not knowing what a computer was to teaching yourself to design web sites. Then a few years ago you built your business enough so you could retire from your job and do Andyy Barr full time."

I looked at Dorothy. "Can I tell you where he got the name Andyy Barr?"

"Sure," she says.

I turn around and face the room. "It's spelled A-N-D-Y-Y B-A-R-R. He came up with it when he was teaching himself to do graphics back when Andy was a baby. He made this floating candy bar and thought it was funny to call it an Andy bar instead of candy bar. He put it on the label and would make it spin and float around on the monitor. One day I went to see what he was doing and noticed he'd added and extra Y to Andy and an extra R to bar. I asked him about it and he said he spelled Andyy that way because Andy has an extra Y." Everyone's smiling politely and I know they don't get it. "Down syndrome is Trisomy 21, meaning there's an extra chromosome on the twenty-first pair. The extra chromosome is a Y instead of an X. That how it is with everyone who has Down syndrome. So the candy bar became Andy Bar and that became Andyy Barr. When he started doing web site development he named his company Andyy Barr Productions."

I turn back to my father who's seems happy and a little embarrassed. "I'm so proud of you, Daddy. I know you don't think you're smart, but you are. Look at what you've done." Tears are sliding down his cheeks but he's happy, and mouths the words "Thank you."

I move my chair over in front of my mother who's sitting stoically with her hands folded neatly in her lap. She has the same look on her face she used to have when my dad would disappear and she'd sit at the kitchen table robotically chain smoking. Her ice blue eyes reflect none of what's just happened. She's all business and I'm in trouble. If she were allowed to speak right now, she would call me Kimberly. She doesn't smile but seems to sigh as I begin.

"Mom. I want you to know how much I love you too. I'm sorry for lying to you all these years. I didn't know until I came here that there was such a thing as lying by omission. I always thought of myself as a very honest person, but I guess I have been lying by not telling you what's been going on with me. First of all, I want you to understand that this isn't your fault. I'm not an addict because you're a bad mother, and I didn't do drugs to hurt you. When you say you must be a bad mother because, after all, look at how Chuck and I turned out, how do you think that makes me feel? What am I supposed to do with that? I know you wanted this perfect family but we never were and we sure as hell aren't going to change at this late stage of the game." She's still sitting there, unmoving. "You did the best you could and you need to stop blaming yourself because I know this.

"I know you're wondering, even though you haven't asked, so I'll just tell you that I never used drugs when I was pregnant. Hell, I didn't even smoke cigarettes or drink soda. I didn't start using again until around Andy's third surgery." I try to smile at her but she's just sitting there. I don't know if she's really hearing me or if she's just pissed about being here. "You know when you said you had no idea what was going on with me? Didn't you ever wonder where the money was coming from? You knew I was paying all the bills and that I paid for Allan and me to go to Cabo last year. Didn't you ever stop to think how I was doing all that writing bonds and making gift baskets? Or did you tell yourself I was doing that well? You would have been happier never knowing the truth.

"I'm most proud of you, Mom, for finally quitting the job you hated. You started at that company as a bookkeeper when you were nineteen and retired at forty-seven as vice president. All those years you worked for that company and for a man you hated because that's what you had to do. I remember, though, you coming home after work, exhausted. I would make dinner and then you and Dad would fall asleep in your chairs in front of the TV while I did the dishes. Your misery was contagious. I'm so proud of you for finally deciding to take care of yourself and retire." She hasn't moved, but one corner of her mouth curls slightly upward. I'm not sure anyone else has noticed except me. "I also want you to know how grateful I am to both of you for being such wonderful grandparents. Regardless of any mistakes you made when I was growing up, I could never ask for Andy to have better grandparents than he does.

"I have to tell both of you, though, that I need for us to be open with each other. I need for us to be able to be honest and to be able to talk about things rather than just ignore them. If you can't do that, I can't include you in my recovery." It feels awkward, asking for what I need. My biggest fear is that they won't be able to follow through and I'll lose them. I've thought long and hard about this, and I know I have to be prepared to follow through if they're not willing or able to do as I've asked. I'm afraid of them hating me for everything I've just said. I'm sick of being afraid all the time. I'm hoping they'll be willing to try.

We sit and listen as the other families, one by one, take their turn. I'm listening but I'm also thinking how I feel much calmer. I feel like I've opened a doorway and can see a window just beyond, lit and shining brightly. Still, I wish Allan were here with me. I would feel more normal- less like a little girl if I had a significant other with me like everyone else in the room. I know he wouldn't have come even if I wanted him to. In my heart I know what I am to him.

I started out feeling positive and now, with these thoughts racing through my head, wishing things were different between Allan and me, I feel stupid and needy and childish. Mom reaches over and takes my hand, holding it for a few minutes, and I let her. I'm grateful to both of my parents and at the same time I long to be normal, like everyone else. All my life I've wanted to belong instead of feeling weird and separate from the rest of the world, and I've always felt just off center instead.

The good feelings that elated me just a few minutes ago are replaced with self-doubt. I spend the remainder of the session inside my head telling myself I'm weird and wondering what's wrong with me. By the time we've finished and our families have gone, I feel worse instead of better.

The family sessions were a beginning for my parents and me. Like my recovery, it took a while to get on track, but it began at the Walker Center. The first couple of years I was sober, we all made a concerted effort to talk to each other instead of keeping silent. Now it comes more naturally to us, but it's something we have to work on. In early recovery, when the cravings were so bad and I was having using dreams almost every night, I talked to my parents. I didn't need them to do anything, I just needed to be heard, and for the first time in my life, my parents listened. That may be the most important thing I took away from the Walker Center.

Chapter 27

Rene and I are sitting on her bed and she's showing me these hand warmer things she uses. She's gotten so skinny since her bariatric surgery and she's cold all the time. She's always bundled up in scarves and sweaters, even when we're inside. I can't get my mind around the fact that she used to weigh over three hundred pounds.

"Are you nervous about going home?" she asks me.

"It's not for a few more days, but yeah. I feel so safe here in my little rehab bubble," I tell her. "I don't have to deal with anything here, you know, like on the outside, with Allan and everything."

"You know what they say about playgrounds and playmates? Well, it's true. You need to get away from Allan. He's not good for you."

"How am I supposed to just walk, Rene? After all I have invested in the house and everything." I look down, picking non-existent lint off her plum-colored comforter. "I know it's stupid, but I love him. Maybe when I go home and I'm sober, things will be different..." I trail off. I know I sound pathetic and I hate it, but I can't help it. It's what I want.

"Well, I don't know much. I mean, look at me. I was home for two weeks and almost killed myself drinking before coming back here, so I'm no expert, but I don't think it's good for you to walk right back into the situation you came from. You need to cut your losses, Kim, and take care of you and Andy."

"I know. I need to sell the house and just be done with it, but it's not that easy." I can feel the tears and they make me angry. Why do I cry all the time? Why am I so damn emotional? "We used to have so much fun together. We both like really good guitar players and he'd play Stevie Ray Vaughn and Pink Floyd for me on his guitar. We both love the blues." I watch Rene as she gets up and starts fixing her hair. I covet her natural curls. "We used to spend hours just talking and..."

"And what?"

"I don't know. We watched a lot of porn together. Back when we were sleeping together." For the first time, it occurs to me that maybe we don't have as much in common as I thought.

"I don't know. It just seems like you'd be better off without him. I'm just thinking of you, you know."

"I know. Thanks."

"So when are you going home?"

"A week from Tuesday. What about you? You came before I did, right?"

"I did, but I'm going to stay an extra week. I want to get it right this time. If I don't...this is life or death for me. Besides, I don't have much to go home to. It's just me and my cats."

I come back from an A.A. meeting to find a message that Allan called. I double check with the staff to make sure they got the message right. I'm flooded with all these emotions, mostly hope and elation, and that irritates me. Why does my happiness hinge on this person? I hate it that a single word from him excites me so much because deep down I think I know that whatever we might have had years ago, real or drug induced, has been gone for a long time. I'm starting to wonder if I've spent so much time trying to make something out of nothing that I don't know how to give it up. With Allan, as with gambling and meth, I'm constantly chasing the dragon in search of that first, perfect high.

I call him and we talk. We talk about the house, mostly, and what to do with it. Then he hits me with the real reason for the call. He's decided to accept a job offer in Twin Falls. "Why don't I just sign the house over to you?" he asks me. "We'll figure out a price and you can buy me out. That way you and Andy don't have to move." Buy him out? What the hell is he talking about?

"What are you talking about, Allan? I don't want the house. I never would have bought it alone and I don't want it now." Can't he see? Doesn't he understand? Maybe it's me. Maybe my thinking is warped. It has to be because we are on two different planets when it comes to our relationship. Of course we are. What am I, new? "We need to just sell it. Have you looked into that Assist to Sell thing? Or contacted a realtor?"

"No, but I will."

"When do you plan to move to Twin?"

"The end of January. Maybe February."

"Allan, what if it hasn't sold by then?"

"It'll have to be."

"Allan...nevermind," this is how he always is: Kim will take care of things or else they'll just fall into place. I'm beginning to get a little pissed off. "So what about the money you owe me? There's no way we're going to walk away from this with twenty grand."

"I know that. I figure we'll just split whatever we make from the sale," he says, in a cheerful voice. I don't get it. I just don't. Then it occurs to me that maybe he never intended to pay me back.

"What do you mean split it? You've always said you would pay me back and that the house was the only way you could see to do that."

"I'll need money to move and get set up in Twin."

I'm speechless. I don't have a clue how to respond to this. He's so matter of fact about it that I begin to think I must be a real bitch. I feel like a greedy pig because I keep asking about the money, but it was his idea in the first place for me to keep track of everything. I don't know why, but I'm confused. I don't know if my feelings are justified. I try to step outside myself and see things objectively. When I do, it seems like my feelings are valid, but he's so matter-of-fact and nonchalant about the situation. Maybe I am wrong.

That night, I write in my journal:

"Funny thing, right after the meeting tonight, I received a message that Allan had called. I called him back later and we had a good conversation. He actually talked, which was nice. I asked him to please call Assist to Sell today and find out about their services for selling the house. He said he would. I hope he does.

As far as what he owes me, I've stated my case clearly. He disagrees and thinks we should split whatever we make from the sale. I don't want to get into attorney fees and all of that, so I think what I'll do is re-state my opinion and then when the house actually sells, (because the check will be in both our names) tell him that I'm leaving it up to him to be man enough to do what's right.

Otherwise, I could end up losing most of the money just to fight for it and we would end up hating each other. I don't want either of those things.

The whole situation, though, has been a huge blow to my self-esteem, which was fragile to begin with. How the hell am I supposed to take it when he decides to sleep with a dog rather than me??!"

Dorothy says my two biggest problems are that I don't set boundaries and I don't ask for help. "You need to start putting your needs first, Kim," she says. "You need to stand up for yourself and set clear boundaries with people right from the beginning. You never set boundaries with Allan. That's what's gotten you into this situation and it's what has kept you in it. You need to accept the fact that you will probably never see that money. It's a painful lesson, but there's no reason for him to pay you back. All he's done is promise, right?"

"He's always said that he will pay me back one day."

"And has he done anything to that end?"

"Well, no, I guess not."

"You guess not? Didn't you tell me that just before you came here he bought himself a new snowboard package, complete with a new outfit and boots?"

"Yes." That had really pissed me off. I hope you don't mind, he said, but I'm taking the bong you bought me. I just stood there in disbelief as he loaded his dad's truck he'd borrowed and drove off.

"I don't understand," I say to Dorothy. "Does he just hate me or am I reading too much into these things?"

"Kim! Think about what happened. What would you tell a friend if she were in the same situation?"

"I guess I'd tell her she was an idiot to let anyone treat her like that. I'd tell her to leave him...or hock all his equipment while he's at work one day." This makes me smile.

"Why can't you treat yourself as well as you do other people?" she asks me.

"I don't know, Dorothy. I guess I don't think I'm worth it. If I were, other people wouldn't treat me so bad," I say. "Shit! I'm a fucking pussy, huh?"

Dorothy laughs.

My inability, or refusal, to ask for help is the next thing Dorothy wants to address. She gives me an assignment. For one day, I'm supposed to ask a different person at each meal to fix my tray for me. As soon as she says this, I cringe, but do as I'm told. The next day I write:

"Laurie did my breakfast tray and while I felt awkward, she was happy to do it for me. At lunch Cheryl kind of spazzed out when I asked her for help because she already had her tray, so Jessica did it for me. Dinner was most interesting. I asked Jen, who was very willing and excited saying this would be great therapy for her as well since she tends to be a little narcissistic. When we got to the cafeteria, however, she started talking to one of the men and completely forgot about me until one of the other women reminded her. She was so sweet and fixed my sandwich perfectly and had me sit down. Then she asked if I wanted chips or something to drink. I said yes, raspberry ice tea and two bags of chips. She asked if I wanted ice. No thank you, I said, and off she went. She returned with two cups of the tea brimming with ice. No chips. She was so proud of herself that I waited until she had fixed her tray to ask for the chips again. I think she came away from the experience feeling philanthropic, and I was glad to be there for her."

The closer I get to my last day, the more I want to stay here forever, protected and supported in my bubble-world. I wish someone would just pack my things at home for me and move me so I could come back to a brand new life. But I know that's not going to happen. I have to go tie up all these loose ends and I've got sentencing the week after I get home.

Dorothy arranges for me to attend relapse prevention when I go home, with Sarah, a private therapist. The Walker Center sometimes refers patients to her after they leave rehab, so there will be other alumni in the sessions. I'll also see her for one on one therapy. I've scheduled my first session for early afternoon on the day of my release.

The night before I leave, I'm catching a last cigarette before curfew, outside by myself. It's the second day of December and the air is frigid, but the moon makes me forget how cold I am. I've never seen a moon like this. It's the color of embers and covers a quarter of the sky. It's so big, I feel like it's barely out of my reach. It looks like a world all by itself - like in the movie *James and the Giant Peach*. This moon holds sway over the flat land and I am in awe of it. I think of how small I am in this universe and how there has to be something bigger than me to create such beauty. I fall asleep with that moon in my heart, spilling over with gratitude for everything I've received here and for my new life that awaits me.

Mom and Dad come to drive me home. Andy's in school and we decide it's best for him to stick with his routine. I'm so happy even if I am a little nervous and the three of us talk all the way to Boise about my progress and my plan for recovery. It's close to eleven in the morning when they drop me off at my house. I'll meet Sarah at 1:00, so I've got time to unpack and just breathe. The house is silent and still. Allan's at work. I walk back to my bedroom and it's just as I left it. It's a mess. The disarray and clutter disgust me. I decide I will spend the next hour or so cleaning. I sit down on my bed and light a cigarette and twenty minutes later, I relapse.

Chapter 28

Playgrounds and playmates. You won't stay sober if you go back to the same environment and associate with the same people as you did when you were using. The concept is stressed in A.A. and in rehab, and it's been the most important factor in my recovery. If I had to name the number one thing that helped me get and remain sober, it's changing playgrounds and playmates. There's no doubt in my mind.

I knew the pipe was there, loaded and ready to go. I tried to tell myself I forgot about it, that I was shocked to find it, but the truth is, I never forgot about it or the two rocks I'd stashed away.

Seeing the pipe again, holding the crystalline rocks of meth in my hand, I was overwhelmed with guilt. I sat there for what seemed like an agonizing stretch of time wrestling with a decision I'd already made. I thought about all I'd accomplished in rehab. I thought about my parents and how proud they were of me. I considered flushing the drugs down the toilet but I knew I wasn't going to do that. I thought about Andy, and I loathed myself for what I was about to do. *It will just be this once. I'll just finish what's here and that will be the end of it. No one will ever know, except me, what a weak person I am.* I'd only been home for twenty minutes and I was right back where I started: alone with the horror of being me.

In retrospect, it was the worst thing I could have done. I walked right back into what I left: filthy, cluttered bedroom in the house that made me miserable, and the only thing to welcome me home was my meth.

If I were serious about recovery, I would have moved in with my parents, but I think I knew I wasn't ready to quit. I saw rehab as a thirty-day break. What I wanted, when I started looking for help online that day, and even before that, was for someone to take care of me. The thought of being locked away in a mental hospital appealed to me because I just wanted to be done. I didn't want to have to make decisions, I didn't want to have to do anything, and I only wanted to be taken care of. Rehab was the closest I could get to that.

My parents have said since then that they considered moving all my things into storage while I was gone and bringing me home with them. They talked it over, they said, and decided against it because I'm an adult and should make my own decisions. Allan said later that he considered going through my room to make sure everything was gone, but decided not to invade my privacy.

I cried as I smoked, shaking so badly it was difficult to keep the flame on the bowl. I thought about what I'd heard so many times at A.A. meetings: going to rehab will fuck up your high. I quit crying, and continued smoking until it was time to meet with Sarah, my therapist and relapse prevention facilitator. I smoked what was in the bowl and one of the rocks. I decided to save the other one for when I got back from my meeting.

I was high again and the feeling completed me, pushing aside the guilt. Meth made me feel like I'd found what I'd been searching for all my life. It was as if I were made of brittle coral, and the smoke from this drug billowed down my porous shell filling in all the nooks, crannies, and holes I thought I was born with. Doing meth made me a complete person.

That's how it felt. That's how seductive meth is. Meth tells you it loves you. It says you don't need anyone or anything else in the world, because it loves you unconditionally. Eventually, though, you start to come down, and after a while, when you've fucked up every relationship in your life, meth *is* all you have.

Sarah's office was downtown just a few blocks from where my office was. I was right on time and for some reason that made me feel better about showing up high. Her office was small with barely enough room for her desk, a little couch and a chair. We sat down and I looked around. There were little trinkets here and there that told me she was new-agey: a glass ball in a pedestal with water running over it, little angels here and there on the bookcase and Tarot cards on an end table. Burgundy satin hung as drapes and covered throw pillows. There were accents of gold. I tried to act like I wasn't high on meth. I was careful about keeping my mouth still and not jiggling my legs or wringing my hands the way I do when I'm nervous or wired. I was very conscious of sitting still and speaking slowly, trying not to come across as chatty as I felt.

Sarah and I talked about my time at the Walker Center and my upcoming sentencing. She asked me a few questions about my drug use and if I accept that I'm an addict. We talked about my past.

"It sounds like you had an important position when you

were dealing drugs," she said. "Do you think you were a successful dealer?"

"I know what you want me to say," I told her, draping an arm across the back of the couch. "You want me to say that, of course I wasn't successful because look where it got me."

"What do you really think?"

"I *was* successful. I supported myself, my son and Allan for a long time. I got arrested, that's all. It's an occupational hazard." The meth made me cocky.

She was writing in a notebook, but didn't comment. We talked about the relapse prevention group, which was every Wednesday at 6:00. We discussed fees and I paid her for eight sessions in advance. The only comment she made about the stack of bills I was holding was something about how nice it would be to have a client pay with cash. The bills were part of what I collected the night before I left for rehab: three thousand dollars in hundreds, fifties and twenties. She didn't seem to give a second thought as to why I was carrying so much money. We had just finished talking about me being a dealer, then I whipped out a fat stack of money and started peeling off bills, paying for sessions in advance, and she said nothing. It made me wonder about the woman who would oversee my relapse prevention.

I think about that day now, and it makes me wonder about *me*. I could have brought out only a few bills. I could have simply paid for the current session. What I chose to do, though, was expose over three grand to someone who should have questioned me about it. I remember other things I did, little things, that may have been cries for help. At the Walker Center, Dorothy asked me one day if I had anything stashed at home. I told her about the pipe and the rocks and she said, "We need to come up with a plan to deal with that. It's important."

It was never mentioned again. She probably forgot. I didn't forget, and I specifically didn't mention it to her again. If I were serious about my recovery, I would have. Then again, as the counselors kept telling us, "You're not in recovery. You're in rehab. Recovery starts out *there*."

There are so many places where I slipped through the cracks in one way or another. All the times I was pulled over and had drugs on me; the alcohol and drug evaluation; Dorothy knowing about my stash; my parents thinking twice about moving me; Sarah and the money. It happens all the time, all the way through the system addicts slide when the opportunity is there to stop them. A huge factor is because we're such good liars. It took me a long time to accept the fact that I was a liar. I thought of lies only as outright, spoken untruths. But I lied all the time. I lied by omission and I lied by conning people. I relied on my unassuming demeanor and the fact that I'm well spoken to fool people into thinking I was innocent and harmless. I got off on it.

When I was a teenager, I did the same thing with my friends' parents. They trusted me. "You keep an eye on her, Kim," they'd say. "If you're going with Kim, well then, okay." Parents loved me. Then my friends and I would go out drinking, taking acid or whatever else we were doing that we shouldn't have been.

I've always seemed trustworthy to authority figures, and I've always betrayed that trust. It's in this way that I've been dishonest most of my life.

I don't think slipping through the cracks is anyone's fault. I think it happens because the addict isn't ready to quit, because if I'd been caught any of the times I slipped, it wouldn't have made a difference. I wasn't ready.

When I got home after seeing Sarah, I immediately loaded the pipe with the last rock. After two hits, I knew what I was going to do. I called Josh.

"Hey! Welcome back. How you doing?" He was thrilled to hear from me.

"I'm good. I just got back a few hours ago."

"How was it?"

"Good. It wasn't bad once I got used to it."

"So you're all rested up, huh? Great! I've been hurting. People out here are ripping me off and the shit's bad - all cut up and everything. You ready to make some money?" I thought about it briefly. What else was I going to do for money? Jill gave me another month off so I could ease back into things. She was very supportive of me. I'd just gotten out of a mental hospital, after all, just like Mariah Carey. She was being very considerate.

"Sure. I need you to come over, though. I don't have anything."

"Yeah! Sure. I'll be there in twenty minutes."

Josh came over and we got high, picking through what he had to find the good stuff, leaving the rest for whoever he would sell to next. We spent the next couple of hours talking and getting high. With every hit off the pipe, my guilt evaporated. Josh wasn't even irritating me. I was actually having a good time with him, joking about things that happened while I was away.

He left just before five. Allan wouldn't be home for another hour and I sure as hell didn't want him know I was using again. I assumed he'd be happy to see me, and I thought he would probably take me to dinner to celebrate my homecoming.

I called Mario while I waited.

"Keem! You back. How are you?"

"I'm good. I missed you. How are you?"

"Okay, okay. You want to see me?"

"Si," I said.

"How much?"

"Mmmm, un libra." I always get libra and libro mixed up. One is "book," the other means "pound." Mario laughs. He knows I have trouble with this, but he understood what I meant.

"When?"

"Later tonight. I'll call you, okay?"

"Okay, Keem. I miss you, too. Good you are home. No more, right? You don't use, right?" *Of course, I don't use anymore, Mario. I'm a good girl now.* That's what I wanted people to think. I didn't want them to know how weak I was.

I was even with Mario. I paid him before I left. I would give him fifteen hundred and he'd float me the rest.

I was in my room listening to Neil Young and unpacking. I hadn't heard music, other than Enya and recordings of the sounds of nature, for a month. I smoked another bowl, blowing it out the window on that crisp December day, just before Allan got home. I was excited to see him, but I couldn't let him know I was using again already. I brushed my teeth, used mouthwash and was still unpacking when I head his truck pull into the driveway. *Any minute now he'll come back to my room and welcome me home. Any minute now.*

My bedroom door was open and I heard the TV click on. *Any minute now.*

He had to know I was home. He knew when I was getting back and he could definitely hear my music. *Any minute now.*

An hour passed before I realized he wasn't coming. I felt stupid, foolish and embarrassed thinking he'd be happy to see me and maybe take me to dinner. I turned off my music so I could hear better. Maybe he was in the shower. I heard nothing but the drone of the TV. I didn't want to be the one to go to him, but I felt like a jackass sitting there in my quiet room listening for him.

I really was right back where I started. I wanted to cry but I didn't want him to hear me so I fought back the tears and waited. All I heard was the sound of the television. Slowly, I walked down the hall and peeked around the corner. Allan was asleep on the couch. I walked past him to the kitchen to get something to drink thinking the noise would wake him, but he was still asleep when I went back to my room. I was devastated and pissed off that I still had hope for us.

Playgrounds and playmates. The definition of insanity is doing something the same way over and over, expecting different results. I walked right back into what I left when I went to rehab. Of course nothing changed, but in my addict fantasy world, I'd convinced myself that if I quit using, things between Allan and I would be different. But the truth was, Allan didn't love me. He never did. There was no reason for me to have expected anything other than what happened that night

I sat by my bedroom door all evening, waiting. Finally, I heard him turn off the TV and go to the bathroom. The next thing I heard was his bedroom door close. I went out to the living room and found all the lights were off and the front door locked. He'd gone to bed.

I couldn't help crying. I felt so stupid for hoping things would be different. Back in my room, I closed my door, pulled out my pipe and got high before calling Mario to arrange our meeting. I changed clothes, still listening for any sign of Allan. Finally, I left the house, slamming the front door behind me. It was a childish thing to do, I know, but I was furious. And hurt.

Chapter 29

"Shadoe, what the hell? Are you kidding me?" He was my first stop after seeing Mario.

"I'm not kidding. It's fine, though. Don't worry about me. I've always said I don't care about dying."

"When did you find the tumor?"

"A couple of weeks ago. I was in the shower and washing down there and something didn't feel right. By the time I went to the doctor it was the size of a grapefruit."

I felt sick and tried not to envision the scenario. "So now what?"

"They took a biopsy and it's cancerous. The doctor wants to remove it, but I said no way. I'm not going to a hospital. You know I don't trust doctors. All they want is my money."

I couldn't believe he was so stubborn. "Shadoe, you don't just walk around with a fucking grapefruit sized tumor in your testicles. How the hell do you even sit?"

He chuckled. "Don't worry about it. If I die, I die." He was so cavalier about the whole thing and it made me want to slap him on his stupid face. I felt dirty just being in the same room with him knowing that, over there in that damn patio chair, between his legs, there was a monster growing. I needed to get high.

"Well, I just want to go on record as saying you're a complete idiot," I said, loading my pipe. "You don't take care of your diabetes. You never did what the doctors told you about your foot and it damn near fell off. Now this." I shook my head. I weighed and packaged the crystal and tossed it to him.

"Thanks. Looks good," he said, loading a bowl himself. "So what's going on with the house?"

"Nothing. Allan didn't do shit while I was gone. Well, that's not exactly right. He finalized his plans for moving to Twin Falls. He'll be leaving the end of January."

"What if the house doesn't sell by then?"

"Oh, he's still leaving. He's got a new life to start, you know."

"Are you and Andy going to stay there?"

"No. That's not the plan, anyway. I guess it's up to me to sell it. I don't know what I'll do if it doesn't sell in six weeks. I hate the stupid thing." I could feel myself getting angry. I didn't want to talk about this anymore.

"I'm sorry, Kim. Is there anything I can do?"

"No. Don't worry about me. I'll figure it out. I always do. Take care of yourself, though, as much as you can anyway."

I checked into a hotel that night and stayed there for two days getting high and trying to figure out what to do. I couldn't bear being in the house with Allan ignoring me. Andy was still with Mom and Dad. They wanted to keep him until after my court date. They were convinced I was going to prison and didn't want to uproot him just to have him move back in with them when the guards hauled me out of the courtroom in shackles.

The Saturday after I got home from rehab, I was playing pool with Mitt, another of Kilo's cousins.

"I need to go home, Mitt. I haven't even been horizontal in, what?" I counted on my fingers "In five days! How the hell did that happen?"

"Yeah," he said. "That'll happen when you quit for a while." I vowed to sleep. As soon as I'd met with Josh and then Mario again. I was a hamster in a cage running in my little wheel again.

In the early hours of Monday morning, I finally quit running and lay down in my bed. Sentencing was Tuesday morning at ten, so I figured I should sleep some before then. I curled up in my fluffy down comforter, creating a cocoon around me. I watched *The Deer Hunter*. I love falling asleep with a movie playing. The background noise is like a lullaby. When my sleep is fitful, as it is after I've been awake for a long time, it's comforting to hear voices when I drift between dream and reality. It soothes me and makes me feel not so alone.

I'd been home from the Walker Center just over a week on December 13, my sentencing date. I'd been high every day since I got home and I was high in the courtroom that day. My parents and lawyer were so proud of me for getting clean and staying sober and even as they congratulated me, I was high on meth.

I let everyone down but no one knew. How could I tell anyone? Even if I wanted to stop, there was no one I could turn to. No one I could admit to throwing thirty days away in less than half an hour. I didn't understand it. I didn't want anyone to know what a shitty person I was.

Before I left for rehab, my attorney told me I'd probably get probation. I was a little nervous, but mostly I was depressed. Allan hadn't done anything about the house while I been gone so I had that to deal with by myself.

Three days after I got home, Allan finally acknowledged my presence as if nothing had happened. As if he didn't know I'd been home for three days. I'd been moving from hotel to hotel at night, working harder than ever. All my boys were back, except Johnny who was in jail on multiple felony drug charges, so things were just clicking along. Everything except me. I was a robot going through the motions and the meth wasn't even getting me high anymore. After years of daily use, meth had become a maintenance drug. I needed it to get through the day. I couldn't function without it.

They told me in rehab that when you relapse, it's not like starting over. Almost immediately, you're right back at your tolerance level. I'm told that this is the case for years after quitting.

The judge sentenced me to three to five years, but gave me a withheld judgment with seven years' felony probation. The prosecution had no problem with the decision considering my immaculate record, the fact that I've always been gainfully employed (on paper anyway), and the two and a half years I'd spent as a foster mother for the state of Idaho.

Mom and Dad wanted to take me to lunch to celebrate, but I begged off saying something about meeting Jill. I hugged and kissed them both and went straight home to get high. I was numb. I didn't feel happy about the sentencing, nor did I feel sad. I didn't feel anything anymore.

The judge ordered me to go to orientation at the Probation and Parole office and said they would assign a P.O. to me soon. I was late for orientation because I had to make a delivery to Shadoe and meet Josh on the way. I was sitting at probation and parole with five grand in my purse, a trunk full of evidence in the parking lot and I was going to meet Mario right after the meeting. The orientation was brief but I was impatient. *Let's wrap this up, guys*, I'm thinking. *I have things to do, places to go and people to see.* I signed a piece of paper to show I'd been there, took the packet the facilitator gave me - sort of a "How to be on Felony Probation 101," - threw it in the backseat of my car and headed to Canyon County to meet Mario.

The packet was mostly a list of Thou Shalt's and Thou Shalt Not's: thou shalt not use drugs or alcohol, thou shalt submit to search and seizure at the request of any law officer, thou shalt not leave the area without permission, thou shalt attend all classes as specified by thou's p.o., thou shalt not fail UA's or thou shalt go to jail, thou shalt not be in possession of firearms, thou shalt not be a pain in the ass...

The whole thing pissed me off, because most things at that time, especially authority, pissed me off. I was a sad, angry meth addict on the loose and things would only get worse before they finally got better.

Chapter 30

Christmas, 2006.

I was adamant about buying a tree and decorating the house. "Kimbo," my mom pleaded with me, "don't do this to yourself. You and Andy just come here and have Christmas Eve with us. Spend the night and let's have a nice Christmas together. Why get a tree and put yourself through all of that when you know it's just going to make you feel worse? Honey, *please* don't do that to yourself."

I knew I was just going through the motions, but I kept telling myself that if I could just make Christmas perfect, maybe everything would be all right, and it's here that I must pause...

What the hell was it about Allan? Had he ever done anything to warrant my frenzied obsession? What was I trying so hard to hang on to and why couldn't I let go?

I didn't love Allan. I may have been in love with him at one time, but that was long past. I was angry: With him, with myself, with my situation, with the world. I don't know what I would have done if he suddenly said, "You know what? I love you. You and I were meant for each other. Let's live happily ever after." I think that may have pissed me off more than what was happening at the time.

I think Allan was my tweak.

Tweak is a lay term used to describe the uncontrollable, subconscious repetitive behaviors that all meth users, in one form or another, engage in. The one most people are familiar with is picking. You've seen the scare-tactic pictures of meth addicts who have sores on their faces and arms. The user will pick incessantly at something that's not there. They'll pick and dig at their skin until it bleeds and scabs and then they'll pick some more. They can't help it. It has to do with the massive amounts of dopamine the brain produces with meth use. You only need look at the pictures to know they're unable to control the picking behavior. No one - in *or* out of their right mind - wants to look like that. Years ago, when I was in my twenties and using crank, I went through my own picking phase. The scars on my face are my permanent marks of shame that I'll wear for the rest of my life.

Tweaking isn't limited to picking. "Tweakers" rock, make jerky, twitchy body movements, clean obsessively, take things apart, draw the same thing over and over, play a certain video game, shop compulsively...gamble compulsively...and maybe even obsess over a person compulsively.

The few people who knew what my situation was back then always asked me, "why?" Why didn't I leave? What was so intoxicating about him that made me want to stay? Until now, I've always said, "I don't know," because that was the truth. Even with all I've learned about my addiction and about meth itself, "I don't know," was my honest answer, which always left me feeling weak. "I don't know," is a child's answer. "Allan was my tweak," is the best I've come up with, because there had to be a reason and it certainly wasn't that I was madly in love.

I was scared. Good or bad, my relationship with Allan was the longest I've ever had with a man. I thought it was my last chance. It's the same reason I married so many years before. I was afraid that it was the best I could do, and that if I didn't have a man who loved me, I must not be worthy of love.

That's a heavy load to pin on someone whether I was conscious of what I was doing or not. I wanted so desperately to be loved, and felt so unworthy of it, that I clung to whatever shred of hope I might have of finding love. It took a long time for me to begin to understand that what I needed most was to love myself.

I knew I had to get out of the house and away from Allan. The situation was toxic and it was killing me. I knew this, but I still couldn't let go. I didn't want things between Allan and me to end. I didn't want to lose him, but I knew that's what was best for me. As depressed as I was, he was just the opposite, buzzing around making plans for his move to Twin Falls with anticipation and excitement, and the happier he seemed, the more betrayed and angry I felt.

We'd always divided Christmas Day between our families' homes, but that year, there was no discussion of our plans for the holiday.

On Christmas morning, I sat in my rocker drinking coffee and chain smoking, waiting for Allan to get out of the shower. Andy was in his room watching *Star Wars*. He spent the night at home so we could enjoy Christmas Eve together and go to Grandma and Papa's for the day. All my gifts for Andy were at Mom and Dad's, so we were just waiting for Allan, who was getting ready to pick up his son on his way to his parents' house.

While Allan dressed in his room, I could hear him on the

phone with his son saying, "Merry Christmas," and finalizing plans to pick him up for the day. When he hung up, he knocked on Andy's door. "Hey, man. Come on out here."

"Oh, I coming, Allan!"

"Merry Christmas, man," he said, giving Andy a big hug. He pulled a present from the pile of gifts under the tree. It was wrapped in typical Allan fashion: too much tape and no bow. I usually did the wrapping for both of us, but not that year.

"Oh, it's a movie! Enna *Star Wars?*"

"No, man. It's *Gremlins,*" Allan tells him. "You'll like it."

"Uh, no fanks," Andy said, waving his hand dismissing the unfamiliar movie. Allan wasn't offended. It takes Andy a while to get used to a new movie. "Allan come Gamma Papa's?"

"Not this time, man. Have a good day." He gathered his things and he walked out the door.

Andy returned to Darth Vader and the Death Star as I sat stunned and fuming before screaming, "You rat-bastard, son of a bitch!" at his truck as he drove off down the street. I was enraged and seething with anger as I stormed around the house cursing him under my breath. I was pissed that he didn't get me a gift, but I felt blindsided by his cavalier attitude. The fact that I didn't get him anything was now justified by his negligence.

I was in my room furiously getting high when an idea popped into my head. The more meth I smoked, the more brilliant I felt until I knew what I was going to do. I don't consider myself a vengeful woman, but the more I thought about what is probably the stupidest, most ass-jacked thing I've ever done, the better I felt.

I finally put my pipe down and went to the basement, bringing back the biggest box I could find - about two-and-a-half feet square - and set it in the middle of the living room floor. From my room, I gathered all the porn tapes, DVDs, books and magazines I'd bought over the years that we used to share. I went to Allan's bathroom and, using a stepladder, collected all his magazines on the top shelf of the cupboard where he kept his towels. I put all these things into the box, carefully wrapped it complete with a jaunty red velvet bow. I wrote, "Merry Christmas, Allan," on a gift tag, set the box dead center of his bed and stood back to admire my work. I felt elated and justified.

Christmas Day at my parents' house was all holiday cheer and merriment. The house smelled heavenly with a ham in the crock-pot and Mom's traditional cinnamon rolls fresh from the oven. There were cold cuts and crackers, cookies and fudge, nuts and candies in little dishes all over the tables and counters. All I wanted was to go home and get high. I didn't want to be around anyone. I only wanted the day to end.

When I got home, Allan was already there, sitting on the couch, as usual, watching television. "Hey," he said. "How was your Christmas?" I didn't know if he'd opened his present yet, but he was acting normal, so I guessed he hadn't.

"Fine. How was yours?"

"Pretty good." I stood there in the living room for a few seconds, watching him load his bong and take his first hit, filling the room with the pungent smell of pot. Then he laid down, turning his attention to the television. I felt stupid standing there, like a pitiful third wheel sitting in the front seat of a car while her best friend and her date are making out in the back.

I went to my room, pulled out my pipe and bag of meth and spent the rest of Christmas getting high and playing black jack online until the next morning. Andy was still staying with my parents. One way or another, I had to sell the house and we'd have to stay with them for a while, at least, until I figured out where we would go. There was no point, my mother reasoned, to move Andy until I had settled down. She was right. I'm so grateful to my parents for taking care of Andy through those final weeks of my addiction. I was in no shape to take care of him and he didn't need to be any closer than he already was when I finally hit bottom.

Allan didn't say anything about the gift I left him. I didn't know if he'd even seen it yet, but I decided he must not have. Maybe he was too busy getting stoned and holding down the couch.

Chapter 31

A few days after Christmas, I received two phone calls. The first came at 12:30 in the afternoon as I was leaving Lou's, where I'd been playing the machines. It was a beautiful day, but the sun stung my eyes as I emerged from the darkness where I had spent my morning. I won close to a grand that day, but even that windfall brought me no pleasure. I planned to stop at Rite-Aid on my way home to make my daily deposit of two hundred fifty dollars to someone on the Isle of Man via Western Union so I could play slots online at home. I had three thousand dollars in my online account but it wouldn't be enough to get me through the day. When it came to my addictions, there was never enough.

Gambling was something I didn't discuss much at the Walker Center. I mentioned it in group a couple of times and it was always treated as a joke by the other clients, and ignored by the staff other than an occasional comment segueing into cross-addiction that had nothing to do with gambling. Maybe because the Walker Center is a drug and alcohol rehab, they don't focus on other addictions such as sex or gambling. All I know is that is was never addressed, and being an addict, I certainly wasn't about to give up all my vices.

The first phone call was from Probation and Parole informing me of my meeting with my P.O. the next day. I was beginning to hope I'd been lost in the system, but of course, that didn't happen. The second call was from a friend of a friend who heard the house was for sale and wanted to look at it that night. I would have to cancel my relapse prevention group, but everyone there knew what was going on. I had to sell the house and this was the first time anyone had shown interest. Allan was all set to leave at the end of the month come hell or high water.

I was high for my first meeting with Julie, my probation officer. She was icy, and I tried not to appear loaded. She asked me questions in a staccato, monotone voice that I would come to loathe, looking at me only a few times as she clicktey-click-clacked on her computer keyboard. Her demeanor was as rigid as her voice as she gave me the address of the building for my first urinary analysis. I had to be there by 5:30.

I went directly to GNC to get a cleansing formula - the same one I bought for Allan when he was on probation, and for a couple of my boys who needed to pass drug tests. It always worked for them and I had no doubt it would work for me. At home, I drank the thick, grape-flavored syrup and filled the bottle with water according to the directions. The formula made my mouth and throat tingle, but I gagged it down anyway. I had to. I was detoxing.

I finished what was in the bottle and filled a gallon jug with water, as I needed to drink that amount to get the desired results. I still had a few hours before the test so I played online slots, drifting away from myself into a separate reality where nothing else existed.

When I realized it was time to get tested, I'd only consumed about a quarter of the water in the jug. I took two long drinks but the container was still more than half-full. *Fuck it*, I thought. *I'll be okay.* Some was better than none.

It was my first U.A. but I knew what to expect. I'd heard about the process from enough people, but it was humiliating sitting on the toilet, holding a plastic cup between my legs while someone watched my every move. At first, I had stage fright and couldn't pee despite my full bladder. When I was finally able to go, I kept missing the cup and I could feel my face flush as I moved it back and forth between my legs attempting to provide enough of a sample for the test. I glanced at the half-filled cup as I handed it to the woman before washing my hands. My urine was cloudy, but yellow. At least it didn't look diluted. A diluted sample is the same as failing. There are no do-overs on felony probation.

The meeting that night at the house went well. The man seemed interested and told me he'd give me a call early the next week.

The day after my U.A., I was sitting on the floor of my living room, getting high with Mike, the son of a man I knew who'd spent his whole life in and out of prison. I bonded him out of jail a couple of times and he recommended me to his son when he needed a friend bailed out.

I began spending a lot of time with Mike when I got out of rehab. Life made him tough and street smart and I felt safe knowing that even when he wasn't with me, he was only a phone call away if I needed him. He was in his early twenties and had the most striking blue eyes I've ever seen. In a box of crayons, they would be cornflower blue, and I swear they could pierce your heart. He and his girlfriend drifted from house to house, because neither of them had a place to stay. Mike started selling meth for me to make enough money to keep them in dope.

We were in my living room getting high while I weighed out a quarter ounce for him, when my phone rang. I checked the caller ID.

"Oh, shit!"

"Who is it?"

"I think it's my P.O., Julie."

"You better answer it," he said, blowing out a huge hit from the pipe. "If you don't, she'll come here and probably kick the door down."

"Shit."

"Kim," she said in that clipped, monotone voice. "You had your U.A. yesterday. You want to tell me what happened?"

I felt the color drain from my face as I sat frozen with the phone to my ear. I tested positive for meth. There was silence while she waited for me to answer.

"I...I don't know what to say, Julie."

"You need to come see me. When can you be at my office?"

I looked at the clock. High noon. "I can be there at 2:00."

"Fine. I'll see you then." My stomach was churning with slithering eels.

"What did she say?" Mike asked, loading another bowl.

"I failed my U.A. and I have to go see her at two."

"Who do you have?"

"Julie Bryant."

"She's my P.O., too. She's tough, but you do what she says and you'll be okay."

"Jesus, Mike. What's she going to do? Am I going to prison?"

"Naw. She'll probably just give you a warning. Everyone fails the first U.A. and she knows that. She's just letting you know what's up."

"Fuck, man. I don't want to see her."

"If you don't, she'll come here and arrest your ass. Just go. Everything will be okay. Don't worry about it. Here," he handed me the pipe. "You already failed. She knows the drug isn't out of your system yet so you might as well smoke up." I took the pipe and spent the next hour and a half getting high and worrying.

I was in the lobby at P & P when Julie opened the door and called my name. Walking down the hall, I had to ask where to go.

Walls and dividers that all looked the same to me separated the offices, and I knew if I had an aerial view, the place would have looked like a rat maze.

Back in her office, I started bawling when she said she was sending me to jail for two days as punishment for the failed drug test. She was smug as she asked why I was crying. *You fucking bitch*, I think. *Why the hell do you think I'm crying?* She called and arranged for me to check myself in that Friday. I'd be spending the weekend in jail. I was surprised she was giving me until Friday and that I was to check myself in. I assumed she thought spending a weekend in jail would be more of a punishment than a couple of weekdays would, but it made no difference to me. My days were all the same, running together as I went through the motions of being a person.

I told Allan, when he got home, about my failed U.A. and impending weekend in jail. All he said was, "I thought you were done with that shit."

Julie ordered me to check myself into Ada County Jail at nine in the morning that Friday, but as usual I couldn't get high enough to leave my house. At 11:00, I decided I'd better get going or Julie would show up and take me herself.

Just as with my arrest, I was booked, fingerprinted and strip-searched, but I was too depressed and exhausted to care. I planned to sleep the weekend away, assuming I wouldn't be in long enough for them to put me on any kind of schedule. It was all I could do to stay awake as I waited in a tiny room in the booking area. I waited over an hour and a half before a guard finally took me to the dorm. My bunk was right across the aisle and one bed over from the one I slept in then. I took off my white Keds with no laces and lay down where I immediately fall asleep.

I woke once, sometime around midnight, stumbled to the toilet and drank greedily from the water fountain before falling back into bed. I slept through breakfast. Someone woke me to tell me I'd been assigned to sweep my quadrant of the dorm. I fought to keep myself awake long enough to finish my chore, and was drifting off again when I heard a guard at the foot of my bed telling me to get my ass up for head count. Through bleary, unfocused eyes, I saw everyone standing at the foot of their bunks staring at me. I dragged myself to a standing position long enough to be counted. I slept through lunch and dinner, waking only a couple of times to use the toilet.

I was processed out by eleven thirty Sunday morning. I drove home, got high and took a shower. Allan was away for another snowboarding weekend with friends, so I didn't expect him back until night. I called Mike and arranged for him to meet me after I checked into a hotel. I didn't want to be there when Allan got home. I didn't want to sit in my room listening to him watch TV until he went to bed. I decided I'd work all night and go home after he left in the morning. It was too painful being at home.

I had to meet Julie on Monday. Back in her office, she asked me how my weekend was and I just sat in the chair, silently wishing she would die. I hated her and I blamed her for putting me in jail. I may have been the one who failed a UA, but she was the one responsible for me spending two days and nights locked up. That's the way my mind was working - or not - at the time. Obviously, I was the one responsible for landing my ass in jail, but I didn't see it that way at the time. The whole world was against me and I was a victim.

She ordered me, as part of my probation, to move in with my parents, effective immediately. My living situation was affecting my mental health and my recovery, she said, and if I didn't move in with my parents, she would impose more jail time.

Families and friends so often want to fix things. It's agonizing to watch someone you love fall, but until the addict/alcoholic hits bottom, there's nothing to do but wait. You wait and hope that the person you love is still alive when that happens. That's the reason it's so important not to rescue an addict from legal trouble. Don't bail them out. Don't pay for attorneys, because getting involved with the legal system is very often the only thing that separates an addict from that fatal fall.

I hated the system. And it saved my life. As I said before, an addict's emotional maturity stops at the age they were when they started using. I was a child: willful, stubborn and egocentric. Julie, my P.O. was, in a way, a surrogate parent. She force-fed me my broccoli and though I still loathe the vile weed, I'm alive because of it.

She made an appointment for me to go to the meth clinic for more intensive outpatient treatment, because my relapse prevention group and therapy sessions with Sarah obviously weren't enough to keep me sober. The plan was for me to begin attending classes three nights a week at the clinic, starting with my intake the next day. She also signed me up for Cognitive Self Change. CSC is a program offered through the Department of Corrections designed to help people change their thinking errors. I immediately renamed the class "How to Quit Thinking Like a Criminal." I left her office pissed off at the world. I hated everything and everyone, but mostly I hated myself.

Leaving Julie's office, I got a phone call from the guy who came to see the house. He made an offer and I immediately accepted. After closing costs, the profit would be just over three thousand dollars, but I didn't care. I just wanted it done. It was January 15, 2007 and Allan was moving out at the end of the month whether the house sold or not. Time was my enemy so I took the offer, glad to be near the end.

After that, things happened fast. We closed on the house on January 26 and had to be out by the end of the month. Meanwhile, I was supposedly staying with my parents, although I spent most of my time at the house packing. At least that's what I told myself. The closer I got to the deadline, the more paralyzed I became. I couldn't do anything but get high and gamble. I was free falling into an abyss and the soundtrack for my life was a requiem.

Allan was gone, Andy was still with my parents and I spent long days and cold nights in the house by myself. The only people I saw were Mario and my boys, and the quantities of meth I was moving was increasing. I was on a rollercoaster barely hanging on while the cars careened around the track, and I had no way to stop it.

So many years. What the hell happened? All I'd wanted originally was a little help getting through finals. Five years later, there I was; alone, without my son, sitting in the dark in a house I was trespassing in, looking down the barrel of three to five years in prison, sucking on a glass dick, and inconceivably, I was still certain that I could quit at any time.

I knew the end was near. I could feel it hovering like an enormous vulture blocking out the sun. I felt it, but couldn't envision it. The picture was fuzzy. I think I saw the end as moving in with my parents, because I still didn't intend to quit using meth. The move only meant figuring out logistics. As far as my legal issue, I kept telling myself that I could pass the UA's if I set my mind to it and followed the instructions on the bottle from GNC. I was smarter than they were. I'd fake my way through probation just as

I'd essentially faked my way through rehab. Just as I'd faked my way through the last five years of my life. *Fuck you all. If I want to quit, I'll quit, but nobody's going to make me.*

Finally, I hired movers to come pack everything and move it to a storage unit, but not all of it fit. Every day I told my parents I was packing the last of my things and cleaning the house, and every day I sat there getting high, selling drugs and gambling. On February 4, my parents had enough. I was trespassing. The house sold days ago and I was supposed to be out by the end of January, but I was still there, unable to move or even think clearly. They came moved the rest of my things to their garage. I was so far gone I couldn't even make simple decisions, like which things to put in which box. Mom did the cleaning, and on Sunday night, I left the keys in the mailbox for the new owner, and officially moved in with my parents.

In the meantime, I failed two UA's at the meth clinic. I didn't even try to detox. I kept hoping the intake woman wouldn't test me. Nothing mattered except selling and smoking meth, but I still didn't see it as my problem. I saw it as my salvation. I lost Allan, I lost the house, I lost my downtown office, I'd been without Andy for months and I was being forced to move in with my parents. All I wanted was to smoke meth. I loved my drug and everyone was conspiring to tear us apart. I couldn't see anything in front of me but the clouds of smoke I was constantly blowing.

Chapter 32

The third time I failed a UA, the director of the meth clinic sat me down.

"Kim, I'm sorry but I can't accept you into the program."

"What?" I wasn't sure I'd heard her correctly. I thought she was telling me there's no room at the inn right *now* but as soon as there is...

"I can't allow you to be here at the clinic. I'm sorry."

I stared at her stupidly. I'd just come from seeing Mario, and I had half a pound of meth in the trunk of my car. I was also extremely high. "Why not?" I asked her.

"It's obvious you can't stay clean. You don't have any sober time, and I can't allow you to put the others who come here at risk. You need more help then we can provide for you."

"So what am I supposed to do?"

"First thing you need to do is call Julie and let her know of our decision."

"What will she do?" I panicked. Things were moving too fast and none of this fit into my plans for the rest of the day. I had to meet Shadoe, Mike and Josh. I had dope to drop off and money to collect. I didn't know what was going to happen. I just kept thinking this was really going to mess up my schedule.

She looked at me and I could see the sadness and pity in her eyes. "It's likely she'll put you in jail until you can get into another rehab program. That or she'll pull your probation and impose your prison sentence."

And that was when it finally hit me like every cliché ever written. That was my bottom. An intensive outpatient treatment program for meth addicts refused to accept me because I was so fucked up that I was too much of a risk to the other clients. How bad off was I that a clinic designed to treat meth addiction won't accept me because I'm too far gone? I was facing prison and I couldn't stop. I could lose my son. I *couldn't* stop on my own. I really was a meth addict.

I'm terrified. I know I won't quit using on my own and I'm scared to death. My sentence was seven years' probation or a minimum of three years in prison. I can't imagine being locked up for that long. I can't imagine being away from Andy that long. I can't get my mind around what's happening. I know, though, that I can't go to jail in my condition.

"Can I go to detox?" I ask her. I'm not even crying. I'm just numb from shock and the realization of what I've done to myself. "Can I check myself into Port of Hope?"

"That's up to Julie, but I think it's a good idea regardless of what happens afterward. Do you want me to call her?" I nod.

She calls Julie and tells her what's going on. I can't get into the meth clinic, I've failed another UA and I've asked to go to Port of Hope, a detox clinic. They talk for a couple of minutes, and then Julie wants to talk to me. She's furious, but gives me permission with the caveat that I see her immediately when I get out.

We call Port of Hope and there's a bed available, but I have to be there in two hours or they won't take me. The director of the clinic wishes me luck and stresses the importance of getting to detox on time. This is my last chance, she says, so don't blow it.

I call Mike, tell him what's going on, and ask him to help me. I've got half a pound of meth I need to get rid of and all my paraphernalia. My things are with him in a locked box at the hotel where he's staying. On my way there, I call Josh and Shadoe and arrange to meet them at different places between the hotel and my parents' house. I can't even think about how I'm going to tell my parents. I have to deal with all this before I pack a bag to take to detox. Andy's birthday is tomorrow, February 13, and I'm going to miss it. I've always had so much fun planning his birthday and making his cake. This year I haven't even bought him a present. How the hell have I ended up here? How could I have risked everything for this drug?

"Mike, I'm dropping two ounces on you, okay?" I'm at the hotel, frantically smoking meth and I've got all my things laid out on the floor. I'll meet Shadoe in half an hour in the parking lot of a grocery store. He's got the money for the two ounces I'm giving him, and I'll give the other four ounces to Josh. "Can you move it, or is it too much for you?"

"I can take it. I don't have any money, though," Mike says.

"It's okay, don't worry about it. When you get it, call Josh and leave it with him. He'll get it to me." For all Josh's faults, I trust him completely. He's the one who will take everything else. I've got two scales, pipes, my bubbler and over six hundred zip lock baggies in various sizes for packaging meth. I gather everything and put it in a small duffle bag.

I'm panicky and my hands are shaking as I continue to

smoke. I know that whatever happens, this is it. I'm giving everything away and I'm done. Not because I want to quit, but because I'm at the end of the line and I have no choice if I want to keep my son and stay out of prison. I don't know what's going to happen after detox, but I don't want to think about that right now. I just have to get rid of everything, collect as much money as I can and get to Port of Hope on time.

I'm shaking so bad and I start to cry a little, tears rolling down my cheeks. Mike hasn't said much. He's just making sure my pipe is loaded while I get everything together. When I'm done, I take three huge hits - maybe the biggest I've ever taken. I fill the room with white smoke and my head is swimming. I feel like I'm going to pass out. I put my head down for a few seconds as the feeling fades.

"Fuck, Mike," I say, looking up at him. "I don't want to be a fucking addict."

"None of us do."

I look at him in awe. This is the first time in all these years that anyone I've been associated with has ever said anything like this. His words pierce my heart and as I look into those amazing blue eyes, I see a deep sadness. I've always just taken it for granted that some people were more gone than others and some couldn't handle their high but none of us have ever mentioned the word addiction. Even when I got back from rehab, Mario and the boys treated it as if I were on a mini vacation just taking a break from everything. People always assumed I would start rolling again when I got out, and they were right. Planned or not, that's exactly what happened. Hearing Mike sum up, in four little words, all the hidden pain and sorrow that's within us is sobering.

"I won't be back, Mike," I tell him. "I have to be done. I can't risk everything anymore."

"I know," he says. "You take care of yourself. I love you," he says awkwardly.

I hug him as I hand him the pipe. "I love you, too. Thank you for everything. Thanks for being there for me." I stand and look at him. "You take care of yourself too, okay?"

"Yeah," he says. "I'll try."

"Be safe." I walk out the door, leaving him for the last time.

After I see Shadoe, I meet Josh at the gas station just a few blocks from my parents' house. "I'm done, Josh," I tell him.

"No! No. Where am I going to go? I don't have anyone to help me out."

"I talked to Mitt. You can go through him."

"Aw, shit," he says. "Mitt will tax me big time."

"Josh, I don't have time for this right now! Quit fucking whining. I didn't even have to do that for you, but I did, so show some gratitude, for Christ's sake."

"Sorry," he says handing me an envelope. "There's three grand in there. I still owe you six. What do you want me to do?"

"Just hang on to it. Mike's going to drop money for me with you, okay?" I look him in the eyes. "I'm trusting you, Josh, so pay attention. I'm changing my phone number when I get out, but I'll call you and you better have my money."

"I will, Kim. I swear."

"I know, but listen. All you know is that I went to detox, okay? You don't give anyone my number when you get it, or I swear to God I'll have someone drive you out to the desert, and you don't want to go there, do you?"

"Don't worry. You know you can trust me."

"That's what I'm counting on. Everything is in there," I nod toward the bag. "Don't say I never did anything for you."

At my parents' house, I'm running around getting my things together.

"Kimberly, what are you doing?" Dad asks me.

"I have to go to detox! I have to be at Port of Hope in twenty minutes." I'm talking so fast that I'm tripping over my own words.

"What? What are you talking about?"

"I failed another UA," I yell at him, "and I have to go to detox. What don't you understand?" I have never spoken to my parents like this and even with all that's going on, I feel a little scared to be doing so.

Mom comes to my room where I'm jamming things into a bag. "Kimbo, slow down. Tell us what happened."

"I don't have time to slow down, Mom! I have to be there right now, don't you get it? Jesus!" I'm frantic and confused. I don't know what to pack so I just throw a nightgown, clean shirt and some toiletries in the bag. My head is buzzing and I feel like I'm going insane. This is too much. Everything is too much and I feel like I'm splitting apart. I feel like a Picasso painting. "I just have to go, okay?"

"Kim, you can't drive in the condition you're in," my dad says. "Let me drive you."

"No! I can fucking do this myself!"

"Kim," mom says. "Let your father drive you there. There's no reason for you to have your car there. How long will you be gone?"

"Until I'm detoxed! Shit!" I'm angry and I don't know why. It's not because I'm going to Port of Hope. I don't know why I'm so mad, but I feel like the world is ending. I just want to get the hell out of here. I need to make the deadline. I need this last chance. "Fine. Dad can drive me."

We don't talk on the way except when I give him directions. In the parking lot outside the clinic, I'm calmer. "Thanks, Dad," I say. "I'm sorry."

"Just call when you're ready to come home. I'll come get you. I love you, Kimbo." He looks defeated and worn out and I know it's because of me.

"Tell Andy I love him and I'm sorry I can't be there on his birthday, okay?" I start crying. "Hug and kiss him for me and tell him I'm sorry. I love you, Daddy." I walk up the stairs to the office to check myself in and watch him from the window as he drives away. I spend five days at the Port of Hope, sleeping and detoxing, just as I did when I first went to rehab.

It's February 12, 2007, and it's the last day I use meth. It's the last day I used any drug. February 13 is my sober date. It's also my son's birthday.

Chapter 33

Meth primarily affects dopamine, the chemical in the brain that allows us to feel pleasure. The release of dopamine reinforces naturally rewarding experiences such as sex or enjoying a good meal. A shortage of dopamine results in lack of motivation and drive, severe fatigue and depression.

For example, during sex, dopamine is released into the synapse. The feelings of pleasure occur when the dopamine finds and attaches to its receptors. Any excess in the synapse when all the receptors are full is either recycled for later use or destroyed by special molecules in the brain. With long-term over-stimulation, the brain permanently destroys the dopamine receptors.

The meth molecule is almost identical in shape to that of dopamine. When meth is ingested, it stimulates the brain into releasing massive amounts of dopamine into the synapses while the meth molecule attaches itself to the dopamine receptors. That's what causes the high. Between the dopamine and the meth molecules, the synapse becomes over-populated. Meth, then, is recycled and dopamine, destroyed. Quite simply, long-term, heavy meth use not only permanently depletes dopamine, but also destroys its receptors.

The result is self-induced mental illness resulting from physical changes to the brain. The damage can be repaired, but it takes time. The brain will eventually create new pathways, using other existing receptors, but the production of dopamine is a long process. The brain wasn't designed to produce large amounts of the chemical. Studies show that it takes eighteen months before recovering meth addicts regain eighty percent of their normal dopamine levels. This is why the relapse rate is so high with meth addicts. It takes a long, long time before we begin to feel anywhere near normal again.

Dopamine also controls the flow of information from other areas of the brain, especially memory, attention and problem-solving tasks.

When I woke up after detoxing at the Port of Hope, I didn't remember much of my stay other than the nurse taking my vital signs. The first time I got up to use the bathroom was the third day. On the fifth day, I dressed and went to the cafeteria to eat. The condition for my release was that I eat a meal and attend an A.A. meeting, so I did both.

Eating was difficult, not only because I had no appetite but also because my motor skills were so impaired. I was weak and shaky from five days of inertia, and performing the simple task of dining was like a comedy of errors without the comedy. I was so weak I had to hold a glass with two hands to avoid spilling. Cutting the sandwich in half was so exhausting I didn't bother. As before, when I detoxed at the Walker Center, my eyes were bleary, as if a thin film covered them. I was a mess, but I was sober, and I was going home.

When I read memoirs about addiction, I'm interested in the *how's* of people's recovery. How did you get sober? How did you stay sober? How is your life in sobriety?

How did I finally get sober? I started by admitting to myself that my life had become unmanageable, that I'm an addict and I needed help.

I chose to go the Port of Hope. Not because I wanted to get clean, but because I was at a dead-end. At first, my recovery was all about avoiding prison. I was sober a year before I *wanted* to be sober.

The first thing I did when I got home was ask my mother to drive me to GNC to buy meth test strips. I gave them to her and told her to test me whenever she wanted. I used one immediately when I got back and tested positive for meth. Meth leaves the system within 48 to 72 hours. My body was so poisoned, I didn't test clean for six days.

Julie gave me one last chance. I saw her twice a week for the first month and a half, and then once a week for the following five months. She UA'd me every time I saw her.

The other thing I did the day I get out of detox was change my phone number. The clerk at the store transferred all my settings, including my phone book, and with my dad watching, I deleted all the numbers that had anything to do with my old life. I also had my car painted and changed the license plates. My parents' last name is different from Andy's and mine because of my brief marriage, so I knew that no one would be able to track me down. I broke all ties to my past life. Playgrounds and playmates.

With time, my body healed, but my cognitive functioning

took longer. I couldn't retain information long enough to copy a sentence from one piece of paper to another and I'd forget things that happened just minutes before. It was difficult to concentrate and it took weeks before I was able to focus enough to read a book.

I went to relapse prevention group every Wednesday with seven or eight other Walker Center alums. I began to understand that my addiction is only a symptom of much larger issues, namely lack of self-esteem and a lack of self-worth. It wasn't that I didn't like myself - I hated myself. I spent a year and a half in those once-a-week sessions before I began to accept the fact that I might actually be worthy of kicking it on this spinning rock.

I had weekly one-on-one therapy sessions with the facilitator of our group, Sarah, and in her new-agey way, she helped me come to terms with my past and start to forgive myself. Babies are born perfect, she'd tell me, and with everything they need. All babies deserve love just for *being*. Why did I think I was any different? That was the hardest concept for me to grasp. I've never felt I deserved anything, let alone love. I agreed that other people did, but I thought so little of myself, how could anyone else love me? In time, though, Sarah led me from the darkness that filled me, into the light of possibility. "The things you are most embarrassed or ashamed about within yourself, Kim, are the things that make you so special," she told me one day in a therapy session. I thought about that for a long time. Slowly, with help, I began to understand what she meant.

The other addicts and alcoholics in my relapse prevention group nourished me as I'd never been before. Even when I was at my most difficult - refusing to engage with people, bursting into tears, putting up my wall in attempt to shut everyone out - they gave me unconditional love. They called me on my bullshit and they pointed out the good in me and, slowly, I began to believe them. They didn't lift me up only to drop me on my face, laughing about how stupid I was. They didn't want anything from me. They didn't have ulterior motives for the kindness they gave. They helped me begin to recognize the beauty that's within me.

One night, in front of the group and without provocation, one of the men told me I was beautiful. He was happily married. He didn't want sex, he didn't want something from me and he wasn't lying to me just so he could say, "Gotcha'! Ah ha ha ha...I can't believe you're so dumb that you fell for that. Hey, guys, she fell for it again!"

The night, for the first time in my life, I accepted the compliment rather than negating it. I felt like the little girl in *Little Miss Sunshine*, when her grandpa tells her he thinks she's the most beautiful girl in the world, "and it's not because of your brains or personality," he said. I choked on my tears when I heard those words.

Jill, my boss, is probably the most confident woman I've ever met. She's the smartest, prettiest, most fascinating person in the room. Just ask her. One day I said to her, "I'd give anything to have a tenth of the confidence you have, Jill. Where does that come from?"

"When I was growing up," she said, "my parents always told me I was the smartest, prettiest, most wonderful little girl in the world, so I believed them."

When she told me that, my heart clenched in my chest and crept into my throat. I believe it's possible to mourn the loss of something you've never had. It wasn't that my parents told me otherwise, it's that they told me nothing. And in the absence of anything, I assumed the worst.

Every day since he was born, I've told Andy how handsome he is. I tell him he's the smartest, funniest, strongest little boy (and now man,) in the world. I tell him I love him multiple times a day, and I shower him with hugs and kisses. I'm conscious of what I'm doing, but it wasn't a decision I made. I can't imagine withholding that from him. It comes so naturally, it would be alien for me not to. Andy's a lot like Jill. He has no doubts about himself, no insecurities, no self-loathing. He's the smartest, handsomest, most fascinating guy in the room. Just ask him.

The group reminded me of my best qualities. Hearing everyone's story and encouraging each other through recovery made me feel not so alone. People in the group relapsed and came back. They went to jail and came back. We called each other when we were having a hard time or when the cravings got particularly bad. We helped each other heal. We loved each other.

They helped me understand what Sarah meant about my best qualities being those of which I'm most embarrassed by. I've always been ashamed of my lack of control over my emotions. I've always suppressed my intelligence, worried that people would think I was pompous or arrogant. I cry and laugh more easily and more often than anyone know. I constantly worry about what other people think of me and I base my self-worth on the acceptance of others. If someone likes me, it means I'm okay. If someone doesn't, it's because I'm disgusting, stupid or just a plain old geek. It doesn't even matter whether or not I like them.

I just want to be like everyone else. I look at people walking around at the mall or sitting in restaurants and they all seem so at ease with themselves. It's as if everyone else has figured out the secret to life, and I'll never be privy to it. I've always compared the way I feel on the inside to how other people seem on the outside, creating unrealistic expectations.

Julie ordered me to take Cognitive Self Change, a two-part, long term series of classes designed to help a person change present thinking patterns that can lead to anti-social behavior. The focus is on taking responsibility for one's behavior. It doesn't matter what's happened to me as much as how I've chosen to act and react to the world. There are three parts to any behavior: the antecedent, or what happened immediately prior to the behavior; the behavior itself; and the consequence, or outcome. The goal in CSC is to examine past behavior in order to anticipate and plan for future behavior. For example, if I spend time with people I know who are still using meth, and someone pulls out a pipe and hands it to me, I have the choice to smoke or not smoke the drug, but the first mistake I've made is putting myself in the situation to begin with.

It doesn't matter how I was potty trained, how my parents punished me when I was a little girl, or whether or not I have an Oedipus complex. What matters is that I am responsible for my behavior and I need to be conscious and purposeful about the life I want to live.

In essence, I got sober by giving up my perceived control, and doing what people told me to do. I kept doing the next right thing.

How do I stay sober? I respect my addiction.

I make it a conscious decision every day. With four years of sobriety, am I cured? Not by a long shot. I can honestly say that I don't know what I would do if I were in a situation where someone passed me a loaded pipe. I'd like to think I could just say no, but I'm not sure.

I respect my addiction by not becoming complacent. I don't associate with people who use, I don't allow myself to be in a situation where there's any chance of drugs being present, and I don't forget how difficult it was for me to get clean. The day I say,

"I'm no longer an addict. I'll never touch meth again," is the day I'm in trouble. So I don't think that way. I'm honest with myself: I don't know what I'd do, so I do everything I can to keep from having to make that decision. That doesn't mean my sobriety is weak, far from it. It means I'm strong enough to take care of myself. Finally.

What's my life like now? Better, of course. What would you expect me to say? It's true, though. I finally have a semblance of peace. But quitting meth was by far the most difficult thing I've ever done.

I nearly destroyed my brain, and since I had a chemical imbalance to begin with (depression/bi-polar) the results were catastrophic.

Sarah referred me to a psych nurse who worked with me to find the right combination of mood stabilizers and anti-depressants. It took months to get the cocktail right, and there were times I was suicidal. Four years later, I still see her regularly and sometimes my meds need to be adjusted. It's an ongoing process and I'll need medication for the rest of my life.

I still have using dreams. I had them nearly every night for the first year. In them, I'd be in the middle of using or on a binge, when I realized I'd blown it. All the progress I'd made, all the hard work, gone. I would be terrified and wake up sweaty, shaking and crying, sometimes for a couple of hours afterward. I was still with my parents then, and they were my saviors. As heart wrenching as it was for them, they listened to me. They listened as I described my dreams. They let me talk until the images and feelings of failure faded away.

They listened without comment when I had cravings, which were continual for months. I still have cravings for meth and using dreams sometimes. I don't know that they'll ever go away, and maybe that's a good thing. They're reminders of what's waiting for me if I were ever to go back to using. They help me to remember and respect my addiction.

The best thing that happened at the Walker Center was that we began to work, as a family, on being honest and talking with one another. That's been hard, especially for my parents, but I'm so proud of them for trying. I love them so much, and I'm eternally grateful for them. I don't think I'd be sober without them. Not only did they make it possible for me to go to rehab where, at the very least, I had my first taste of sobriety, but they also took care of my son when I couldn't even take care of myself.

They gave Andy and me a safe place to stay, and the support I needed when I was falling apart. None of this was easy for them. They really were disgusted, not so much with me, but by the very thought of meth and what I'd done to myself. Somehow, though, they were able to put that aside and just love me while I tried to learn how to love myself. We have a better relationship than ever. It's a far cry from perfect, but as they say in A.A., "progress over perfection."

The best part about being sober is that I'm fully present for Andy. I'm so proud of the person he is, and I know how fortunate I am to be his mother.

We moved into an apartment in March of 2008 and we're still here. Andy rules over his kingdom from the window of his second story bedroom, playing his harmonica and shouting quotes from his movies to anyone passing by. Sometimes, just to the empty parking lot. He doesn't care. I think he figures that somewhere, someone might be listening, and it's his duty to share his talents with the world. We live a simple life and we're dirt poor, but we have each other and that's all I've ever really wanted. We're happy.

I still go to therapy and see my psych nurse. I'm still working on loving myself and forgiving myself for my past. I often wish I could be done with it, but I'll never be done with it. I'm a work in progress.

Epilogue

I've been working on this book for a few of years. Being a writer is a dream I've always had, but it was akin to wishing to be a movie star - something nice to think about, but too out of reach for the average mortal. I've been lucky enough to have the time to work on it, though. It's difficult finding employment when you're a felon.

Julie didn't want me to work for the first few months. She wanted me to focus on my recovery instead. Since then, I've had a couple of jobs, the most recent I lost because of my drug charge. I drove for a van service once in a while, but when my unemployment ran out, I got scared.

Every employer these days asks about criminal history and most do background checks. In the rare cases when I got an interview or call back, the result was always the same. No thanks.

So in December of 2010, with five dollars to my name and bills to pay, it just popped into my head that maybe I could make and sell fudge, because I happen to make the best fudge on earth. I posted on Face Book what I was doing and ended up selling 39 pounds of fudge that month. That got me through December but, of course, the bills keep on coming. So I stated making other things and sharing the pictures with my friends.

Then someone hired me to do a Super Bowl party - just a little light catering. Then someone wanted to know if I could do a birthday cake for her son. I'd never done a "real" cake before but I needed the money so I casually said yes while frantically searching the Internet for blogs and tutorials about cake decorating. I really liked the creativity of cake decorating and was surprised at how well it turned out.

On February 13, 2011, I celebrated four years of sobriety. My son, Andy, was turning 19 and kept telling me he was getting married. He watches a lot of movies and *Mama Mia* was one of his many obsessions as is *The Sound of Music*. He told me he was going to marry Maria in a church and have seven children, but that Captain VonTrapp could live with them, which I think is very generous of Andy considering he'd be breaking up the family.

Just before his birthday, I asked him what kind of cake he wanted. He kept saying, "Mamma Mia, Mamma Mia," until I got so frustrated, I did a Google search for cake images and we looked at them together. I'd only scrolled down a little when he made me stop and pointed to the one he wanted. "That one."

"Honey, that's not a birthday cake. That's a wedding cake."

"Oh, yeah. Essa Mamma Mia. Inna get married. Enna Sophie."

He kissed me on the check and left the room. He'd made his decision. It was my fault. I was the one who gave him a choice.

So I ended up making him a two-tiered wedding cake complete with white chocolate flowers and leaves. The bottom tier was chocolate fudge with Oreo butter cream filling and the top was white with raspberry filling - just like a real wedding cake. I figured, why not do this for him? As much as I refuse to limit my son's future, the reality is that he's never going to get married, so if he wanted a wedding cake for his birthday...I'd do anything for my son. Andy was beside himself. I posted pictures of the whole ordeal online and people were very responsive. I got more orders here and there for cakes.

The chocolate flowers really caught my interest and I began researching more about working with chocolate as edible art. This led me to chocolate stilettos. Life size, 3-D chocolate stilettos. Now *those* were fun to make and the sky's the limit as far as design. I could do very plain or fabulously funky.

I was fascinated by chocolate and spent hours studying and experimenting. I started getting sales within a couple of days for candy barks and hand dipped chocolates. Then I got an Easter order for three stilettos from a woman who wanted to give them to her daughters as baskets. When they arrived in Texas, one of the shoes was nothing but a puddle of chocolate.

Shipping chocolate would require ice packs and insulation which would result in higher costs. I was back to square one, except that I still had local orders trickling in. One day I was just sitting at my desk doing nothing when out of the blue I thought, "I wonder how those professional companies make those really cute cookies?"

Again, I started reading blogs, looking at thousands of pictures and YouTube tutorials, and again I started experimenting and sharing pictures. Today I work for myself at my own company, Kimbo's Cookies, making custom designed sugar cookies.

During the time I've worked on this book, Andy's become quite a writer himself. He makes what he calls his lists, which are actually endless pages in a notebook filled with his writing. At first, he was copying words out of magazines, but he quickly grew bored with that. Lately, he'll pop in a DVD with the sub-titles on, press "pause," and copy down the words on the screen - complete with cues.

"Luke," *mechanical breathing,* "I am your father."

Every few paragraphs or so, he comes to me and has me read aloud what he's written. The problem is that in the past few weeks, he's started turning on the foreign language sub-titles. The Spanish I can work through phonetically. When it comes to French or Italian, I just fake it.

Lately, he's been watching *The Rocky Horror Picture Show,* which makes for very interesting "lists" indeed.

These days, I bake and I write. I sit upstairs in my little writing room every day, looking out on the commons and the playground, and most days I think of how lucky I am to have made it through those years and come out the other side largely intact.

When I work on this book, I write until the memories are too painful, then I bake until the pain passes and I can move on. My days are quiet. Andy still has long days with school and therapy, so from seven in the morning until shortly after six, it's just me.

I'm actually pretty good company.

It's Friday, and the playground is full of children. I write sporadically because the flippers are out. That's what I call this group of little boys who seem to defy gravity. They flip everywhere: Off the playground equipment, off the sides of trees, off the ground and out of each other's hands. Over and over again, they spend close to an hour flipping. I watch this little flip-clique and try to imagine Andy as one of them. Sometimes I wonder what he would be like if he didn't have Down syndrome. I think he'd be pretty much the same, but easier to understand. I think he'd make a fantastic flipper.

He'll be home soon, so I go downstairs to pre-heat the oven for his little pizzas. I take a bag of frozen peas and pour some into a pan, and as I shut the freezer door, I hear the best sound in the world: "Oh hi, Mom. It's me. I'm home."

Acknowledgments

Thank you to my editors Paula Berinstein and Eliza Dreier for making this book better and helping me become a stronger writer. Thank you to Jeff Yeager, my mentor. Thank you, Brad Peachey (the only man I know who can rock a bow tie five days a week) for your critical eye. Thank you to all the writers and artists who've shared their own struggle and in doing so inspired me to keep going. Thank you to all my friends who've been so supportive throughout my journey. Thank you so much, Mom and Dad, for always being there for me and not giving up on me. Most of all, thank you to my bug-in-a-boy-suit, my perfect person and the best human I've ever known: Andy. Being your mom is the best thing I've ever done or will ever do. I love you, sweetheart.

Made in the USA
Monee, IL
27 June 2024

60850581R00156